Modula-2 Made Easy

Modula-2 Made Easy

Herbert Schildt

Osborne **McGraw-Hill**
Berkeley, California

Osborne **McGraw-Hill**
2600 Tenth Street
Berkeley, California 94710
U.S.A.

For information on translations and book distributors outside of the U.S.A., please write to Osborne **McGraw-Hill** at the above address.

Modula-2 Made Easy

234567890 DODO 89876

ISBN 0-07-881241-0

To my brother, Dave

CONTENTS

Please send me ______ copies, at $29.95 each, of the listings in *Modula-2 Made Easy*. For foreign orders, please add $5.00 for shipping and handling.

____

Name

____

Address

____

City State ZIP

____

Telephone

Method of payment: Check ____ Visa ____ MC ____

Credit card number: ______________________________

Expiration date: ______________________________

Signature: ______________________________

Send to: Herbert Schildt
RR 1, Box 130
Mahomet, IL 61853

INTRODUCTION

Programming definitely is best learned by doing. Therefore it is recommended that you acquire or have access to a Modula-2 compiler. There are several available both for microcomputers and mainframes; however, you should make sure that the one you are using is a complete and standard implementation. All the examples in this book will compile and run on any standard Modula-2 compiler.

This book assumes that you have some knowledge of programming. You should understand the general concepts of variables, assignment statements, and loops. Don't worry—your programming experience need not be extensive; in fact, if you have written even a few short programs in any other language, you will be able to use this book.

A note to Pascal programmers: Although at first glance Modula-2 may appear to be simply an expanded Pascal, you are cautioned against jumping to this conclusion. There are several subtle and not so subtle differences between the two. Appendix A, which outlines these differences, has been added to help you make the switch, but you are urged to read the entire book to avoid misunderstandings.

example, you can create and use disk files without knowing what controller or disk drives are being used.

Modula-2's second language is more closely connected with the actual physical devices that comprise your computer system. After you have mastered the fundamentals of Modula-2 you will be ready to use the language in this second way. At this level, you as the programmer have access to many system-specific functions and much information. This second language has less error-checking facility and makes you responsible for keeping things straight, but it allows specialized programs to be written. These specialized programs are usually systems programs, although occasionally they may be applications programs that must interface to a unique device—for example, to a speech synthesizer or digital plotter.

Part of Modula-2's uniqueness is that it allows both applications and systems programs to be written with the same ease. A *systems program* is simply a piece of software that is, is part of, or is closely aligned with the operating system and, in part, requires knowledge of the physical machine executing it. *Applications programs* generally perform a specific user task, such as accounting, and interface with the computer as a logical device. Here are some examples of both applications and systems programs:

Applications programs	**Systems programs**
• General ledgers	• Operating systems
• Mailing lists	• Compilers
• Loan amortization	• Text editors
• Payroll programs	• Print spoolers

The chief difference between the two is that applications programs do not require an intimate understanding of the workings of the actual machine that is executing them, whereas systems programs do.

Modula-2's Level

It is common to classify computer languages in yet another way: by level. The *level* of a language is determined by its distance from the circuit structure of the computer that will process the code. The lowest level is *machine* code, the actual binary instructions that the computer executes. Only in the very earliest days of computing have people actually written programs directly in binary codes, because this is extremely tedious, time consuming, and prone to error. The next level up is *assembly language,* which is simply the symbolic representation of machine code. Assembly language is a little easier for programmers to use, but it is still very difficult and demanding. At the next level the so-called *high-level languages* begin to appear.

Although you will hear the term *high-level language* applied to any programming language above assembly language, there is actually a broad spectrum of levels to which a language can belong, with the lowest level being closest to assembly language and the highest being the most abstracted and distant from the computer. A high-level language substitutes logical programming constructs, such as loops, input and output statements, and IF/THEN/ELSE statements for their multi-instruction equivalents in machine code. Some of the more common languages and their relative levels are listed here. It is important to notice that Modula-2 is listed twice—once because it is a highly abstracted language like Pascal or Ada, and a second time because it can be used in many situations as a substitute for assembly code.

The Language Spectrum

Highest level:	Ada
	Modula-2
	Pascal
	BASIC
	COBOL
	FORTH
	Modula-2
	C
	Assembly language
Lowest level:	Machine code

Modula-2 as a Structured Language

Modula-2 is a *structured language.* In contrast, BASIC is a nonstructured language. The two most distinguishing features of a structured language are its use of *subunits* or *blocks* and its inclusion of loop statements based on a boolean test. A block is an indivisible set of statements that are logically connected—that is, if one statement in a block is executed, all the other statements in the block will also be executed. For example, imagine an IF statement that, if successful, will execute three discrete statements. If these statements can be grouped together and referenced easily, and if they form an indivisible unit, then they form a block. Skipping ahead just a little, note that the following Modula-2 program fragment will always print the number **123** on the screen if **X** is less than 10.

```
IF X<10 THEN
   WriteString("1");
   WriteString("2");
   WriteString("3");
END;
```

There is no situation in which only 1 or 2 or 23 or any number but 123 will be written on the screen, because the statements between the words **THEN** and **END** form a block, and if **X** is less than 10, they will all execute; otherwise, none of them will execute.

Also implicit in the concept of a structured language is the availability of both *local* and *global* variables. Although later in this book you will learn more precisely the differences and benefits of each of these types of variables as they relate to Modula-2, the following definitions will be helpful. A *global variable* is known throughout the entire program during its entire execution. For example, all variables in BASIC are global. On the other hand, a *local variable* is known only to a small portion of the program, and it may go in and out of existence many times as the program executes. The reason that local variables are considered important in a modern, structured programming language is that they allow small units of code to be written, debugged, and altered without accidental side effects elsewhere in the program. If you have ever written a large BASIC program you surely understand how frustrating these side effects can be—and how difficult they are to find.

Another attribute of a structured language is the removal of **GOTO** as the common form of loop control. In these languages, **GOTO** is either prohibited or discouraged and is not the common form of program control in the same way that it is in BASIC or FORTRAN. The reason for this has to do with algorithmic clarity. Routines written using **GOTOs** are often difficult to understand and to verify. Also, there is no routine that requires **GOTO**; thus, it is not often used in structured languages.

A structured language often allows separately compiled subroutines to be used without be ing in the program proper. This means that you can create a subroutine library that contains useful, tested subroutines that can be accessed by any program you write. In Modula-2 these are called ***MODULE***s, and you will learn more about them and libraries as you progress. Finally, a structured language allows you to indent statements and does not require a strict field concept (as in FORTRAN). Hence, your programs will look clearer and will represent more fairly your underlying algorithms.

Here are some examples of structured and nonstructured languages:

Nonstructured	**Structured**
FORTRAN	Modula-2 (and Pascal)
BASIC	Ada
COBOL	C

Structured languages tend to be more modern, and nonstructured languages are older. In fact, a mark of an old computer language is that it is not structured. Today it is widely considered that structured languages are not only easier to program in, but the programs written in them are much easier to maintain because the code is clearer and less prone to error.

Although you may be able to think of languages that are not structured and yet still appear to satisfy the previous requirements of a structured language (such as advanced BASICs), a structured language is based on the compartmentalization of code and data; that is, the reduction of each task to its own subroutine or block of code. As you learn the Modula-2 programming language, the difference between a structured and nonstructured language will become quite clear. In fact, Modula-2 is probably the most structured of the structured languages.

Compilers Versus Interpreters

If you are a beginner, then the terms *compiler* and *interpreter* may be unfamiliar to you. They refer to the way in which a program, written by you, is actually executed by the computer. Any programming language can, in theory, be either compiled or interpreted, but some languages are usually executed one way or the other. The way a program is executed, however, is generally not defined by the language in which it is written. Interpreters and compilers are simply sophisticated programs that operate on your program source code.

An interpreter reads the text to your program one line at a time and performs the specific instructions contained in that line. On the other hand, a compiler reads the entire program and converts it into a form that the computer can execute.

Therefore, because Modula-2 is generally compiled, your programs will consist of both *source code,* which is the program text that you actually write, and *object code* (also referred to as *binary* or *machine* code), which is your program translated into instructions the computer can execute. Once the program is compiled, a line of source code is no longer meaningful to the execution of your program.

An interpreter must be present each time you wish to run your program. In BASIC, you must first execute the BASIC interpreter, load your program, and then type RUN each time you want to use your program. A compiler, by contrast, converts your program into object code that can be directly executed by your computer. Because the compiler translates your program one time, all you need do is execute your program directly, generally by simply typing its name.

Compiled programs run much faster than interpreted ones. The compiling process itself does take extra time, but this is easily offset by the time you save while using the program. The only time this is not true is if your program is very short—say, less than 50 lines—and does not use any loops. In this case, it could take a very long time to make up the difference in execution speed.

In addition to speed advantages, compilers protect your source code from unauthorized tampering and theft. Compiled code bears no resemblance to source code. This is the main reason that compilers are used almost exclusively by commercial software houses.

Two terms that you will see often in this book and in your Modula-2 compiler manual are *compile time* and *run time.* Compile time refers to the events that occur during the compilation process. Run time refers to the events that occur while the program is actually executing. Unfortunately, you will often see them used in connection with the word *errors,* as in *compile-time errors* and *run-time errors.*

The Modula-2 Philosophy

It will be helpful to your study of Modula-2 to understand the philosophy behind the language. In general, language influences the way we think. This is true for human languages, the language of mathematics, and programming languages. For example, it has been said that French is a poetic language, that German is an engineering language, and that English is a poor blend of these. More seriously, consider the language of calculus. Both Isaac Newton and Gottfried Leibniz independently developed the basis for calculus. However, Leibniz's notation, or language, was clearer and easier to understand and use than was Newton's. Hence, it is Leibniz's notation that is still in use today. Even though the problems both Newton's and Leibniz's calculus could solve were the same, Leibniz's *language made it easier to solve them.* The same situation exists in programming.

Computer science is still a very young endeavor, and it is not only programming languages that are evolving and progressing, but also the way we think about problems and their solutions. When Wirth created Modula-2, he actually also defined an approach to problem solving. The essence of this method is *modularity,* and it is embodied in the Modula-2 language. A modular approach to problem solving suggests that every problem consists of one of two elements: two or more subproblems, or a solution. Therefore, any problem can either be reduced into its parts, or solved.

In terms of programming, every programming problem can be broken into smaller pieces (subproblems). These smaller pieces can then be separated into even smaller pieces or into individual statements or subroutines (solutions). The advantage of reducing a problem into its parts is twofold. First, it lets you more clearly see all elements and facets to the task—in essence, it allows you to better understand the problem. Second, it enables you to code and debug pieces of the program a little at a time. This is important because it has been postulated that debugging time is an exponential relationship based on the size of the routine or program. Therefore, the smaller the pieces are that you are working with, the less time you spend correcting your work.

The Modula-2 language very strongly encourages the concept of task reduction by allowing you to easily create separate logical routines that you later combine to make your program. Therefore, a Modula-2 program can

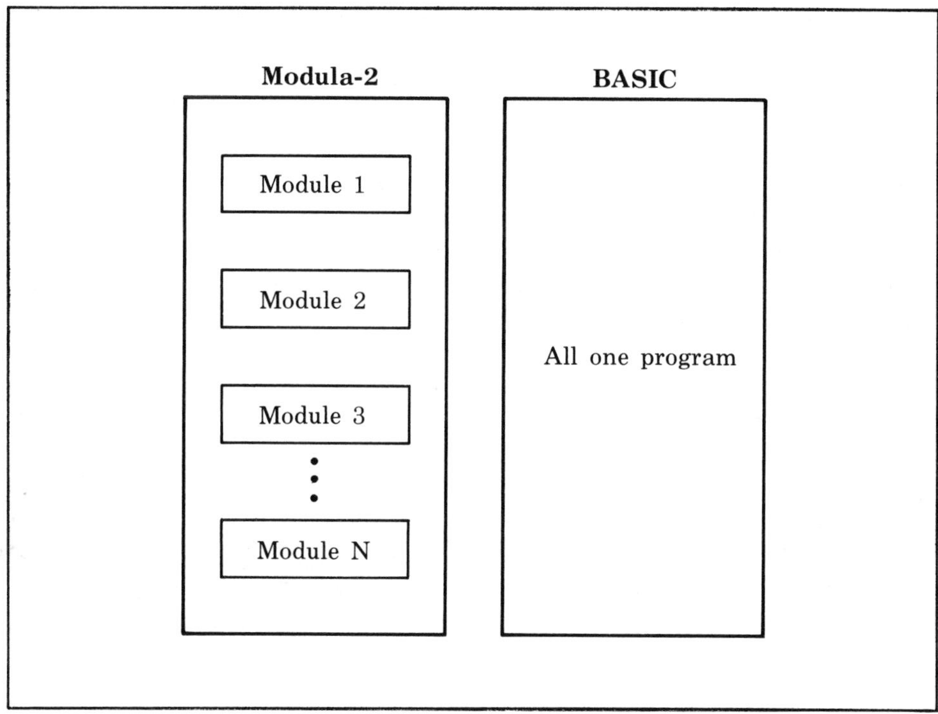

Figure 1-2. A Modula-2 program compared to a BASIC program

be thought of as a collection of small pieces, as shown in Figure 1-2. The form of a normal BASIC program is included for comparison.

Notational Conventions

For clarity, all Modula-2 keywords will be shown in boldface, as will all program variables, procedures, and module names.

From time to time, notes will be directed to Pascal programmers. If you are not familiar with Pascal, then you may ignore these notes. If, however, you have a background in Pascal, you may find helpful the differences in the basic syntax of Modula-2 that are pointed out.

Your First Modula-2 Program

By now, you are probably curious about what a Modula-2 program actually looks like. The very simple one shown here will print the message "Hello" on the screen. You should enter this program into your computer and compile it according to the method described by your compiler. Once you have done this you will be ready to proceed with the rest of the book.

```
MODULE Sample1;
  FROM Terminal IMPORT WriteString;
BEGIN
  WriteString("Hello");
END Sample1.
```

All programs are called ***MODULE***s, although there can be special kinds of **MODULE**s that are not actually programs by themselves. All programs (**MODULE**s) have names; in the example here, the program name is **Sample1.** The next line instructs the Modula-2 compiler to include a procedure called ***WriteString,*** found in the library called ***Terminal,*** and add it to the program. You will learn much more about the Modula-2 libraries and their contents as you progress through this book, but generally, a library is a file that contains many procedures that can be used by your programs. (A procedure is simply a subroutine that performs a specific function.) The keyword **BEGIN** signals the start of the actual program, which in this case is simply a call to the procedure **WriteString** with the message "Hello" as an argument. The program ends with an **END** statement, the **MODULE** name, and a period.

Two more points about this program: First, in Modula-2 upper- and lowercase letters are distinct. Therefore, **WriteString** and **writestring** are not the same. Second, all Modula-2 keywords—for example, **BEGIN, END,** and **IMPORT**—are in uppercase letters.

Overview of Modula-2

CHAPTER 2

This chapter will familiarize you with the basics of Modula-2. One of the hardest problems encountered while learning a programming language is that you have to know something about it in order to learn it. This is because each aspect of the language does not exist in a void, but rather in relation to the entire language. This chapter will give you the necessary background for the rest of the book. Most of the topics discussed here will be examined in much greater detail later on, and if you already have some knowledge of Modula-2, then you may wish to advance to Chapter 3 at this time.

Modula-2 Reserved Words

The Modula-2 language, like all languages, is comprised of *reserved words* and the syntax rules that apply to them. (Sometimes the term *keywords* is

AND	ELSIF	LOOP	REPEAT
ARRAY	END	MOD	RETURN
BEGIN	EXIT	MODULE	SET
BY	EXPORT	NOT	THEN
CASE	FOR	OF	TO
CONST	FROM	OR	TYPE
DEFINITION	IF	POINTER	UNTIL
DIV	IMPLEMENTATION	PROCEDURE	VAR
DO	IMPORT	QUALIFIED	WHILE
ELSE	IN	RECORD	WITH

Figure 2-1. Modula-2 reserved words

used instead of reserved words; however, we will stick to Wirth's terminology.) Figure 2-1 lists the Modula-2 reserved words. All Modula-2 reserved words must be in uppercase letters. As mentioned in Chapter 1, Modula-2 is case sensitive; therefore, the words IMPORT and Import are different, and only the first is a valid reserved word. The reserved words are reserved and may not be used as variable, procedure, or **MODULE** names.

In addition to the reserved words, your Modula-2 compiler supplies a set of *standard identifiers*.These standard identifiers are recognized by the compiler and are used to do various things, such as declare variables and perform type conversions. They may be used as if they were part of the language—even though, for technical reasons, they are not. As with the reserved words, you should not use them as names for anything else. The standard identifiers are listed in Figure 2-2.

Data Types

Modula-2 supports a wide variety of different kinds of data. This differs from a language like BASIC, which only handles numbers and strings.

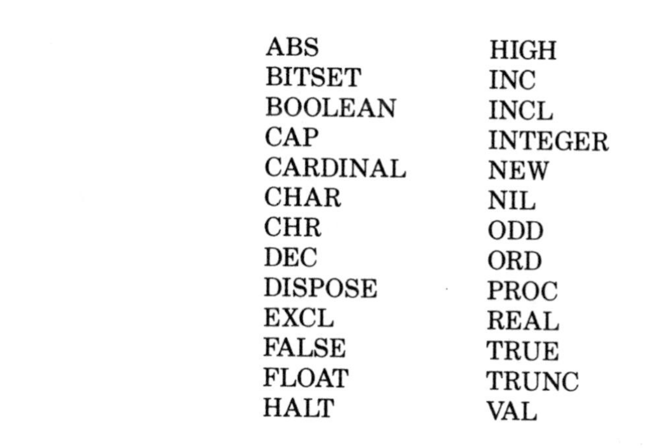

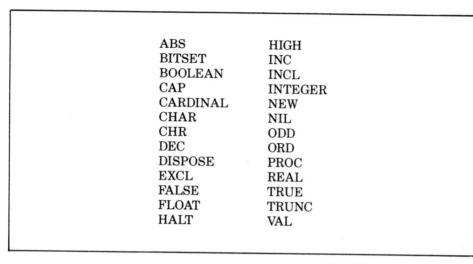

ABS	HIGH
BITSET	INC
BOOLEAN	INCL
CAP	INTEGER
CARDINAL	NEW
CHAR	NIL
CHR	ODD
DEC	ORD
DISPOSE	PROC
EXCL	REAL
FALSE	TRUE
FLOAT	TRUNC
HALT	VAL

Figure 2-2. Modula-2 standard identifiers

The availability of many different data types makes it possible to write programs that are efficient and lessens the programmer's frustration in trying to shoehorn one thing into another (which is so often the case in BASIC).

Modula-2 has six elementary data types, shown in Table 2-1. Each of these may be arrayed, and as you will learn later, you can also create custom types that add even more flexibility.

Table 2-1. The Modula-2 Elementary Data Types and Ranges

Data Type	Range (assuming 16-bit word size)
BOOLEAN	TRUE or FALSE
CHAR	ASCII character set
CARDINAL	0 through 65535
INTEGER	−32768 through 32767
REAL	Varies with implementation
BITSET	0 through 15

BOOLEAN data can have only two values: **TRUE** or **FALSE**. **CHAR** data is a single ASCII character. You may find that in some Modula-2 implementations a **CHAR** may also be able to hold special characters, such as graphics characters. **CARDINAL** data may have only the positive values between 0 and the largest integer. On most 16-bit computers, this is 65535, although you should check your user manual. An **INTEGER** may take any value between the smallest negative number and largest positive number. Because of the way numbers are represented in the computer, the largest **INTEGER** will be one half the value of the largest **CARDINAL**. For most 16-bit systems, the **INTEGER**s range is −32,768 to 32,767. **REAL** data may have floating-point values; the exact range and precision will vary with the implementation. **BITSET** data can have a value of 0 through N−1, where N is usually, but not necessarily, the number of bits in a word. For 16-bit systems, the range is 0 through 15.

Modula-2 is a *strongly typed* language. This means that data of one type may not be directly mixed with data of another type. For example, an **INTEGER** cannot be assigned to a **CHAR**. Modula-2 supports various conversion procedures to allow this sort of thing when necessary. (Later on, you will learn that it is possible to bypass most of Modula-2's type checking rules when working in system mode—but this is for advanced users only.)

Constants

A *constant* is a value that is fixed throughout the life of a program. There can be constants of any elementary data type. For example, in the expression

```
X:=100-10;
```

100 and 10 are constants, whereas X is a variable. The single most important constant is a string. A string is an array of characters enclosed between either single or double quotation marks. In programming terms, the string is said to be *delimited* by single or double quotation marks. For

example,

"Meet me at midnight"

is a string. If you wish to use double quotation marks in the string, then you must delimit the string with single quotation marks, as shown here.

'She said, "this is a test"'

The reverse is also true, if the string is delimited by double quotation marks, then single quotation marks may be contained in the string.

It is possible to give a constant a name, and this is done in the constant declaration section of the program.

Variables, Operators, And Expressions

For a programming language to be useful, it must support variables that can be acted upon by operators to form expressions.

Variables

A Modula-2 program can use several different types of variables. If your previous programming experience is limited to BASIC, then different kinds of variables is a new concept. In a language like BASIC, all variables are either numeric or string variables. This is one of the features of BASIC that makes it easy for beginners to learn. However, limiting all variables to only two types greatly restricts the control you, the programmer, have over the way your program works and can reduce its efficiency. This is the reason that most other high-level languages, including Modula-2, offer a wide range of variable types.

Variables can be of any type supported by Modula-2, including the six elementary data types discussed earlier. As you will see later, it is possible to declare arrays of variables and to define custom data types. *Custom* data types are defined in the type declaration section of a **MODULE**. Conglomerate data types, called **RECORD**s, may also be used. A **RECORD** is a variable that is actually a combination of other variables, grouped together and referenced under one name. Another kind of variable is a *pointer.* A pointer holds the address of the actual variable used. (Pointers are so important that Chapter 7 is devoted exclusively to them.)

All variables must be declared before they are used. To declare a variable, you place its name and type in the variable declaration section of a **MODULE**. This section begins with the keyword **VAR**. For example, to declare three variables, **X** through **Z**, with types **BOOLEAN**, **INTEGER**, and **REAL**, you would write

```
VAR
   X: BOOLEAN;
   Y: INTEGER;
   Z: REAL;
```

This tells the compiler to create three variables, named **X, Y,** and **Z,** as **BOOLEAN, INTEGER,** and **REAL,** respectively, and to make them known to the rest of your program. (Technically, variables may be known to selected portions of your program, as you will learn in subsequent chapters.) If you try to use a variable before it is declared, you will get a syntax error message, and your program will not compile. A variable can be of one and only one type—it is not possible to create a variable that is both **INTEGER** and **REAL**, for example.

All variable names in Modula-2 must begin with a letter followed by letters or numbers. They cannot include spaces, underscores, dashes, or other special characters. Also, no reserved words (Modula-2 commands) can be used as variable names. The maximum length of a variable name is determined by the compiler you are using, but it is safe to assume at least eight characters. Within these limits, you can call a variable by whatever name you like. Some valid and invalid variable names are shown here.

Valid	**Invalid**	
Rex	first time	(Can't use spaces)
FirstTime	start_count	(Can't use underscore)
X2	2E	(Must start with letter)

Because variables may have long names, you can add clarity to your programs by choosing meaningful ones. For example, here are two different ways to represent the same formula.

```
X:=Q*P*U;
CubeVolume:=Side1*Side2*Side3;
```

Both versions assign the volume of a cube, but the second makes it clear to anyone reading the program what is happening. A word of warning: Don't make your variable names so long that they are laborious to type and cause unusually long lines. For example, instead of **Employee TerminationDate**, you will be better off with **EmpTermDate**.

A last point: In Modula-2 programming, a convention generally followed calls for the capitalization of the first letter in each word of a multiword variable name. For example, instead of using **initheadoflist**, you would write **InitHeadOfList** to make the name more readable.

Operators

Modula-2 supports a wide array of operators, as shown in Table 2-2. Notice that the standard arithmetic operators +, −, *, / have a dual function as set operators. (Sets will be discussed in Chapter 3.) Also, the not-equal operator may be either a # or <>, whichever you choose. As with Pascal, there is no exponentiation operator in Modula-2. (BASIC programmers note: The ^ is used in Modula-2 to reference pointer variables and is not comparable to the exponentiation operator in BASIC.)

As in Pascal, but unlike most other languages, the assignment operator is the character pair :=. Therefore, to assign the value 10 to the variable **COUNT**, you would write

```
COUNT:=10;
```

However, determining whether one value is equal to another requires the use of the single = sign. For example,

```
IF X=10 THEN WriteString('equal') END;
```

will print the message **equal** only if **X** is equal to 10.

Table 2-2. The Modula-2 Operators

Operator	Function
+	Addition or set union
−	Subtraction or set difference
*	Multiplication or set intersection
/	Division or symmetric set difference
DIV	Integer division
MOD	Modulus
:=	Assignment
AND	Logical AND
NOT	Logical NOT
&	Logical AND
=	Equal
<> or #	Not equal
<	Less than
>	Greater than
<=	Less than or equal
>=	Greater than or equal
^	Pointer operator
IN	Set member

Expressions

An expression is any valid combination of operators, variables, and constants. Like most other computer languages, all Modula-2 expressions must follow the rules of algebra. This means, for example, that

```
Z:=Y*/10;
```

is incorrect because the multiplication and division operators are adjacent to each other.

The order of evaluation in expressions is determined by the *precedence* of the operators and the existence of parentheses, if any. Where precedences are equal, evaluation is left to right. The precedence of the operators is shown in Figure 2-3.

Highest	NOT
	* / DIV MOD AND &
	+−OR
Lowest	= # <> < <= >= > IN

Figure 2-3. Operator precedence

For example, the expression

10*(6−2)

produces the value 40, not 58, because the parentheses override the higher precedence of the multiplication operator.

Simple Form Of the ***IF*** *Statement*

Although the **IF** statement will not be covered in complete detail until Chapter 4, it is so useful in presenting some of the concepts in Chapter 3 that its simplest form will be introduced here. The general form of the **IF** statement is

IF *<condition>* THEN *<statement>* END;

Here, *<condition>* must be a **BOOLEAN** expression—that is, **TRUE** or **FALSE**—and *<statement>* can be any valid Modula-2 statement. The **IF** works in Modula-2 just like it does in any other programming language—indeed, just as it does in English. For example,

IF 10<11 THEN WriteString("is less than") END;

will print the message **is less than** on the screen because 10 is, in fact, less than 11. On the other hand,

```
IF 10=11 THEN WriteString('is equal') END;
```

will print no message on the screen.

Comments

If you wish to place a comment in a Modula-2 program, you do so by enclosing the message between two symbols, (* and *), which are the comments symbols. For example, here is a correct comment.

```
BEGIN
(* this section finds the area of a circle *)
   area:=pi*radius*radius;
END;
```

Comments may not be inserted into the middle of reserved words, variable or procedure names, or operators, however. The following comment will cause a syntax error:

```
IF Z<100 TH(* this will not work*)EN WriteString('wrong') END;
```

Good comments add so much to the readability and, hence, the maintainability of a program that their importance cannot be overemphasized. However, poorly thought-out comments can clutter a program and lead to confusion. A good general practice is to use a comment that explains what is happening at the start of each section or routine. A line-by-line commentary generally should be avoided. A header comment at the start of your program is a good idea. For example, a **MODULE** header like

```
(*
Author: <your name>
Purpose: <what your program does>
Date last modified: <when did you last change it>
Comments: <any special information>
*)
```

is a good idea—especially when you are working on many different or large programs.

BEGIN, END, And Semicolons

Three elements appear again and again in Modula-2 programs: the reserved words **BEGIN** and **END**, and semicolons. The correct use of these is very important for both the logical correctness and the readability of your programs.

The words **BEGIN** and **END** are used to open and close the main block of code that forms a **MODULE**. However, many other statements use **END** without **BEGIN**. You have seen a few examples of the **IF** statement all terminated with **END**, even when there was only one statement. In general, many statements in Modula-2 can be used to begin a block of code, so **BEGIN** is not necessary. However, because a block of code has been started, **END** is needed for termination. (Pascal programmers: This differs from Pascal.) In essence, **END** is used to conclude a block of code.

Semicolons are used to separate statements. In a way, they are to a statement what **END** is to a block. The semicolon tells the compiler that the statement has ended. This is different than in languages like BASIC, FORTRAN, and COBOL, where the end of the line is used to terminate a statement. There are two main advantages to using a semicolon instead of the end of a line to signal the end of a statement. The first is that multiple statements may be placed on a single line. For example,

```
X:=10;  Y:=0;
```

is functionally identical to

```
X:=10;
Y:=0;
```

The second advantage is that long lines may be broken, eliminating annoying wraparound.

Technically, not all statements need to be terminated by a semicolon, because a syntactically correct reserved word can also end a statement. However, a semicolon can still be used, even if a reserved word follows. For example, both

```
IF X<10 THEN WriteString("less than"); END;
```

and

```
IF X<10 THEN WriteString("less than") END;
```

are valid and functionally equivalent. The reason you may use a semicolon after all statements is that Modula-2 allows *empty statements;* hence, in the first version the semicolon after **WriteString** simply implies an empty statement before the reserved word **END**.

Although Professor Wirth's own examples tend to reflect a very pure use of semicolons (as in the second version), most Modula-2 programmers tend to use a semicolon after every statement out of habit. In this book, both methods will be used, so that you will become accustomed to seeing them. In terms of the efficiency of the code produced, the two approaches are equivalent.

Libraries and ***IMPORT***

As stated earlier, a Modula-2 compiler comes with a set of libraries that contain many functions necessary to make the language useful. This introduces an important point about Modula-2: There are no built-in commands to do input/output (I/O) processing of any sort, including console and disk files; extended math functions, such as sine and cosine; screen handling routines; and string functions. Procedures for these and many other functions are found in the libraries supplied with the compiler. In short, without libraries, Modula-2 would not be a generally usable language. In essence, the Modula-2 language and its libraries have a symbiotic relationship—neither can truly exist without the other, yet they are distinct entities. For your programs to run, they need both the compiler and the libraries, as shown in Figure 2-4. This approach differs radically

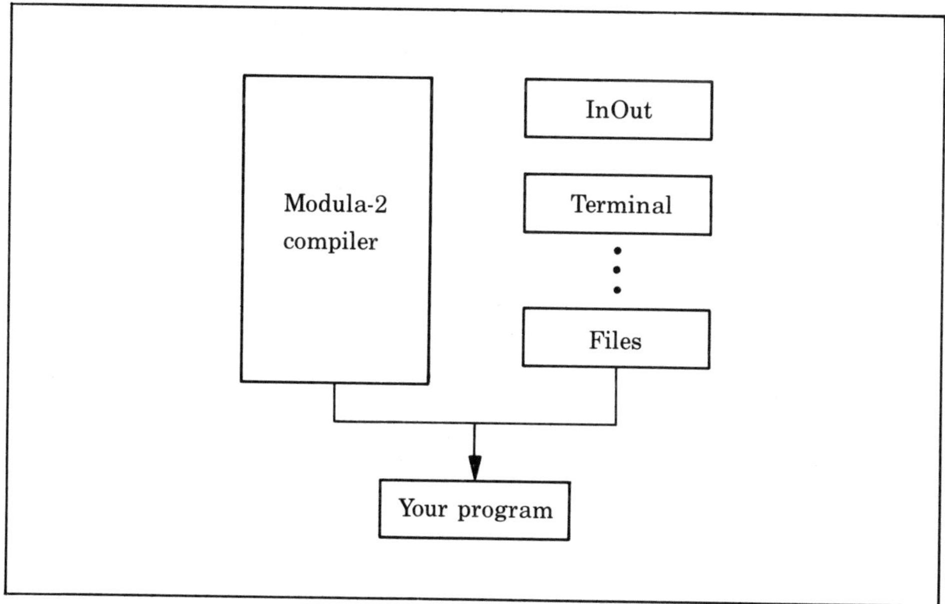

Figure 2-4. Modula-2 compiler with its libraries

from that of most other high-level computer languages (the major exception is C). For example, in BASIC, all necessary functions are actually part of the language and are inseparable from it; that is, you would never find a BASIC that did not include a PRINT command. Modula-2, on the other hand, has placed these types of operations into various libraries that can be linked to your program.

The names of the libraries and the names of the procedures they contain have, in part, been defined by Wirth, but there is nothing that stipulates that additional libraries, different names, or different procedures cannot be used. For any implementation of Modula-2 to be successful, however, it must follow Wirth's standard. Therefore, you should have at least the common Modula-2 libraries shown in Table 2-3. (Remember, some implementations may use slightly different names.)

You are probably asking yourself why Modula-2 is separated in this way. The answer lies in the two benefits this separation yields: portability and extensibility. Although a Modula-2 compiler, with its libraries, is a very complex bit of software, the compiler alone is fairly straightforward.

Table 2-3. Common Modula-2 Libraries

Library	Function
FileSystem	Disk file routines
InOut	High-level I/O
MathLib0	Extended math functions
NumberConversion	Convert among INTEGERs, CARDINALs, and strings
Processes	Support multiprocessing programs
RealConversion	Convert between REALs and strings
Storage	Dynamic allocation management
Strings	Various operations on strings
Terminal	Console I/O

This means that a new version can be written for a new computer system (or operating system) quickly. Because most of the libraries are written in Modula-2 (using some advanced, system-dependent features you will learn about later), the entire library system can then be modified and recompiled for the new environment. This process is *much faster* than writing the entire language in assembly code, for example.

The second reason many functions have been placed into libraries is to enable the language to be flexible. In fact, because Modula-2 supports—indeed encourages—separate compilation and linking, it is possible to extend the language through the creation of additional library functions. For example, an engineer working with CAD/CAM may have a specialized library of graphics functions, while an artificial intelligence researcher may have a speech synthesis library. Such flexibility cannot be achieved in languages like BASIC.

IMPORT

Before library procedures can be used by your program, they must be included with it. This inclusion is not completely automatic. You, as programmer, must specifically instruct the compiler to add the needed library procedures to your program by using the **IMPORT** *statement.* (This is not the only use of **IMPORT**, as you will soon see.) The general form of the **IMPORT** statement is

FROM <*library-name*> IMPORT <*list-of-procedures*>;

where <*library name*> is the name of the library that contains the procedures you wish to use in your program, and <*list-of-procedures*> is a comma-separated list of those procedures. For example, to **IMPORT** **ReadInt** and **WriteInt** from library **InOut**, you would write

```
FROM InOut IMPORT ReadInt, WriteInt;
```

There can be as many **IMPORT** statements as necessary in your program—unless your compiler sets some arbitrary limit.

In addition to procedures, it is also possible to import variables found in a library. Sometimes these variables are used to provide status information about the operation of various procedures found in that library.

Some Common Library Functions

Because the library functions are so important to the language and are needed by most examples in this book, a few of the most common ones will be discussed here. Others will be discussed throughout this book as they are needed.

You should keep in mind that several libraries and procedures are supplied with your compiler. Some of these will be, as described here, those defined by Wirth when he created Modula-2. However, you may also have several other libraries that are not discussed in this book. This is fine—there is nothing that says a Modula-2 compiler implementor cannot supply *extra* libraries and functions, just that those defined by Wirth must be supplied. You should explore your user's manual to see what "goodies" have been given to you.

WriteString The procedure is found in both the **InOut** and **Terminal** libraries. As stated before, capital and lowercase letters are treated differently by Modula-2; therefore, the exact spelling of both procedures and libraries is critical. As you know, a string is an array of characters.

For now, only string constants will be used. **WriteString** takes as its only argument a quoted string—either single or double quotation marks may be used. If single quotation marks are used, then double quotation marks may be used as part of the string. If double quotation marks delimit the string, then single quotation marks may be part of the string. The string cannot contain *both* single and double quotation marks. Here are some examples.

```
WriteString('Hi there. ')
WriteString("Pick up the ball. ");
WriteString("That's Joe's ball!");
```

These display

Hi there. Pick up the ball. That's Joe's ball!

Note that no carriage return, line-feed sequence is output by a **WriteString** call.

WriteLn **WriteLn** takes no arguments and is used simply to output a carriage return, line-feed sequence. Like **WriteString**, it can be found in both the **Terminal** and **InOut** libraries. For example, the sequence

```
WriteString('Hi there');
WriteLn;
WriteString("Tom.");
```

displays

Hi there
Tom.

Write **Write**, found in the **InOut** library, is used to write a single character to the screen.

WriteInt **WriteInt**, found in the **InOut** library, displays an integer value. The general form of the procedure is

WriteInt (*value, minimum-width*);

where **value** is the integer value and **minimum-width** is the minimum field width. The minimum field width specifies the least amount of space the output number will use, but more will be used if necessary. If the number is not large enough for the space specified, then leading blanks are supplied. Also, no carriage return, line-feed sequences are output. For example,

```
                           Displays
WriteInt(100,3)            |100|
WriteInt(100,4)            | 100|
WriteInt(100,2)            |100|
```

It is, of course, possible to use an **INTEGER** variable as an argument for **WriteInt**, as shown here.

```
X:=100*3;
WriteInt(X,5);
```

This will display **300** on the screen.

WriteCard **WriteCard**, found in the **InOut** library, is exactly like **WriteInt**, except that it is used only for **CARDINAL** numbers.

Read **Read**, found in the **InOut** library, is used to read a single character from the console. This character is not echoed automatically to the screen, however.

ReadInt **ReadInt**, found in the **InOut** library, reads an **INTEGER** value from the keyboard, echoing each digit as it is typed. For example, to read an **INTEGER** value into the variable **X**, you would write

```
ReadInt(X);
```

ReadCard **ReadCard**, found in the **InOut** library, is the same as **ReadInt**, except that it works with **CARDINAL** variables.

User-Defined ***PROCEDUREs***

As has been discussed, Modula-2 allows you to create subroutines—called **PROCEDUREs**—give them a name, and then use them in your program. This is one of the most important and powerful features of

Modula-2. A complete discussion of **PROCEDUREs** is deferred until Chapter 6, after you know more about the language.

Creating and Compiling A Program

Many Modula-2 compilers come with more than just the compiler and its libraries. For example, many have utility programs, such as debuggers and source file managers, to aid in the programming process. These make nice additions and are generally useful—and not really new. One utility you may have received with your compiler that is new is a *syntax-directed editor.* This is a special text editor specifically designed to help you write Modula-2 programs. Also, some implementations have a unique approach to the software development environment, while others are more standard. These innovations and differences will be briefly discussed here.

A Syntax-Directed Editor

A syntax-directed editor is simply a text editor that "knows" a computer language. Most Modula-2 compilers supply one, either as a standard feature or as an option. Although this utility may be quite new to you, it is the outgrowth of research done in the late 1970s that focused on programmer productivity.

There are really only three ways to increase programmer efficiency:

1. Reduce syntax errors (this shortens compile time and thus increases throughput).
2. Reduce program bugs (this shortens testing time).
3. Improve program design (this reduces the number of rewrite cycles).

Methods 2 and 3 fall more into the realm of art than science, making them difficult to effect, but approach 1 is a completely mechanistic process that, in theory, can be achieved simply by not making typing errors. Since excellent typing has never been a prerequisite for becoming a programmer, a different method was sought.

The answer is a syntax-directed editor designed for the language in which you are programming. With a syntax-directed editor, you can issue special commands that instruct the editor to prepare a skeleton for any specific statement. For example, control-I might be used to provide a skeleton for the **IF** statement, as shown here.

IF <*condition*>THEN<*statement*>END;
↑
Cursor positioned here

In this case, the entire statement is roughed in, the cursor is positioned at the first character position of the conditional test, and you are prompted by the message <**condition**>. When you begin to type, the prompt disappears, and your text takes over. Once the condition is entered, you then move to the <**statement**> prompt and fill it in. Each syntax-directed editor performs slightly differently, however, and this is just an example.

The main advantage of this method is that much of the typing is done for you, so you avoid the normal misspellings and forgotten semicolons. A side benefit is that the uppercase, reserved words are filled in for you. (After all, no programmer likes using the shift key!)

If you do not have a syntax-directed editor or choose not to use one, this is fine; simply enter the programs using your favorite text editor. However, if you are going to do a lot of Modula-2 programming, a syntax-directed editor is definitely worth considering.

Compiling Your Program: Batch Files

The Modula-2 compilers currently available use two general methods to compile a program once it is written. The first method uses a batch file to invoke the compiler and then the linker. This is the standard method used by most language compilers. Some Modula-2 systems come with a complete development environment, which allows you to edit, compile, link, and run programs simply by selecting options from pop-up menus. With this second approach, you never leave the programming environment, and many systems allow multiple windows, concurrent compiles, and other time-saving features. Both approaches have their merits.

If you simply have a compiler and a linker, then you will want to use a *batch file* to help compile your programs. A batch file is a series of automated commands that you can create. Your operating system manual will contain a full explanation. The following batch file is approximately what you will need to compile your program using PC-DOS (or MS-DOS):

```
Modula %1
link %1
```

To use this file, you would simply type the name of the batch file followed by the name of your program on the command line of the operating system. Then your program would automatically be compiled and linked for you. To be certain you are using the correct procedures for compilation, consult your compiler manual.

In the integrated software development environment, you use menus to issue instructions to compile, link, edit, and run programs. The development system will help you along and often will even answer questions about Modula-2 and about the environment itself. The exact method of operation will be explained in your user's manual.

Neither the more traditional compilation method nor the integrated development environment is a clear winner in terms of ease of use. If you have programmed for years, then the more traditional approach may be easier for you because it is familiar. However, if you are willing to invest the time to learn to use a complete development system, then the fully integrated method may provide better throughput. The only qualifier is that if you don't like the "personality" of the integrated system, then you may find yourself fighting it more than working with it. It is a good idea to try out a system prior to purchasing it if you have any doubts about whether this approach is right for you.

What the Compiler and Linker Do

The Modula-2 compiler converts your source code into *relocatable object code.* Relocatable object code is very similar to machine code (the actual instructions executed by the computer) with one major exception: It has no fixed addresses. The reason for this is that the code for the library procedures used by your program have not yet been included, so the compiler has no way of knowing where in memory they will be located. Hence, all the addresses are stored as either offsets or unknowns.

When the linker is executed, it combines the object code of your program with the object code of the necessary library routines and fixes the addresses. Once this is done, the linker writes the entire, executable program to a disk file. As mentioned earlier, Modula-2 also allows you to break your program into pieces and compile each one separately. It is the linker that combines the pieces of your program.

General Form of a Modula-2 Program

Now that you know some of the fundamentals about Modula-2, it is time to learn the general form of a Modula-2 program. All Modula-2 programs take the form shown in Figure 2-5.

All programs begin with the keyword **MODULE**, followed by the **MODULE** name and a semicolon. This constitutes the *MODULE header.* Next follows the *declaration section,* where you declare and define various elements used in your program. All of the entries in the section are optional and can be left out. The *import list* (**IMPORT**) tells the compiler to include the specified procedures with your program. These external procedures are found either in the standard libraries provided by your compiler or in other **MODULE**s that you create. For now, you will only be

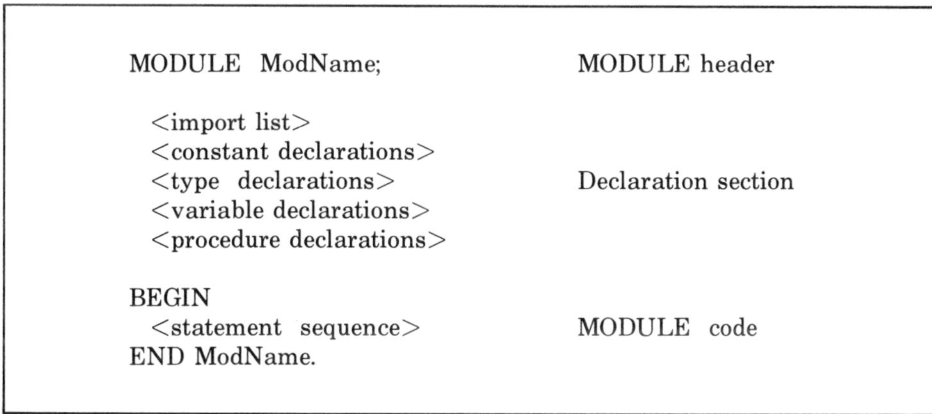
MODULE ModName;
MODULE header
<import list>
<constant declarations>
<type declarations>
Declaration section
<variable declarations>
<procedure declarations>
BEGIN
<statement sequence>
MODULE code
END ModName.

Figure 2-5. Format of a Modula-2 program

concerned with **IMPORT**ing procedures from the standard libraries. *Constant declarations* (**CONST**) are used to assign names to constants. The *type declarations* (**TYPE**) allow you to create custom data types. The *variable declaration* section is where variables are declared prior to use. Remember: In Modula-2, you must declare all variables before they are used. The *procedure declaration* (**PROCEDURE**) section is where subroutines that your program will use are defined. The keyword **BEGIN** signals the start of the **MODULE** code section, where the main **MODULE** program statements are located. It is this code that is executed when you run a program. The last line, which concludes the program, ends with a period.

At this point, a question is commonly asked: "Why are programs called **MODULE**s instead of PROGRAMs?" The answer is that, in Modula-2, a program is defined as *one or more **MODULE**s*. Therefore, a program can be simply one **MODULE**, or it can be several combined. The **MODULE** that is described here is commonly called the *program **MODULE***. You will learn later that there are two other types of **MODULE**s, but for the first part of this book, only program **MODULE**s will be discussed.

An Example

Now that you have the necessary background information, it is time to look at a real program. The program shown here will first print the message **Enter a number** on the screen. It will then accept an integer entered from the keyboard and display its square.

```
MODULE  SquareInteger  ;                        <---- MODULE header

   FROM InOut IMPORT ReadInt,WriteInt,          <---- IMPORT list
      WriteString, WriteLn;

   VAR                                          <---- Variable
      I:INTEGER;                                      declarations

BEGIN                                           }
   WriteString('Enter a number ');              }
   ReadInt(I);                                  }
   WriteLn;  (* blank line *)                   } <---- MODULE code
   WriteInt(I*I,5);                             }
END SquareInteger.                              }
```

As you can see, the program is called **SquareInteger**, and it **IMPORTs** four procedures from the **InOut** library: **ReadInt**, **WriteInt**, **WriteString**, and **WriteLn**. There are no constant or **TYPE** definitions. **I** is declared to be an **INTEGER** variable. The main code uses **WriteString** to print the prompt message on the screen and **ReadInt** to accept an **INTEGER** entered from the keyboard. After the number has been entered, the cursor is still on the same line, one space after the last digit of the number entered, so a call to procedure **WriteLn** is made to cause a carriage return, line-feed sequence to be sent. Finally, the square of the number is output with a minimum field width of 5 using **WriteInt**.

As a point of interest, because there is no range checking in the program, it is possible to generate a run-time error by entering a number whose square is greater than the largest integer allowed by the system. For most 16-bit computers this will be 32,767. In this case, the standard procedure, **WriteInt**, cannot output the number because it is not technically an integer.

Indentation Conventions

There is a rhyme and a reason to the indentation of Modula-2 program statements. The reason is very simple: It makes the logic of your programs *much more readable.* But to do this, the indentation must follow a fixed form—the rhyme. In essence, each new block is indented one level, and this indentation level stays in effect until an **END** is reached. Each **END** causes the indentation to be moved in one level. An exception to this occurs in the declaration section of a **MODULE**; here, each section starts one level in from the **MODULE** header. This indentation scheme will seem natural to you before you proceed very far in this book, because every example in this book is properly indented.

There is a storm raging over how many spaces should constitute an indentation level. Some programmers think two spaces are enough, and others want three or more. You can use as many spaces as you choose.

*A Program With an **IF** Statement*

The following program uses a simple form of the **IF** statement:

```
MODULE  TestInteger  ;
   FROM InOut IMPORT ReadInt,
      WriteString, WriteLn;

   VAR
      I:INTEGER;
```

```
BEGIN
   WriteString('Enter a number ');
   ReadInt(I);
   WriteLn;   (* blank line *)
   IF I<10 THEN WriteString('I less than 10') END;
END TestInteger.
```

Much of this program is the same as the **SquareInteger** program shown before. The major difference is the inclusion of the **IF** statement. In this case, if the number entered from the keyboard is less than 10, then the message **I less than 10** will be displayed on the screen; otherwise, no further action is taken.

If you feel comfortable with these two examples, then it is time for you to proceed with the rest of this book.

EXERCISES

1. What are the six elementary data types found in Modula-2?
2. What does the following line of code do?

```
WriteString("Let's go to Joe's!");
```

3. Which of the following are valid Modula-2 variable names?

a. First_Time	b. count
c. EmpHireDate	d. X123
e. Big$ForMe	f. RedDelicious

4. Given the following variable declarations

```
VAR
   ch:CHAR;
   I:INTEGER;
```

is the following statement valid?

```
ch:=I;
```

5. What is the difference between **DIV** and /?

6. What do the compiler and the linker do?

7. Write a short program that enters two **CARDINAL** numbers and tells whether they are equal.

ANSWERS

1. BOOLEAN, CHAR, CARDINAL, INTEGER, REAL, BITSET.

2. It prints the message **Let's go to Joe's** on the screen.

3. B,C,D,F

4. The assignment is not valid because **ch** and **I** are not of the same type.

5. **DIV** is used when dividing **INTEGER**s or **CARDINAL**s, whereas the normal division sign, /, is used when dividing **REAL**s.

6. The compiler converts source code into relocatable object code. The linker adds in any library or separately compiled procedures that a program uses and creates an executable file.

7.
```
MODULE  TestIntegers  ;
   FROM InOut IMPORT ReadInt,
      WriteString, WriteLn;

   VAR
      I,J:INTEGER;

BEGIN
   WriteString('Enter first number ');
   ReadInt(I);
   WriteLn;  (* blank line *)
   WriteString('Enter second number ');
   ReadInt(J);
   WriteLn;  (* blank line *)
   IF I=J THEN WriteString('The numbers are equal') END;
END TestIntegers.
```

Variables, Constants, Operators, and Expressions

CHAPTER 3

Variables and constants are manipulated by operators to form expressions. This is the basis of all programming and the subject of this chapter.

Data Types

As you learned in Chapter 2, all variables in Modula-2 must be declared prior to use. Explicit in the declaration is a variable's *type*—that is, what kind of data it is capable of holding. There are six elementary data types found in Modula-2, as shown in Table 3-1. These types are built into the Modula-2 compiler and may be used freely when needed. It is also possible for you to define custom data types, but a discussion of this is deferred

Table 3-1. Modula-2 Elementary Data Types and Ranges

Data type	Range (assuming 16-bit word size)
BOOLEAN	TRUE or FALSE
CHAR	ASCII character set
CARDINAL	0 through 65535
INTEGER	−32768 through 32767
REAL	Varies with implementation
BITSET	0 through 15

until Chapter 5. A variable's type determines what it can be used for; therefore, we will begin with a discussion of the six elementary types.

BOOLEAN Data Type

A **BOOLEAN** value is either **TRUE** or **FALSE**. **BOOLEAN** values are used both for loop control and for conditional statements, such as the **IF/THEN**. In most implementations, a byte is used to store a **BOOLEAN** value.

CHAR Data Type

CHAR data may consist only of ASCII characters. However, some implementations allow any 8-bit value to be represented by type **CHAR**, thus enabling its use with special graphics characters and extended keysets, such as Chinese. Each **CHAR** data is one byte long.

CARDINAL Data Type

CARDINAL values are positive whole numbers—decimals are not included. The range of **CARDINAL** values normally is 0 through the largest number that can be represented by one word (two bytes). In 16-bit systems this normally is 0 through 65,535; however, you should check your user's manual. A **CARDINAL** value requires a word for storage.

INTEGER Data Type

INTEGERs are positive and negative whole numbers—decimals are not included. The range of an **INTEGER** is determined by the word size of the computer. For most 16-bit implementations, an **INTEGER**'s range is −32,768 through 32,767. Like the **CARDINAL** type, the **INTEGER** type uses one word for storage.

REAL Data Type

A **REAL** value is a floating-point number. Values of this type can have decimal parts and may be either positive or negative. The actual range and precision vary with each implementation, so check your user's manual. Storage for **REAL**s also varies, but a safe guess is eight bytes.

BITSET Data Type

A **BITSET** value may be between 0 and N−1, where N is the number of bits in a word. For 16-bit systems, N is 16; hence, the range is 0 through 15. **BITSET** data requires one word for storage.

Variables

As you probably know, a variable is simply a named location in the memory of the computer, known to your program, that is used to hold different values as your program is executed. In Modula-2 all variable names must begin with a letter, which is followed by letters or digits. No special characters are allowed. This means that underscores and other punctuation marks may not be used as part of a variable name. The maximum length of a variable name is determined by the actual compiler, but eight characters is a safe bet.

All variables must be declared before they are used. If you fail to do this, an error message will be displayed during compilation, and your program will not compile. Variables are declared in the variable declaration section of your program. This section is signaled by the reserved word **VAR**. The general form of variable declaration is

```
VAR
        <variable-list> : <type>;
```

where ***<variable-list>*** is a comma-separated list of variable names, and ***<type>***) is a valid Modula-2 type. For example, the following code fragment declares variables of each of the elementary types.

```
VAR

    count, limit  : INTEGER;
    DollarValue   : REAL;
    done          : BOOLEAN;
    i,j,k         : CARDINAL;
    Indexer       : BITSET;
    ch            : CHAR;
```

Notice that commas are not needed when only one variable of a type is being declared.

Why Are There Different Variable Types?

At this point, beginning Modula-2 programmers often ask the following question: Why are there so many different types of variables? If your previous experience has been with a langauge like BASIC that has only two (sometimes three) data types, you may not see the benefit of having more than these. The answer to the question is efficiency and flexibility. Let's see why.

First, variables play many different roles in a program. Consider an accounting program. Some variables hold financial information and thus require floating-point (**REAL**) variables. Other variables may be used only to control a loop, in which case it makes no sense to use a floating-point variable, which is about eight bytes long, to do the job that an **INTEGER** could do with just two bytes. Also, any arithmetic done with an **INTEGER** will be *much faster* than that done using a **REAL**.

Okay, you may say, but what about **CARDINAL**s? Why are they needed? First, occasionally it is helpful to have an integer value that is as large as can be supported by the word size of the computer. As you become more skilled at Modula-2 programming, you will see why. Second, many computers perform arithmetic faster on purely positive integers than they do on numbers that can also be negative. (Technically, this results from the difference between *signed* and *unsigned* arithmetic. For further information, the interested reader is directed to any of a number of good books about assembly language programming.)

The remaining types, **BOOLEAN, CHAR,** and **BITSET**, exist to fulfill their specific roles. The **BOOLEAN** type is used to hold **TRUE/FALSE** information, and it greatly simplifies your programs. **CHAR** is used to hold single-byte characters, and **BITSET** eases the problems of interfacing with special devices and other system-related tasks.

Another way to answer the original question is that Modula-2 gives you, the programmer, the basic construction materials to build highly efficient programs with minimal effort and frustration.

Arrays

Although arrays are covered in greater detail in Chapter 10, basic information about them will be discussed now, because arrays are used to form string variables. An *array* is a set of data elements of like type grouped together under one name. Each element is accessed via an *index*. In Modula-2 all arrays have a fixed size, which is specified at the time the array is declared. The actual starting and ending indexes for the array, or the array *bounds,* as they are called, are part of the declaration. Arrays of any valid data types may be used. Arrays, being variables, are declared in the variable declaration section. The general form of a single-dimension array declaration is

```
VAR
    <array-name> : ARRAY [<start> . . <end>] OF <type>;
```

where **<*array-name*>** is a comma-separated list of array names, and **<*type*>** is any valid Modula-2 variable type. The boundaries of the array, which define the array's length, are placed within square brackets, with two periods separating the *start* and *end* values. Hence, **<*start*>** is the lowest element in the array, and **<*end*>** is the highest.

Arrays need not start at 0 or 1, but may start wherever you like, according to the needs of your program. For example, the following code fragment declares a **CHAR** array, called **StudentsGrades**, with thirty elements.

```
VAR
    StudentsGrades: ARRAY [1..30] OF CHAR;
```

This means that array **StudentsGrades** has thirty elements, with the first element indexed at 1 and the last at 30.

When an array is indexed, a specific element is referenced. The number of the desired element is placed within square brackets directly after the array name. For example, to assign student 3 a grade of B, the following statement is used.

```
StudentsGrades[3] := 'B';
```

Further, to display the grade for student 17, you could write

```
Write(StudentsGrades[17]);
```

The array **StudentsGrades** would appear in memory as 30 contiguous bytes of memory. Figure 3-1 shows how this would appear if the array started at location 2000.

The character array is one of the most important arrays because it is used to hold strings. The lowest index of all character arrays used to hold strings must start at 0, and the largest index must be at least one less than the length of the largest string that it is intended to hold. For example,

```
VAR
    Message : ARRAY [0..79] OF CHAR;
```

declares an array called **Message** that can hold a string of up to 80 characters.

A character array can be assigned strings several different ways. First,

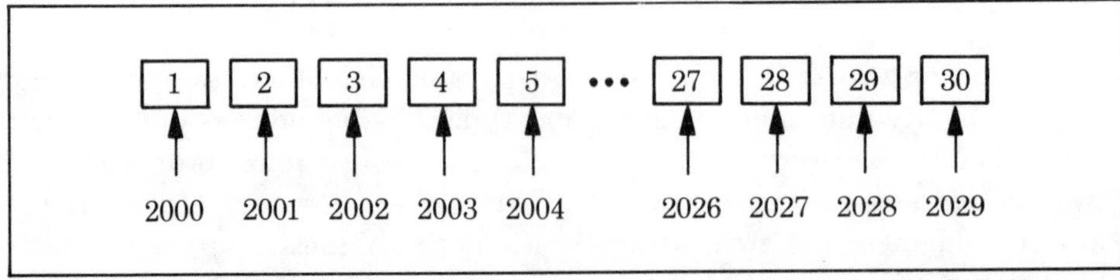

Figure 3-1. Array of **StudentsGrades** in memory, starting at 2000

you can manually enter each string character using individual assignment statements—this way is not recommended. Second, you can assign the entire string all at once. For example, to assign the array **Message** the string "this is a test," you would write

```
Message := "this is a test";
```

The array **Message** now contains the string with location 0 holding a "t," location 1 holding an "h," and location 13 holding the final "t" in **test**.

A string array can be used with any of the standard string procedures, such as **WriteString**. For example,

```
WriteString(Message);
```

will print *"this is a test"* on the screen.

Another standard procedure, found in the Modula-2 library **InOut**, is **ReadString**, and it is used to read a string of characters entered from the keyboard into a character array variable. (Remember, the character array variable must have a lower bound of zero.) Each character is echoed as it is typed, and input is terminated by striking any character that is less than or equal to a space in the ASCII code, including carriage returns, tabs, and control characters. However, because this tends to limit the application of the function, some implementations terminate input only when a carriage return is struck (this is similar to BASIC and most other languages), so you should check your user's manual. The following program will read and write a string from and to the console.

```
MODULE ReadWrite ;

  FROM InOut IMPORT ReadString, WriteString, WriteLn;

  VAR
     Message : ARRAY [0..79] OF CHAR;

BEGIN
   ReadString(Message);
   WriteLn;
   WriteString(Message);
END ReadWrite.
```

Constants

As you saw in Chapter 2, a constant is a fixed value—that is, it remains unchanged throughout the life of a program. There can be constants of each elementary data type. Also, string constants, which simply are character arrays that follow a few special rules, are supported.

Constants can be represented in your program in two ways. The first way is to use the constant value each time it is needed. The second way is to give the constant a name and then use that name each time the constant value is required.

Like variables, constants are of different types, and Modula-2 enforces its type-checking rules on them. Table 3-2 shows examples of constants of each of the elementary data types as well as of strings. Let's look at each in turn.

BOOLEAN constants may have only the values *true* and *false* and are represented by the reserved words **TRUE** and **FALSE**.

Constants of type **CHAR** can have any ASCII character value. A **CHAR** constant is, therefore, any single character enclosed by either single or double quotation marks.

INTEGER and **CARDINAL** constants are virtually the same with the exception that **CARDINALs** may not be negative. These constants can have no fractional part, and they cannot contain a decimal point.

REAL constants must contain a decimal point. It is the decimal point that tells the compiler that a floating-point number, rather than an **INTEGER**, is being used. There are two ways to represent floating-point constants: by using standard notation and by using scientific notation. When using standard notation, you must remember that a decimal point must be used even for whole numbers. For instance, when the value 10 is

Table 3-2. Examples of Constants

Type	**Examples**
BOOLEAN	TRUE FALSE
CHAR	'A' 'B' 'C'
INTEGER	10 1 −123 32546
CARDINAL	10 1 56342 19
REAL	10.0 1.20E3 1.123E−3 1.1234
BITSET	0 3 13 8
string	"Hello" 'She said, "Hi Jake"'

used as a **REAL** constant, it must be written as 10.0. In scientific notation, a scale factor is added by placing an **E** directly after the number and following this letter with the number of decimal places that the decimal point is to be shifted. A positive scale factor shifts the decimal point to the right (makes the number larger), and a negative factor shifts the decimal point to the left (makes the number smaller). For example, the following pairs of numbers are the same.

10.0	1.0E1
0.1	1.0E−1
121.23	1.2123E2

Constants of type **BITSET** use the values 0 through N−1, where N generally is the word size for the computer.

String constants are defined as ASCII characters enclosed between either single or double quotation marks. If single quotation marks are used to delimit the string, then double quotation marks may be used as part of the string, and vice versa.

To use a constant directly in your program, you simply use its value. For example, in this expression

```
X:=-10 DIV 3;
```

−10 is an **INTEGER** constant because it is a whole number that is negative, and although by itself **3** could be either an **INTEGER** or a **CARDINAL**, it must be an **INTEGER** here because Modula-2 does not allow different data types to be mixed in the same expression.

If **TEST** is a **BOOLEAN** variable, then

```
IF TEST = TRUE THEN WriteString("is true") END;
```

is a valid form of the **IF** statement.

Instead of using the actual constant value each time it is needed in your program, you may give each constant a name and then use these names when constants are needed. The main advantage to this method is in large programs, where the same constant value is used in several places, because each constant can easily be altered throughout the entire program simply by changing its definition. Secondarily, by giving each constant a name, the readability of your program is improved, because it is clear what each constant stands for.

A constant is declared in a program in the constant declaration section, with the following general form.

```
CONST
    <constant-name> = <value>;
```

Here, <***constant-name***> is the name of the constant, and ***value*** is the constant's fixed value. Constant names must follow the same rules as variable names.

For example, to declare three constants to represent the dimensions of a house, you could write

```
CONST
    Length=100;
    Width=23;
    Height=12;
```

Here, these constants may be assumed to be either **INTEGER**s or **CARDINAL**s. To use them in an expression, you substitute the name for the actual value. For example, assuming that **Volume** is an **INTEGER** variable, here is a valid expression.

```
Volume := Length * Height * Width;
```

It is possible to represent constants in octal or hexadecimal instead of decimal form. An octal number is followed by a B and a hexadecimal number is followed by an H. In octal format, only the digits 0 through 7 are used, while in hexadecimal format, the digits 0 through 9 plus the letters A through F are needed. For example, the number 10 in octal and hexadecimal formats is

12B   0AH

As illustrated in this example, a hexadecimal constant must not start with a letter, so a leading zero is added.

Operators

Modula-2 supports a rich variety of operators. These operators can be divided into the following six classes:

- Arithmetic operators
- Relational operators
- Logical operators
- Set operators
- Pointer operators
- Assignment operators.

Table 3-3 shows the operators in each category. A discussion of the set operators is deferred until Chapter 5. The pointer operator is explored in detail in Chapter 9. The arithmetic, relational, logical, and assignment operators are examined here.

Arithmetic Operators

The basic operations of +, −, *, and / are, no doubt, familiar to you. These operators work in Modula-2 the same way they do in all other computer languages. However, because Modula-2 is a strongly typed language, two division operators are provided—one for **REAL** operands and the other for **CARDINAL** or **INTEGER** operands. Two operators are needed because a floating-point division may have a fractional component (that is, digits to the right of the decimal point), whereas integer division can produce only whole-number results—any remainder is discarded. Therefore, in Modula-2 the standard division sign, /, is used only with operands of type **REAL**, and the reserved word **DIV** is used with operands of type **INTEGER** or **CARDINAL**.

To better understand integer division, consider this example:

```
10 DIV 3
=3  (with a remainder of 1)
```

Keep in mind that integer operations can only produce integer results. This means that 10 DIV 3 cannot produce the answer 3.33333... because an integer value must be a whole number. Therefore, the "correct" answer is, instead, the whole number 3, with no fractional part. (If this is a new concept to you, think about distributing 10 ice cream cones among three hungry Boy Scouts. Each will get 3 cones, and 1 cone will be left over—it can't be divided. Of course, perhaps you could eat it!)

Table 3-3. Modula-2 Operators

Arithmetic	**Function**
+	Addition
−	Subtraction
*	Multiplication
/	Division
DIV	Integer division
MOD	Modulus
Relational	**Function**
=	Equal
<> or #	Not equal
<	Less than
>	Greater than
<=	Less than or equal
>=	Greater than or equal
Logical	**Function**
AND	Logical AND
NOT	Logical NOT
OR	Logical OR
Set	**Function**
+	Addition or set union
−	Subtraction or set difference
*	Multiplication or set intersection
/	Division or symmetric set difference
IN	Set member
=	Set equality
<> or #	Set inequality
<=	Is subset
>=	Is superset
Pointer	**Function**
^	Dereferencing
Assignment	**Function**
:=	Assigns value to variable

The short program shown here performs both real and integer division and displays the results on the screen. Notice that the library **RealInOut** is introduced. It contains the procedures necessary to read and write floating-point values to and from the console. The program uses **WriteReal** to display the outcome of the division. The second argument is the minimum field width.

```
MODULE Division ;

  FROM InOut IMPORT WriteInt, WriteLn;
  FROM  RealInOut IMPORT WriteReal;

  VAR
     A,B,C: REAL;
     X,Y,Z: INTEGER;

BEGIN
   A:=10.0;
   B:=3.0;
   C:=A/B;   (* real division *)
   WriteReal(C,6);
   WriteLn;
   X:=10;
   Y:=3;
   Z:=10 DIV 3;    (* integer division *)
   WriteInt(Z,5);
END Division.
```

The **MOD** operator is used to produce the remainder for an integer division. Therefore, continuing the previous example,

10 MOD 3
=1

because 3 goes into 10 three times, with 1 left over. Stated algebraically,

if	X=Y DIV Z
and if	R=Y MOD Z
then	Y=(Z*X)+R

For example,

2=11 DIV 4
3=11 MOD 4

Therefore,

(2*4)+3=11

Here are some more examples.

5 DIV 2=2	5 MOD 2=1
20 DIV 5=4	20 MOD 5=0
19 DIV 5=3	19 MOD 5=4

Remember that **MOD** can only be used with integer values; that is, variables or constants of types **CARDINAL** or **INTEGER**. Both algebraically and in Modula-2, **MOD** is not defined for **REAL** numbers. The short program shown here prints the integer division and remainder on the screen.

```
MODULE ModDiv ;

  FROM InOut IMPORT WriteInt, WriteLn;

  VAR
     X,Y,Z: INTEGER;

BEGIN
   X:=10;
   Y:=3;
   Z:=10 DIV 3;    (* integer division *)
   WriteInt(Z,5);
   WriteLn;
   Z:=10 MOD 3;    (* get remainder *)
   WriteInt(Z,5);
END ModDiv.
```

The *unary minus* is used to reverse the sign of a number. It can be applied to both variables and constants. For example, if **A** is initially equal to 5, then **−A** has the value −5. When using the unary minus in conjunction with other operators, you must use parentheses to avoid having two operators in a row. For example,

X/−Y

is invalid, and should be written as

X/(−Y)

Relational Operators

Relational operators are used to compare one value with another and produce a **BOOLEAN** (**TRUE/FALSE**) result. In essence, they determine what relationship two values have to each other. For example,

10=10 is TRUE
10<10 is FALSE
10<9 is TRUE
10< >9 is TRUE
19<=10 is FALSE

Either operand may be a variable, a constant, or an expression and may involve any of the elementary data types. However, both operands must be of the same type. (In Modula-2 you really can't compare apples to oranges!)

As stated, the result produced using a relational operator is a value of type **BOOLEAN**; therefore, a relational expression can be used whenever a **BOOLEAN** type is required. For example, the following code fragment is perfectly valid.

```
VAR
   B: BOOLEAN;
   X: INTEGER;

BEGIN
   ReadInt(X);
   B:=X<100;
   .
   .
   .
```

As you can see, even though **X** and **100** are not of type **BOOLEAN**, the actual outcome of the operation is and can be assigned to the **BOOLEAN** variable **B**.

The relational operators frequently are used in conjunction with the **IF** statement. In this short program, the number entered from the console is checked for zero before it is used to divide the constant 100.

```
MODULE RelExample ;

  FROM InOut IMPORT ReadInt, WriteLn, WriteInt;

  VAR
     X: INTEGER;

BEGIN
   ReadInt(X);
   IF X<>0 THEN WriteInt(100 DIV X,5);  END;
END RelExample.
```

Logical Operators

Logical operators are used to combine two **BOOLEAN** expressions or values and produce a **BOOLEAN** result. Because of this, they are frequently used in conjunction with relational operators. Each logical operator works in a specific way, following the rules of formal logic. The most common method of illustrating how each operator works is to use a *truth table*—a table that shows the outcome of all possible combinations of **TRUE** and **FALSE** operands.

The **AND** operator behaves as shown here by its truth table.

AND	TRUE	FALSE
TRUE	TRUE	FALSE
FALSE	FALSE	FALSE

As you can see, the outcome of an **AND** operation is true *if and only if* both operands are **TRUE**; otherwise, the operation is **FALSE**. This is exactly the way "and" works in its normal English language usage.

The truth table shown here describes the **OR** operator.

OR	TRUE	FALSE
TRUE	TRUE	TRUE
FALSE	TRUE	FALSE

Like **AND**, **OR** works just as it does in the English language. If either or both of the operands is **TRUE**, then the entire expression is **TRUE**; otherwise, it is **FALSE**.

The **NOT** operator simply reverses the value of whatever it precedes. It is called a *unary* operator because it only needs one operand. Its truth table is as follows:

NOT	TRUE	FALSE
	FALSE	TRUE

Some examples are shown here, with T standing for **TRUE** and F for **FALSE**.

T AND T is TRUE
T AND F is FALSE
T OR F is TRUE
NOT T is FALSE

A series of operations can be strung together to produce more complex logical operations. To do this, however, requires the use of parentheses to enclose each discrete operation. For example,

(F AND T) OR (NOT F) is TRUE

and

F AND (F OR (NOT F)) is FALSE

The ability to combine logical operations allows another common logical operation to be created, even though there is no built-in Modula-2 operator for it. This operation is the *exclusive-OR* operation, and it is **TRUE** if and only if exactly one of the operands is **TRUE**. If we denote the exclusive-OR operation as **XOR**, then its truth table is as follows:

XOR	TRUE	FALSE
TRUE	FALSE	TRUE
FALSE	TRUE	FALSE

It is unclear why Professor Wirth did not include this operator in Modula-2, because it is very useful in many systems programs, but you can easily construct it using the other operators, as shown here, with the traditional variables P and Q from formal logic.

(P OR Q) AND (NOT(P AND Q))

For example, imagine the intersection of two one-way streets with traffic lights. Instead of using the standard time-delay method, the traffic light's operation is based on sensing switches located on the roads. The situation is shown here, with S1 and S2 being the sensors, and L1 and L2 being the lights.

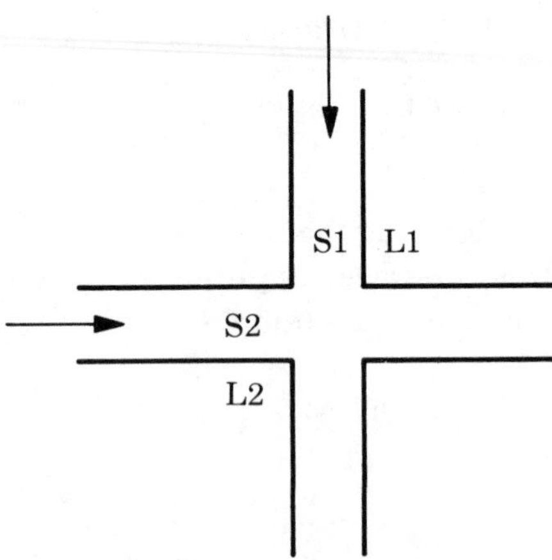

The basic method of operation is as follows. When no cars are present, lights L1 and L2 both are set to RED. If S1 is activated (turned on), then L1 is set to GREEN, and cars are allowed to pass. If S2 is activated, then L2 is set to GREEN, and cars are allowed to pass. However, if S1 and S2 both are activated, then L1 is set to GREEN first, and L2 is left on RED so that cars do not collide in the middle of the intersection. This situation represents the exclusive-OR logical operation: one light or the other can be GREEN, but both lights cannot be GREEN at the same time. The following program fragment shows how this situation could be programmed using a constructed XOR operation.

```
S1:=ReadSignal1;
S2:=ReadSignal2;
IF (S1 OR S2) AND (NOT (S1 AND S2)) THEN DoLights; END;
```

Let's look at another logical operation not found in Modula-2. In formal logic there is an operation called *implication*. Its operation is reflected in our normal English language usage of the term; for example, X<10 *implies* X<11. If we let IMP stand for implication, then its truth table is as follows:

IMP	TRUE	FALSE
TRUE	TRUE	FALSE
FALSE	TRUE	TRUE

At first thought, it might seem hard to justify how a **FALSE** premise can produce a **TRUE** implication; however, in formal logic it can. Once again using P and Q, it is possible to construct the IMP operation using the Modula-2 built-in logical operators, as shown here.

NOT (P AND (NOT Q))

You can use this to create a short program that will tell you if an implication is **TRUE** or not, as shown here.

```
MODULE IMP ;
   (* this program uses the built-in logical operators
      to construct an IMP operation. *)

   FROM InOut IMPORT Read, WriteString, WriteLn;

   VAR
      P,Q: BOOLEAN;
      ch: CHAR;

BEGIN
   P:=FALSE;
   Q:=FALSE;  (*initialize*)
   WriteString("Is Premise TRUE? (Y/N)");
   Read(ch);  WriteLn;
   IF ch='Y' THEN P:=TRUE  END;
   WriteString("Is consequent TRUE? (Y/N)");
   Read(ch); WriteLn;
   IF ch='Y' THEN Q:=TRUE  END;

   IF NOT (P AND (NOT Q)) THEN
      WriteString('Implication is TRUE');
   END;

END IMP.
```

Sometimes programmers, novice or experienced, create overly complex logical expressions because they don't know how to simplify them. Although there are books written on the subject of logic and its laws, there is a very important rule, called de Morgan's Law, after its inventor, that can be used to transform certain logical expressions into simpler ones. Once again using P and Q, de Morgan's law is as follows:

(NOT P) AND (NOT Q) <=> NOT (P OR Q)

and

(NOT P) OR (NOT Q) <=> NOT (P AND Q)

where <=> means equivalent. Not only will using simple logical expressions make your programs run faster, but it will make their logic easier to follow.

Assignment Operators

The assignment operation is used to assign a value to a variable. As you know already, the assignment operator in Modula-2 is :=. Because its use is so fundamental to all programming—and so intuitive—it is often taken for granted that this operator is fully understood. Two points will be emphasized here.

First, the variable being assigned a value must have the same type as the value, or expression, on the right side. For example, here is an invalid assignment.

```
VAR
   X,Y: INTEGER;
   R: REAL;

  .
  .
  .
   R:=X*Y;    (*invalid assignment*)
```

Here, **R** is a **REAL** variable, yet the expression on the right produces an **INTEGER** result. In Modula-2 there is no automatic type conversion.

Second, the left side of the assignment must be a variable. Sometimes beginning Modula-2 programmers think that the assignment operator can also be used to assign a named constant a value, but this is not true. For example, this is an incorrect use of assignment:

```
CONST
   COUNT = 100;
  .
  .
  .
   COUNT:=200;  (* this will not work! *)
```

Remember, a constant's value is fixed throughout the life of the program and cannot be altered.

Expressions

Until now, we have been using expressions without explanation. In Modula-2, an expression is any valid combination of constants, variables, and operators (and later procedure calls will be added). Of course, the question that naturally arises is "what is a valid combination?" Here you will learn the rules that govern Modula-2 expressions.

Algebraic Correctness

First and foremost, expressions in Modula-2 must be algebraically correct. That is, operators and operands must be properly organized. Some improper examples are shown here.

Improper expression	Reason
10 +/ 5	Two operators in a row
10 10 −	Two operands in a row
(10 −5	Unbalanced parentheses
10 DIV −5	Two operators in a row, should be 10 DIV (−5)

The last incorrect example brings up an important point about Modula-2. Remember, unlike some other computer languages, the unary minus must be preceded by a parenthesis if it follows another operator.

Mixed Types

Even though an expression may be algebraically correct, other problems can occur. As you know, all pieces of an expression must be of the same type. However, some complex situations can occur. For example, consider this fragment:

```
VAR
   B: BOOLEAN;
 .
 .
 .
   B:=10<(9+5);
```

This expression is valid because the parentheses ensure that the 9+5 operation is performed prior to the comparison; thus, no type mismatch is produced. However, the statement

```
B:=(10<9)+5;
```

is invalid. The integer 5 cannot be added to the **BOOLEAN** value produced by 10<9 because they are of different types.

Complex Logical Expressions

Modula-2 requires the use of parentheses in complex logical expressions. For example,

```
10<B  AND  C<>21
```

is an invalid expression. To correct it, each operand of the **AND** operation must be enclosed by parentheses. The corrected expression is as follows:

(10 < B) AND (C <> 21)

Neglecting parentheses will cause a somewhat confusing compile-time error message to the effect that there is a type mismatch. The reason for this is that logical operators, including **AND**, have a higher precedence than relational operators. Hence, without the parentheses, the compiler thinks that you are trying to **AND** B and C.

BOOLEAN *Expressions*

If you have only programmed in BASIC before, then you might find the following code fragment a little unsettling.

```
VAR
   B: BOOLEAN;

   .
   .
   .
   IF B THEN WriteString("B is TRUE")  END;
```

Because **B** is a **BOOLEAN** variable and the condition of the **IF** requires a **BOOLEAN** expression, the **IF** statement is perfectly valid. It is not necessary (but not improper) to write it like this:

```
IF B=TRUE THEN WriteString("B is TRUE")  END;
```

Precedence of Operators And Order of Evaluation

Table 3-4 shows the order of precedence of the Modula-2 operators. Expressions are evaluated in order of operator precedence, with the highest first and the lowest last. In the case of equal precedence, order of evaluation is from left to right. Of course, parentheses may be used to alter the evaluation order.

For example, in the expression

10+5*10

the 5*10 operation occurs first, because * is of higher precedence than +. Thus, 5*10=50, which is then added to 10. However, in

10+5+21

the 10+5 calculation is performed first and the result is added to 21, because in cases of equal precedence, evaluation proceeds left to right.

Table 3-4. Sequence of Operator Precedence

Highest	NOT − (unary)
	* / DIV MOD AND
	+ − OR
Lowest	= <> < <= > >= IN

In the following expression, parentheses are used to alter the natural order of evaluation.

```
(10+5)*10
```

Here, the result is 150, not 60, as it would have been if the parentheses had been left out.

Parentheses have another use, however, in very complex expressions: They can clarify the order of evaluation to the reader. For example,

```
100-4/21+45*2
```

is the same as

```
100-(4/21)+(45*2)
```

but it is much easier to read the latter and confirm exactly what is going on.

Type Conversions

Because Modula-2 is a strongly typed language, constants and variables of one type cannot be mixed with those of another type in expressions. The purpose of this restriction is to help prevent programmer errors by forcing all expressions to deal with compatible data. However, in virtually all real programs there sometimes is a justified need to mix data of one type with data of another. As you will see in the next chapter, many loops are controlled using **CARDINAL** or **INTEGER** variables, yet it is common to use the loop counter in other expressions, such as expressions involving floating-point decimals. Fortunately, Modula-2 has several built-in *type conversion* functions, as well as some type conversion functions found in the standard libraries, that allow data of one type to be converted to another type. The standard, built-in type conversion functions are shown in Table 3-5.

In addition, the built-in function ABS, which returns the absolute value of its argument, is sometimes used in type conversions. These functions are not in a library, so they do not have to be **IMPORT**ed and may be used at will. Let's look at each of these in turn.

Table 3-5. Modula-2 Built-in Conversion Functions

Function	Purpose
CHR	Converts a number into a character
ORD	Converts a CHAR or an INTEGER into a CARDINAL
VAL	Converts between CARDINAL, INTEGER, and CHAR
FLOAT	Converts a CARDINAL into a REAL
TRUNC	Converts a REAL into a CARDINAL

CHR Function

The **CHR** function has the general form

```
CHR(C)
```

where **C** is a variable or constant of type **CARDINAL** and the result is its ASCII equivalent—a character of type **CHAR**. (Actually, as you will see in Chapter 5, **CHR**'s usage is more general than this, but this is its main purpose.) For example, the following fragment converts the number 65, the ASCII code for A, into the character A.

```
VAR
    ch:CHAR;
.
.
.
    ch:=CHR(65);
    Write(ch); (* will print the letter A on the screen *)
```

ORD Function

ORD returns a **CARDINAL** value that is equivalent to its argument's relative position in the set of all values of its type. **ORD** is mainly used to return the ASCII code of a character. (However, like **CHR**, its use is not limited to this, as you will see in Chapter 5.) The general form of **ORD** is

ORD(ch)

where **ch** is generally a character. For example, to obtain the **CARDINAL** value (that is, the ASCII code) for the character B, you would write

```
VAR
   C:CARDINAL;
 .
 .
 .
   C:=ORD('B');
   (* C now holds the value 66 - B's ASCII code *)
```

FLOAT Function

The built-in procedure **FLOAT** is used to convert data of type **CARDINAL** to type **REAL**. Its general form is

FLOAT(C);

where **C** must be a **CARDINAL**.

For example, the following code converts the value of the **CARDINAL** variable **Counter** into a **REAL** and assigns it to **R**.

```
VAR
   Counter: CARDINAL;
   R: REAL;
 .
 .
 .
   Counter:=12;
   R:=FLOAT(Counter);
   (* now R=12.0 and Counter=12 *)
```

You must remember that **FLOAT** can only be used to convert **CARDINALs** to **REALs**; it will not work with **INTEGERs**.

TRUNC Function

TRUNC is the opposite of **FLOAT**. It is used to convert data of type **REAL** into data of type **CARDINAL**. The general form is

TRUNC(R)

where **R** must be data of type **REAL**. When the conversion is made, any decimal portion is discarded. Also, **TRUNC** will not work with negative numbers. If a negative number must be converted, then its absolute value must be used.

The code shown here converts the value of the **REAL** variable **R** into a **CARDINAL** and assigns it to **C**.

```
VAR
   R: REAL;
   C: CARDINAL;
 .
 .
 .
   R:=1.123;
   C:=TRUNC(R);
   (* R=1.123 and C=1 *)
```

VAL Function

As you may have noticed, in the type conversion functions described so far, there is no way to convert a **REAL** into an **INTEGER**, or a **CHAR** into an **INTEGER**, or a **CARDINAL** into an **INTEGER**. Also, **INTEGERs** cannot be used as arguments to **ORD** or **FLOAT**. Does this mean that **INTEGERs** cannot be converted? Fortunately, the answer is no. Modula-2 contains one more standard conversion function called **VAL**, which can be used to convert among **INTEGERs**, **CHARs**, and **CARDINALs** (as well as certain user-defined types). The general form is

VAL(*target-type*,*value*);

where ***target-type*** is one the type specifiers mentioned earlier, and ***value*** is the value to be converted. The type produced is ***target-type***.

For example, to convert the **CARDINAL C** into the **INTEGER I**, you would write

```
I:=VAL(INTEGER,C);
```

Therefore, to convert an **INTEGER** into a **REAL**, you would use **VAL** in conjuction with **FLOAT**, as in the following example.

```
VAR
   I:INTEGER;
   R:REAL;
 .
 .
 .
   I:=100;
   R:=FLOAT(VAL(CARDINAL,I));
   (* R now contains 100.0  *)
```

ABS Function

A sometimes frustrating problem is encountered when you attempt to type convert a negative number. Since it is not possible to convert directly from a **REAL** to an **INTEGER** using the standard routines described above, and all **CARDINALs** must be positive, how can negative values be converted? There are two ways. The first is to use a sequence of statements and the **ABS** function, which returns the positive, absolute value of its argument; and the other is to use routines found in the Modula-2 libraries. Because the libaries vary, we will look at both methods.

The standard form of **ABS** is

ABS(*value*)

where ***value*** may be **INTEGER** or **REAL**. **ABS** returns the absolute value, with the type being the same as that of the argument.

For example,

I:=ABS(−100);

places the value 100 into **I**.

Therefore, to convert the **REAL** value −1.123 into an **INTEGER**, you would use code similar to the following fragment.

```
VAR
   Negative:BOOLEAN;
   R:REAL;
   I:INTEGER;
 .
 .
 .
   Negative:=FALSE;
   IF R<0.0 THEN Negative:=TRUE; END;
   R:=ABS(R);
```

```
        I:=VAL(INTEGER,TRUNC(R));
        IF Negative THEN I:=-I;  END;
      .
      .
      .
```

As you can see, this is a fairly large amount of code for a very simple type conversion. This is why you will usually find two additional type conversion routines in the standard libary of your compiler.

***The real** Procedure* Library **MathLib0** contains the procedure **real** that is used to directly convert an **INTEGER** into a **REAL**. It is unclear why this is not a built-in procedure, like those discussed earlier, because it is quite useful. The general form is

real(I);

where **I** is an **INTEGER** value. For example,

```
FROM MathLib0 IMPORT real;

VAR
   R:REAL;
  .
  .
  .
   R:=real(-10);
   (* R = -10.0 *)
```

directly converts −10 into its floating-point equivalent and is definitely easier to use than the version that employs only the standard built-in procedures and **ABS**.

***The entier** Procedure* Library **MathLib0** also contains the procedure **entier**, which is used to directly convert a **REAL** into an **INTEGER**. Its general form is

entier(R)

where **R** is a **REAL** value.

For example, the following code directly converts −123.32 into its **INTEGER** equivalent.

```
FROM MathLib0 IMPORT entier;

VAR
   I:INTEGER;
  .
  .
  .
   I:=entier(-123.23);
   (* I = -123 *)
```

As a final example of type conversions, you might want to type this program and observe its output. You should see the following:

1.30E+001 23B 65 10 10 1.00E+001 1

```
MODULE TypeConversions ;
   (* this program uses the standard type conversion
      procedures plus real and entier. *)

   FROM InOut IMPORT Write, WriteLn, WriteCard, WriteInt;
   FROM RealInOut IMPORT WriteReal;
   FROM  MathLib0 IMPORT real, entier;

   VAR
      ch: CHAR;
      x: INTEGER;
      c: CARDINAL;
      r: REAL;
BEGIN
   ch:='A';
   x:=-10;
   c:=13;
   r:=10.123;
   WriteReal(FLOAT(c),5);
   WriteCard(c+VAL(CARDINAL,ABS(x)),4);
   Write(CHR(66));
   WriteCard(ORD(ch),4);
   WriteCard(TRUNC(r),4);
   x:=entier(r);
   WriteInt(x,4);
   r:=real(x);
   WriteReal(r,5);
   WriteInt(VAL(INTEGER,TRUNC(1.123)),5);
END TypeConversions.
```

Now that you have learned the basic building blocks of Modula-2, you are ready to move on and explore the language's rich and flexible set of program control statements.

EXERCISES

1. What is the difference between a **CARDINAL** value and an **INTEGER**?

2. How would a constant named **COUNT** be declared to have a value of 100?

3. What type of constants are the following:

   a. TRUE
   b. −10
   c. 10.123
   d. 10
   e. "Hi"
   f. 'A'

4. What is the difference between **DIV** and /?

5. Which of the following expressions are **TRUE**?

   a. 10<10
   b. NOT (9<10)
   c. (10=9) OR (10=10)
   d. 19=19

6. What is wrong with the following code fragment?

```
VAR
   I,J,K: INTEGER;
   C: CARDINAL;
 .
 .
 .
   I:=10;
   K:=I*J;
   C:=K MOD 19;
```

7. Write a program that converts a **REAL** value into an **INTEGER** and then back again.

ANSWERS

1. **CARDINAL** values may be only positive whole numbers, whereas **INTEGERs** may be both positive and negative whole numbers.

2. ```
CONST
   COUNT = 100;
```

3. a. BOOLEAN
   b. INTEGER
   c. REAL
   d. CARDINAL or INTEGER
   e. String
   f. CHAR

4. **DIV** is used to divide **INTEGERs** and **CARDINALs**, whereas / is used to divide **REALs**.

5. c and d.

6. The line

```
C:=K MOD 19;
```

is invalid because it attempts to assign an **INTEGER** value to a **CARDINAL**.

7. ```
MODULE CON;

   FROM MathLib0 INPORT real, entier;

   VAR
      R: REAL;
      I: INTEGER;

BEGIN
   R:=100.1;
   I:=entier(R);
   R:=real(I);
END CON.
```

Program Control Statements

CHAPTER 4

Program control statements in many ways are the essence of a computer language. They govern not only the way a program will execute, but also the way a programmer thinks about a problem. There are two types of program control statements: conditional and loop control. Modula-2 has two conditional control statements, **IF** and **CASE**, and four loop control statements, **FOR**, **WHILE/DO**, **REPEAT/UNTIL**, and **LOOP/EXIT**. These statements are the subject of this chapter.

Conditional Statements

Conditional statements are used to cause the selective execution of various parts of a program. The **IF** statement can be used whenever a conditional statement is needed, and the **CASE** statement can replace several **IF** statements in certain situations to create more optimal, efficient code.

*The **IF** Statement*

You learned about the simplest form of the **IF** statement in Chapter 2. Here you will see how much more powerful it can be. The general format of the complete **IF** statement is

IF *<condition>* THEN *<statement-block>*
ELSIF *<condition>* THEN *<statement-block>*
ELSE *<statement-block>*
END;

where ***<condition>*** must be a valid **BOOLEAN** expression, and ***<statement-block>*** consists of one or more statements to be executed. Note that **ELSIF** is spelled without the final "E" in ELSE—this is not an error, but the way Modula-2 requires it. Both **ELSIF** and **ELSE** are optional, and you can have as many **ELSIF** statements as you need. To better understand how the extended **IF** statement works, consider this example:

```
IF A THEN WriteString("A is true")
ELSIF B THEN WriteString("B is true")
ELSIF C THEN WriteString("C is true")
ELSE WriteString("A B C are all false")
END;

WriteString('all done');
```

This will execute as follows: If **A** is TRUE, the message **A is true** will be printed on the screen, the rest of the **IF** statement will be skipped, and then the message **all done** will be printed. If **A** is FALSE, then **B** is checked. If **B** is TRUE, the message **B is true** is printed, the rest of the statement is skipped, and then **all done** is printed. If, however, both **A** and **B** are FALSE and **C** is TRUE, then the messages **C is true** and **all done** are displayed with the **ELSE** clause skipped. In the event that **A, B,** and **C** all are **FALSE,** then the message **A B C are all FALSE** is printed followed by **all done**. The point is that one and only one of the four possible messages found in the **IF** statement will be printed on the screen.

Stated formally, the first TRUE condition causes its block of statements to execute, and the **IF** statement is satisfied. Execution then resumes with the first statement after the **IF** statement's **END**.

As stated, there does not have to be either an **ELSE** statement or **ELSIF** statements. For example,

```
IF Z<100 THEN A:=19
ELSE A:=20
END;
```

does not have an **ELSIF**, and this code

```
IF 'A'<CH THEN WRITE(CH)
ELSIF a<CH THEN ProcessError
END;
```

does not have an **ELSE**.

A program that illustrates the use of the **IF** statement is a simple version of the magic number game, where you try to guess a number known only to the computer. The program, called *Magic,* is shown here.

```
MODULE Magic;

  FROM InOut IMPORT WriteLn, ReadInt, WriteString;

  CONST
    MagicNumber = 73;

  VAR
    guess: INTEGER;

BEGIN
  WriteString("Guess the magic Number!");
  WriteLn;
  WriteString("Enter your best guess between 1 and 100: ");
  ReadInt(guess);
  WriteLn;
  IF guess=MagicNumber THEN WriteString("*** R i g h t ***")
  ELSE WriteString("wrong");
  END;
END Magic.
```

As you can see, there is no **ELSIF** clause, and the objects of both **IF** and **ELSE** are single statements.

Until now, only a single statement has been used as an object of **IF**, but, as shown earlier in the statement's general format, the statement blocks connected to **IF**, **ELSIF**, and **ELSE** may contain multiple statements. Recall from Chapter 1 that a block of code is an indivisible collection of statements—the execution of one implies that they all will execute. Look, for example, at the following code fragment.

```
IF A=100 THEN
  A:=1;
  B:=A DIV 12;
```

```
    WriteString("PROCESS COMPLETED")
  ELSIF A<100 THEN
    WriteString('PROCESS CONTINUED");
    A:=A * 2
  ELSE
    WriteString("ERROR IN PROCESS");
    A:=A DIV 2;
    B:= ResetValue
  END;
```

In this fragment, each clause of the **IF** has a block of code as its object. If the **IF** condition is true, then the three statements

```
A:=1;
B:=A DIV 12;
WriteString("PROCESS COMPLETED")
```

all will execute, and the **IF** statement will be terminated. If, instead, the **ELSIF** condition is true, then the statements

```
WriteString('PROCESS CONTINUED");
A:=A * 2
```

will execute, and the **IF** statement will terminate. Finally, if neither the **IF** nor the **ELSIF** conditions are true, then the **ELSE** block

```
WriteString("ERROR IN PROCESS");
A:=A DIV 2;
B:= ResetValue
```

will be executed.

To improve the magic number program, you can use blocks of code as objects of the **IF** statement, as shown here.

```
MODULE Magic2;
  (* An improved version of Magic that gives hints - and
     advice - to the user. *)

  FROM InOut IMPORT WriteLn, ReadInt, WriteString, WriteInt;

  CONST
    MagicNumber = 73;

  VAR
    guess: INTEGER;

BEGIN
  WriteString("Guess the magic Number!");
  WriteLn;
  WriteString("Enter your best guess between 1 and 100: ");
  ReadInt(guess);
```

```
    WriteLn;
    IF guess=MagicNumber THEN
      WriteString("*** R i g h t ***");
      WriteInt(guess,5);
      WriteString(' is the magic number')
    ELSIF guess<MagicNumber THEN
      WriteString("too low");
      WriteLn;
      WriteString("If you think too small, you will never succeed!")
    ELSIF guess>MagicNumber THEN
      WriteString("too high");
      WriteLn;
      WriteString("Don't overreach - stay within your limits!")
    END;
  END Magic2.
```

This version gives hints—and advice—about wrong guesses. Notice that the **ELSE** clause is replaced by two **ELSIF** clauses. **ELSE** is no longer needed because either **IF** or one of the **ELSIF** conditions will be true.

Nested IF Statements Nexted **IF** statements are easily the most confusing aspect of any programming language. Fortunately, Modula-2 makes it easy to know what is going on. A nested **IF** statement is simply an **IF** statement that is the object of another **IF** statement. Look, for example, at the following code.

```
IF Count=100 THEN
  ReadInt(G);
  IF ABS(G)<10 THEN B:=10
  ELSIF B=11 THEN DONE:=TRUE
  END
ELSE WriteString('Error')
END;
```

Here, the nested **IF** statement will execute if and only if **Count** is equal to 100; otherwise, the **ELSE** statement will execute. Beginning Modula-2 programmers often have trouble telling where one **IF** ends and another begins, even though the rule is quite simple: An **IF** statement ends with its **END**. In this example, you know that the **ELSE** has to be associated with the outer (first) **IF**, because the inner **IF** has been terminated by its **END**. If the **END** had not been where it is, but rather after the **ELSE**, the code would have looked like this:

```
IF Count=100 THEN
  ReadInt(G);
  IF ABS(G)<10 THEN B:=10
  ELSIF B=11 THEN DONE:=TRUE
```

```
    ELSE WriteString('Error')
    END
  END;
```

Here, the **ELSE** is moved inside the **END** statement of the inner **IF** and is linked with it.

The previous examples illustrate how important good indentation practices are. Not only do they help make your programs more readable, but they can help prevent nesting errors. Remember, simply indent one level at the beginning of each block and back up with each **END** statement. If you're still not a believer, examine the following examples. These two code fragments are the same, but the second is much easier to read.

```
IF A=B THEN
IF B=C THEN
A:=D;
D:=F;
T:=A;
ELSIF A=(B DIV C) THEN
WriteString('ERROR');
ELSE B:=100
END;
ELSIF C=10 THEN WriteString('out of bounds');
END

IF A=B THEN
  IF B=C THEN
    A:=D;
    D:=F;
    T:=A;
  ELSIF A=(B DIV C) THEN
    WriteString('ERROR');
  ELSE B:=100
  END;
ELSIF C=10 THEN WriteString('out of bounds');
END
```

ELSIF Versus IF/ELSE IF It may have occurred to you that **ELSIF** is not technically necessary, because the same effect can be created using an **IF/ELSE IF** ladder. An **IF/ELSE IF** ladder is simply a chain of **IF** statements that have **ELSE IF** statements as objects, as shown in this example.

```
IF A THEN a:=1
ELSE IF B THEN
  b:=1
  ELSE IF C THEN
    c:=1
    ELSE IF D THEN
      d:=1
```

```
            END
          END
        END
      END
```

Prior to Modula-2, this was the way a multiple conditional statement using **IF** statements had to be written because there was no **ELSIF** statement. As you can see, the code is quite confusing because, even in this simple example, it is difficult to know what goes with what. (In fact, without the proper indentation, this type of code is virtually impossible to read.) One of the major breakthroughs embodied in Modula-2 is the use of **ELSIF** as a separate clause in the **IF** statement. **ELSIF** eliminates the **IF/ELSE IF** ladder and replaces it with a clear, easy-to-understand construct. For example, the same example coded using the **ELSIF** becomes

```
IF A THEN a:=1
ELSIF B THEN b:=1
ELSIF C THEN c:=1
ELSIF D THEN d:=1
END
```

which is clearly better.

Although the **IF/ELSE IF** ladder may be necessary in other languages, it should be avoided in Modula-2. This does not mean, however, that it is wrong to have nested **IF** statements, because there are many times when they are needed; it means only that when **ELSIF** will do the job, use it.

*The **CASE** Statement*

Even though the Modula-2 **IF** statement is quite powerful, it can sometimes be cumbersome to use, especially when a program presents numerous possible situations to choose from involving one expression tested against various constants. Look, for example, at the following code.

```
IF CH='A' THEN X:=1
ELSIF CH='B' THEN X:=2
ELSIF CH='C' THEN X:=3
ELSIF CH='D' THEN X:=4
ELSE X:=5;
END;
```

Here, the variable **CH** is tested against four different constants. As you can see, a large portion of each statement is the same in each line. Situations of this type prompted the invention of the *multiway decision* statement. In Modula-2 this is called the **CASE** statement.

The **CASE** statement allows the value of an expression to determine which block of statements will be executed by matching the value of the expression with a list of constants. The general form of the **CASE** statement is shown here.

CASE <*expression*> OF
    <*constant1*>: <*statement-block*> |
    <*constant2*>: <*statement-block*> |
    <*constant3*>: <*statement-block*> |
    .
    .
    .
    <*constantN*>: <*statement-block*>
ELSE <*statement-block*>
END;

Here, <***constant***> is a value to be matched by the value of <***expression***>, and <***statement-block***> is one or more valid statements. The vertical bars are actually part of the **CASE** statement and are used to separate each case from the other. (On the IBM PC keyboard, the vertical bar is one key left of the "Z.") The **ELSE** clause is optional. The type of both the expression and the constants must be the same. You may use any of the elementary data types except **REAL**. (Pascal programmers: The Pascal and Modula-2 **CASE** statements have substantial differences, so careful attention to this section is advised.)

The **CASE** statement works like this: The expression is evaluated, and its value is checked against the constants. If the value is found to be equal to a constant, then that block of statements will execute until a vertical bar, **ELSE**, or **END** is encountered. If no match is found and **ELSE** is present, the **ELSE** statements will execute. If no matches are found and **ELSE** is not present, then execution simply begins with the next line of code following the **END** statement (some implementations may generate errors).

To see how the **CASE** statement works, here is the **CASE** statement version of the **IF** example shown earlier.

```
CASE CH OF
  'A': X:=1 |
  'B': X:=2 |
```

```
    'C': X:=3 |
    'D': X:=4
  ELSE X:=5
  END;
```

You can see how much easier this code is both to read and write. Also, the object code for this program should execute substantially faster than that for the corresponding **IF** statement.

It is important to remember that the vertical bar is not used after the last case—that is, the last block of code prior to either **ELSE** or **END** does not have a vertical bar after it.

CASE statements are often found in menu routines that ask for user input and then select one of a number of different options. The simple program shown here prompts the user and then adds, subtracts, multiplies, or divides, depending on the user's selection.

```
MODULE CaseExample;
  FROM InOut IMPORT Read, Write, WriteString, WriteLn, ReadInt,
                    WriteInt;

  VAR
    ch:CHAR;
    i,j: INTEGER;

BEGIN
  WriteString("1. add");
  WriteLn;
  WriteString("2. subtract");
  WriteLn;
  WriteString("3. divide");
  WriteLn;
  WriteString("4. multiply");
  WriteLn;
  WriteString("chose one: ");
  Read(ch); Write(ch);
  WriteLn;
  CASE ch OF
    '1': ReadInt(i);
         Write('+');
         ReadInt(j);
         Write('=');
         WriteInt(i+j,5) |
    '2': ReadInt(i);
         Write('-');
         ReadInt(j);
         Write('=');
         WriteInt(i-j,5) |
    '3': ReadInt(i);
         WriteString(' DIV ');
         ReadInt(j);
         Write('=');
         IF j<>0 THEN WriteInt(i DIV j,5) END; |
    '4': ReadInt(i);
         Write('*');
         ReadInt(j);
```

```
            Write('=');
            WriteInt(i*j,5)
    END (* case *);
  END CaseExample.
```

Notice that the object of each case is a block of statements.

CASE Versus IF

It is sometimes difficult to choose between the **CASE** and **IF** statements; however, a few rules will help. First, you must use the **IF** statement if the condition tested involves variables. For example, there is no way to directly code the following into a **CASE** statement.

```
IF A=B THEN A:=J
ELSIF A=C THEN A:=K
ELSIF A=D THEN A:=L
END;
```

Here, both sides of the equal sign are variables, and the **CASE** statement requires a list of constants.

Second, any condition that does not involve equality must be an **IF** condition. For example,

```
IF CH<'A' THEN S:='IS ACTION'
ELSIF CH<'B' THEN S:='IS STEP ZERO'
ELSIF CH<'C' THEN S:='IS CORRECT'
END;
```

cannot be made into a **CASE** statement, because the **CASE** statement attempts to match a value to a constant—it cannot look for inequality.

A third rule really is more a matter of style and readability than necessity: A **CASE** statement should use only related elements. Thus, each **CASE** statement can be thought of as a unit of code, not as a hodgepodge of unrelated actions.

Loop Control Statements

Modula-2 has four loop control statements: **WHILE/DO**, **REPEAT/UNTIL**, **FOR**, and **LOOP/EXIT**. The combination of these give Modula-2 one of the richest and most powerful set of loop control statements of any computer language. However, the wise use of each statement is crucial to successful programming.

*The **FOR** Loop*

If you have programmed in BASIC, then the Modula-2 **FOR** loop will be familiar to you, because it works in a way very similar to BASIC's FOR/NEXT loop. The general form of the **FOR** is

FOR <*variable*>:=<*expression*> TO <*expression*> BY <*expression*>
  DO <*statement-block*>
END;

where <***variable***> is the loop control variable of type **CARDINAL** or **INTEGER**, <***expression***> is a **CARDINAL** or **INTEGER** expression, and <***statement-block***> is one or more statements to be repeated. The statements that are executed repeatedly are called the *loop body.* The **BY** clause is optional. In general, the **FOR** loop will repeat its code until the control variable's value equals the value of the target expression. If **BY** is absent, then the control variable is incremented by one each time the loop repeats. If **BY** is present, then the control variable is incremented or decremented by the value of the **BY** expression. For example,

```
FOR X:=1 TO 100 DO
  WriteInt(X,5)
END;
```

will print the numbers 1 through 100 on the screen. On the other hand, the following code will print the even numbers 2 through 100 on the screen because the **BY** expression increments **X** by 2 each time through the loop.

```
FOR X:=2 TO 100 BY 2 DO
  WriteInt(X,5)
END;
```

To generate a negative running loop, you must use a **BY** expression with a negative value. For example, this loop displays the numbers 100 to 1 on the screen.

```
FOR X:=100 TO 1 BY -1 DO
  WriteInt(X,5);
END;
```

A very important point about the **FOR** loop is that it does not necessarily execute the loop body. Consider this example:

```
FOR X:= 1 TO 0 DO
  WriteString('this will not be executed');
END;
```

The message will never be printed, because the condition that governs the loop, counting from 1 to 0, is already satisfied, so the body of code in the loop is skipped.

A **FOR** loop is used when you know in advance how many iterations are required. The following program computes the factorial of a number. The factorial of a number is the product of each digit between 1 and the number. For example, 4 factorial is 1*2*3*4, or 24.

```
MODULE Factorial;
  FROM InOut IMPORT ReadCard, WriteLn, WriteString, WriteCard;

  VAR
    count,x,factorial: CARDINAL;

BEGIN
  WriteString("enter number: ");
  ReadCard(x);
  WriteLn;
  factorial:=1;  (* initialize *)
  FOR count:=1 TO x DO
    factorial:=factorial*count;
  END;
  WriteCard(factorial,5);
END Factorial.
```

FOR loops are also commonly used to initialize arrays to some known state. The following fragment will set all elements in **name** to spaces.

```
VAR
   name: ARRAY [1..79] OF CHAR;
   i: INTEGER;
BEGIN
   FOR i:=1 TO 79 DO
   name[i]:=' '
   END;
.
.
.
```

Modifying the Loop Control Variable It is very important that you never alter the loop control variable inside the loop body of a **FOR**

loop. Although the Modula-2 compiler will allow you to do so, it is especially poor programming form, because it completely destructures the loop and makes it difficult for someone reading it to know what is going on. For example, the following code is valid, yet the loop will not repeat 100 times.

```
FOR Count:=1 TO 100 DO
  WriteInt(Count,5);
  WriteLn;
  Count:=Count+1; (* very poor style! *)
END;
```

Instead of repeating 100 times, this loop will only repeat 50 times, because the loop control variable **Count** is incremented inside the loop. This type of coding is very misleading and should be avoided.

Nested FOR Loops Modula-2 supports nested **FOR** loops, which means that you can have **FOR** loops inside of other **FOR** loops. For example,

```
FOR A:=1 TO 100 DO
  FOR J:=1 TO 10 DO
    WriteString('Hello ')
  END;
END;
```

will write the message **Hello** 1000 times. This is because the outer loop will execute the inner loop 100 times, and the inner loop prints the message 10 times each time it is executed.

Be careful when using nested **FOR** loops that you do not accidentally use the same loop control variable for more than one loop. The loop control variable often is simply a temporary place holder, making it easy to use it without really thinking about it, so this type of error is fairly common. For example, in the following program the outermost and innermost loops share the same control variable, **X**, which means that this code will not do what was intended.

```
(* THIS IS INCORRECT *)

FOR X:=1 TO 100 BY 4 DO
  FOR Y:=A TO B DO
    FOR X:=100 TO 1 BY -1 DO
        .
        .
        .
    END;
  END;
END;
```

The ***WHILE/DO*** *Loop*

Although the **FOR** loop is useful when you know in advance how many iterations are needed, it clearly is not designed for situations where an indefinite number of repetitions are required. One loop that can work in this situation is the **WHILE/DO** loop, which allows code to be repeated when a specified **BOOLEAN** condition is **TRUE**.

The general form of the **WHILE/DO** loop is

```
WHILE <expression> DO
   <statement-block>
END;
```

where ***<expression>*** is any valid **BOOLEAN** expression and ***<statement-block>*** is one or more statements.

The following loop will repeat its body of code until the number 100 is entered from the keyboard.

```
ReadInt(num);

WHILE num<>100 DO
  WriteInt(num,5);
  WriteString(' squared is ');
  WriteInt(num*num,5);
  WriteLn;
  ReadInt(num);
END;

WriteString('All done.');
```

Here, the code inside the loop will execute so long as the condition **num<>100** is **TRUE**. If the number 100 is entered, then the condition will be **FALSE**, and execution will continue with the statement immediately following the loop—in this case, **WriteString('All done.');**.

One of the most important points about the **WHILE/DO** loop is that it will not necessarily execute. In the preceding example, if the user entered the number 100 at the first **ReadInt** statement prior to the **WHILE/DO**, then the loop condition **NUM<>100** would be **FALSE**, and the code inside the loop would not execute. This fact makes **WHILE/DO** loops ideal for situations where the initial condition can be **FALSE**, thus avoiding an additional check prior to the loop. For example, the following short program accepts a sentence entered at the keyboard and reports the location of the first space.

```
MODULE FindSpace;
  FROM InOut IMPORT Write, ReadString, WriteString, WriteLn, WriteInt;

  VAR
    Sentence: ARRAY [0..79] OF CHAR;
    i: INTEGER;

BEGIN
  FOR i:=0 TO 79 DO
    Sentence[i]:=' ';   (* initialize array *)
  END;
  WriteString('Enter a sentence: ');
  ReadString(Sentence);
  WriteLn;
  i:=0;
  WHILE Sentence[i]<>' ' DO
  Write(Sentence[i]);
  i:=i+1;
END;
WriteLn;
WriteString('First space at location ');
WriteInt(i,3);
END FindSpace.
```

In this program the character array **Sentence** is first initialized to spaces, and then the input procedure **ReadString** is executed. If the user enters a string of characters, then the loop will execute until a space is found. However, if the user simply strikes the RETURN key, then the loop will be skipped, because the condition will be **FALSE** to begin with—the first element in **Sentence** will be a space (because of the initialization).

It is possible to have a complex expression for the loop test condition. For example, the **FindSpace** program can be modified to find and report the position of any character you choose, as shown here.

```
MODULE FindChar;
  FROM InOut IMPORT Write, ReadString, WriteString, WriteLn,
                    WriteInt, Read;
  VAR
    Sentence: ARRAY [0..79] OF CHAR;
    i: INTEGER;
    ch: CHAR;

BEGIN
  FOR i:=0 TO 79 DO
    Sentence[i]:=' ';  (* initialize array *)
  END;
  WriteString('Enter a sentence: ');
  ReadString(Sentence);
  WriteLn;
  WriteString('Enter character to find: ');
  Read(ch);
  WriteLn;
  i:=0;
  WHILE (Sentence[i]<>ch) AND (i<80) DO
```

```
    Write(Sentence[i]);
    i:=i+1;
  END;
  WriteLn;
  WriteString('First ');
  Write(ch);
  WriteString(' at location ');
  WriteInt(i,3);
END FindChar.
```

Here, you need to check for both the character being found and the end of the array. This brings up a very important point: When using loops that index arrays, always make sure that the array boundaries are not exceeded. If they are, a run-time error will result—that is, your program will crash.

Just because the loop test condition can be a complex **BOOLEAN** expression does not mean that it should necessarily be so. For example, here is a poorly thought out **WHILE/DO** loop.

```
WHILE (A<>B) AND ((C=100) OR (D<10)) AND (NOT B) DO
  .
  .
  .
END;
```

A much better approach is to create a **BOOLEAN** *loop control variable* and use this to control the loop. When the loop is rewritten in this way, the code fragment becomes

```
WHILE NOT DONE DO
  IF A<>B THEN DONE:=TRUE
  ELSIF (C=100) OR (D<10) THEN DONE:=TRUE
  ELSIF NOT B THEN DONE:=TRUE
  END;
  .
  .
  .
END;
```

Using this approach, several different conditions can cause the loop to exit, yet the loop code is kept clean and easy to read.

Although this example does not increase execution speed, in situations where some of the conditions are conditionally checked it will do so, as shown here.

```
WHILE NOT DONE DO
  IF A<>B THEN DONE:=TRUE END;

  IF A=100 THEN
    IF (C=100) OR (D<10) THEN
      DONE:=TRUE;
      ELSIF NOT B THEN DONE:=TRUE
    END;
  END;
  .
  .
  .
END;
```

Here, the tests for (C=100) AND (D<10) and **NOT B** will occur only when **A=100**. Hence, instead of being tested each time through the loop, the conditions are checked only when necessary, thus increasing the overall speed of the code.

*The **REPEAT/UNTIL** Loop*

Unlike the **FOR** and the **WHILE/DO** loops, which do not necessarily execute the body of a loop, the **REPEAT/UNTIL** loop guarantees that at least one iteration will be performed, because the loop test condition is located at the bottom of the loop rather than at the top. The general form of the **REPEAT/UNTIL** loop is

REPEAT
<*statement-block*>
UNTIL <*expression*>;

where ***<statement-block>*** is one or more statements, and ***<expression>*** is any valid **BOOLEAN** expression. The code inside the loop will repeat until the specified condition is **TRUE**. Note that this differs from the **WHILE/DO**, in which the loop runs until the condition becomes **FALSE**.

In this code fragment, the code inside the loop will repeat until the user types a "Q."

```
REPEAT
  Read(ch);
  WriteCard(ORD(ch),5);
UNTIL ch='Q';
```

As you can see, because the loop will execute at least once, it is not necessary to place a **Read** statement outside the **REPEAT/UNTIL** loop, as it would be had a **WHILE/DO** been used instead, as shown in the following example.

```
Read(ch);

WHILE ch<>'Q' DO
  WriteCard(ORD(ch),5);
  Read(ch);
END;
```

One of the most common uses for the **REPEAT/UNTIL** is in accepting user input for menu selection. In this situation, you always want the loop to execute at least once. For example, the code for a spelling checker menu routine might look like this:

```
WriteString('1. Check Spelling');
WriteLn;
WriteString('2. Correct Spelling');
WriteLn;
WriteString('3. Quit');

REPEAT
  WriteLn;
  WriteString('Choose one: ');
  Read(ch);
UNTIL (ch>='1') AND (ch<='3');
```

Another good use for **REPEAT/UNTIL** is to improve the magic number program presented earlier in this chapter. Instead of allowing only one guess, you can cause the program to loop until the correct number is entered. The enhanced version of the program is shown here.

```
MODULE MagicEnhanced;

  FROM InOut IMPORT WriteLn, ReadInt, WriteString, WriteInt;

  CONST
    MagicNumber = 73;

  VAR
    guess: INTEGER;

BEGIN
  WriteString("Guess the magic Number!");
  REPEAT
    WriteLn;
    WriteString("Enter your best guess between 1 and 100: ");
    ReadInt(guess);
```

```
  WriteLn;
  IF guess=MagicNumber THEN
    WriteString("*** R i g h t ***");
    WriteInt(guess,5);
    WriteString(' is the magic number')
  ELSIF guess<MagicNumber THEN
    WriteString("too low");
    WriteLn;
    WriteString("If you think too small, you will never succeed!")
  ELSIF guess>MagicNumber THEN
    WriteString("too high");
    WriteLn;
    WriteString("Don't overreach - stay within your limits!")
  END;
  UNTIL guess=MagicNumber;
END MagicEnhanced.
```

*The **LOOP/EXIT** Loop*

FOR, **WHILE/DO**, and **REPEAT/UNTIL** are Modula-2's structured loop statements. They are called this because both entry and exit from the loops are clearly defined. However, because Modula-2 was designed to meet a variety of programming needs, including systems programming, where execution speed is critical, a fourth, unstructured loop was created. In this loop, the iterative code simply continues to execute until the reserved word **EXIT** is encountered. The general form of the **LOOP/EXIT** statement is shown here.

```
LOOP
  <statement-block>
END;
```

where ***<statement-block>*** is one or more statements, at least one of which must be **EXIT**. For example, the following code will repeat until the user enters 100.

```
LOOP
  ReadInt(X);
  IF X=100 THEN EXIT END;
END;
```

There may be several **EXIT** statements inside a **LOOP**. In fact, this is the reason for its inclusion in Modula-2. Although most loops have a well-defined termination condition, some have numerous termination conditions. When a **LOOP** is used, **EXIT**s may be sprinkled about inside the loop so that various situations can cause immediate termination. This is especially important in system code that may have to be terminated if a user strikes a key, if a disk error occurs, if the printer is busy, and so forth.

Perhaps the main reason for the inclusion of the **LOOP** statement is to avoid the following nightmarish situation involving the exit from a deeply nested loop.

```
WHILE (NOT DONE) AND (A<100) DO
  REPEAT
    WHILE (NOT DONE) AND KeyPressed DO
      IF X=Y THEN DONE:=TRUE END;
        .
        .
        .
    END;
  UNTIL DONE AND OK;
END;
```

Here, it is clear that the outer loops are forced to check for the **BOOLEAN DONE** so that the innermost loop can terminate the entire sequence. This situation is better recoded using a **LOOP** for the outer loop. Then, when the inner loop needs to terminate all the loops, only an **EXIT** command need be executed, as shown here.

```
LOOP
  IF A<100 THEN EXIT END;
  REPEAT
    WHILE KeyPressed DO
      IF X=Y THEN EXIT END;
        .
        .
        .
    END;
  UNTIL OK;
END;
```

This method eliminates the need for the additional variable **DONE** and the checks for it.

Remember that although it is not syntactically necessary, at least one **EXIT** statement must be included inside a **LOOP**. Without this **EXIT** there is no way for the loop to terminate, and an *infinite loop* will have been created.

The following program provides a concrete example of the action of

LOOP and **EXIT**, illustrating an exit from a nested loop. You should type this program and experiment with it.

```
MODULE LoopExample;
  FROM InOut IMPORT Read, Write, WriteLn, WriteString, WriteInt;

VAR
  ch:CHAR;
  i:INTEGER;
  OFF:BOOLEAN;

BEGIN

  LOOP   (* read characters until special condition *)

    WriteString('OFF? ');
    Read(ch);
    WriteLn;
    IF ch='y' THEN OFF:=TRUE
    ELSE OFF:=FALSE
    END;

    REPEAT
      Read(ch); Write(ch);
      IF ch='a' THEN
        FOR i:=ORD(ch) TO 1 BY -1 DO
          IF OFF THEN EXIT END;
          WriteInt(i,4)
        END;
      END;  (* IF *)
    UNTIL ch='q';

  END; (* LOOP *)
END LoopExample.
```

When structured languages were first invented, constructs such as **LOOP/EXIT** were frowned upon because they violated the basic philosophy of one entry point and one exit point for a loop—the basis of a structured loop. However, it eventually became clear that in certain situations the code was actually cleaner and easier to read when such constructs were applied carefully. Also, the **LOOP/EXIT** concept allows high-level languages to approximate certain assembly language coding constructs, which reduces the need to program in assembler. Much credit for legitimizing this approach goes to Dennis Ritchie, the creator of the C programming language, who pioneered this area.

In general, because **LOOP** is an unstructured statement, you should use it only when any other method would reduce the efficiency or readability of your code; it should never be used to "construct" one of the other built-in loops.

Choosing the Right Loop

The loop construct that you use can affect the efficiency of a routine. Each of Modula-2's loop statements has a specific use, and it is not good programming practice to use one when another would do better. For example, here are two ways to print the numbers 1 to 100 on the screen.

POOR	GOOD
`x:=1;`	
`WHILE X<=100 DO`	`FOR x:=1 to 100 DO`
`  WriteInt(x,3);`	`  WriteInt(x,3);`
`  x:=x+1;`	`END;`
`END;`	

Here, **WHILE/DO** was pressed into service essentially to construct a **FOR** statement. Because of this, extra lines of code are needed, and the meaning of the code is not obvious. On the other hand, the **FOR** is doing what it was designed to do: looping a predetermined number of times. Its meaning is clear, and with most compilers it will execute faster and use less memory.

Choose a loop according to the following rules.

1. If the number of iterations is known in advance, use **FOR**.
2. If the number of iterations is undetermined, and if a condition can exist where the loop is not executed, use **WHILE/DO**.
3. If the number of iterations is undetermined, and if the loop will always execute at least once, use **REPEAT/UNTIL**.
4. If a variety of disconnected events can terminate the loop, or if several loops must be terminated from a nest loop, use **LOOP/EXIT**.

If you follow these rules, your code will be better structured, will run faster, and will be easier to read and maintain.

EXERCISES

1. Recode the following **IF** statement to its **CASE** equivalent.

```
IF A=1 THEN X:=10
ELSIF A=2 THEN X:=20
ELSIF A=3 THEN X:=30
ELSE X:=40
END;
```

2. What is wrong with the following code?

```
VAR
  X,Y,Z:INTEGER;
.
.
.
CASE Y+Z OF
  X: Z:=100 |
  X-1: X:=200 |
  X=3: X:=300
END;
```

3. Using a **FOR** loop, create a program that sums the numbers between 1 and N, where N is an integer entered by the user at the console.

4. Explain the two key differences between the **WHILE/DO** and the **REPEAT/UNTIL** loops.

5. Name the four Modula-2 loops.

6. How many times will this loop execute?

```
x:=1;
REPEAT
  x:=x+2;
UNTIL x>100;
```

ANSWERS

1.
```
CASE A OF
  1: X:=10 |
  2: X:=20 |
  3: X:=30
  ELSE X:=40
END;
```

2. Only constants can be used in the list of values to be matched. The **CASE** statement does not allow the use of variables.

3.
```
MODULE SUM;

  FROM InOut IMPORT ReadInt;

  VAR
    i,j,sum:INTEGER;

BEGIN
  ReadInt(i);
  sum:=0;
  FOR j:=i TO 0 BY -1 DO
    sum:=sum+j;
  END;
END SUM.
```

4. **REPEAT/UNTIL** always executes at least once, but **WHILE/DO** may not execute at all, depending on the state of the loop test condition. Also, **WHILE/DO** executes when a condition is **TRUE**, and **REPEAT/UNTIL** executes when a condition is **FALSE.**

5. **FOR, WHILE/DO, REPEAT/UNTIL**, and **LOOP/EXIT**.

6. 50

User-Defined Types

CHAPTER 5

Most of the time, the kind of variable your program requires will be one of the built-in elementary data types. However, occasionally a routine will require data that do not fit easily into one of these standard types. To allow for this situation, Modula-2 enables you to create your own *user-defined*, or *custom*, data types.

In Modula-2, the creation of custom data types takes place in the **TYPE** declaration portion of a **MODULE**. These new data types include *subranges, enumerations*, and *sets*. Also, standard types can be renamed in order to make programs easier to develop and modify and to improve the readability of program code.

TYPE Declarations

All user-defined types are declared in the **TYPE** declaration portion of a **MODULE**. The general form is shown here.

TYPE <*name*> = <*type*>;

Here, **<*name*>** is the new type, and **<*type*>** is either one of the built-in data types or a previously defined type. For example,

```
TYPE
  INDEX = CARDINAL;
  BALANCE = REAL;
  COUNTER = INDEX;  (* notice that COUNTER is of type INDEX
                       which, in turn, is of type CARDINAL *)
```

creates three new types called **INDEX**, **BALANCE**, and **COUNTER**.

Once a new type has been defined, its name can be used wherever a type specifier is needed. For example, given the previous type declarations, the following variable declarations are correct.

```
VAR
  i: INDEX;
  j: INDEX;
  k: INDEX;
  OverDue, PastDue: BALANCE;
  count: COUNTER;
```

Here, **i**, **j**, **k**, and **count** are ultimately of type **CARDINAL**, and **OverDue** and **PastDue** are of type **REAL**.

At this point you may be wondering what, if any, advantage has been gained by declaring **i**, **j**, **k** to be of type **INDEX** instead of type **CARDINAL** and **OverDue** and **PastDue** to be of type **BALANCE** instead of type **REAL**—that is, why create seemingly unnecessary types when the built-in types will do? The answer is that it is much easier to alter the type specifications, should they need to be changed. For example, if negative values are needed for **i**, **j**, and **k**, then only the definition of **INDEX** would have to be changed to **INTEGER**; no further alterations would be necessary. In very large programs, this can save a substantial amount of editing time. Consider these two code fragments:

```
(* Better *)

TYPE
  INDEX = CARDINAL;
  BALANCE = REAL;
  COUNTER = INDEX;

VAR
  first, last: INDEX;
  Count: COUNTER;
  OutStdBalance: BALANCE;
  PastDue, OverDue: BALANCE;
  start, end: CARDINAL;
```

```
(* not flexible *)

VAR
  first, last: CARDINAL;
  Count: CARDINAL;
  OutStdBalance: REAL;
  PastDue, OverDue: REAL;
  start, end: CARDINAL;
```

In this situation, if negative index values were required, the version using user-defined types would require less typing to change. You would simply alter **INDEX**'s definition to

```
INDEX = INTEGER;
```

whereas in the nontyped version, several definitions would require modification, and even more importantly, it would be very easy to accidentally change **start** and **end** into **INTEGERs**, even though this was not required or intended.

Although using new names for built-in types can be helpful, the real advantage to custom types lies not in the ability to rename built-in data types, but in the ability to create new data types—which is the subject of the rest of this chapter.

Defining String Types

Because Modula-2 does not have a built-in string data type, arrays of characters are used. Even though this works fine, keying in the array declaration for each string can be tedious and error prone if several strings are needed. The way strings are generally defined in professionally written Modula-2 programs is through the use of custom data types. For example, the following code defines a new type called **STRING80** and uses it to declare the string variables **Name**, **Street**, and **City**.

```
TYPE
  STRING80 = ARRAY [0..79] OF CHAR;

VAR
  Name: STRING80;
  Street: STRING80;
  City: STRING80;
```

In Modula-2, a string may be any length between zero and the size of the character array used to hold the string. Although certain programming situations require different sizes, 80 characters is a common default length because this is one full line of characters on the display.

Remember, **STRING80** ultimately is an array of 80 characters. Therefore, any variable of type **STRING80** can be used with the standard string functions such as **ReadString** and **WriteString**. For example, the following program fragment reads and writes the string **Name** at the console.

```
ReadString(Name);
WriteString(Name);
```

Enumeration Types

One of the most exciting uses of Modula-2's **TYPE** statement is for the creation of an entirely new data type by specifying the *names of the things* that may belong to the data type. Each name represents a value, although in a somewhat abstracted form. This is called an *enumeration type* because each value (name) is specified in its definition. The general form of an enumeration type is

TYPE
<*Ename*> = (<*N1*>,<*N2*>,<*N3*>,. . .<*Nn*>);

where ***<Ename>*** is the name of the new enumeration type, and ***<N1>*** through ***<Nn>*** are the names of the possible values. Each name must be unique.

For example, a program that keeps an inventory of fruit might use the following definition.

```
TYPE
  FRUIT = (apple, orange, banana, pear, grape);
```

Here, **apple**, **orange**, **banana**, **pear**, and **grape** are the values that a variable of type **FRUIT** can have.

In an enumeration, each name is linked with a **CARDINAL** number; however, your program must use the names, not numbers, when performing operations.

Several types of operations are defined for enumeration values. These include assignment and relational operations. However, the standard arithmetic operators, such as * and **DIV**, have no meaning and may not be used.

Assignment works the same as it does for the built-in types. The following code fragment assigns the value **apple** to **KindOfFruit**.

```
VAR
  KindOfFruit: FRUIT;

BEGIN
  KindOfFruit:=apple;
.
.
.
```

All of the relational operators also may be applied to enumeration values, because the values in the type definition are ordered according to their positions in the list, with *N1* the lowest value and *Nn* the highest value. Therefore, **apple** is less than **orange**, and **pear** is greater than **banana**. For example,

```
IF KindOfFruit = apple THEN
  WriteString('Apples are good today')
END;
```

will print the message **Apples are good today** only if **KindOfFruit** is equal to **apple**.

If this is the first computer language you have learned that allows user-defined types of this nature, you might be unsure about what is actually going on. The short program shown here will let you experiment with enumeration types before continuing.

```
MODULE Fruit;

  FROM InOut IMPORT WriteLn, WriteString, ReadString;

  TYPE
    FRUIT = (apple, orange, banana, pear, grape);
    STRING80 = ARRAY [0..79] OF CHAR;
```

```
    VAR
      KindOfFruit: FRUIT;
      s: STRING80;

  BEGIN
    REPEAT
      WriteString("enter fruit: ");
      ReadString(s);
      CASE s[0] OF
        'a': KindOfFruit:=apple |
        'o': KindOfFruit:=orange |
        'b': KindOfFruit:=banana |
        'p': KindOfFruit:=pear |
        'g': KindOfFruit:=grape
      END;
      WriteLn;

      IF KindOfFruit=apple THEN
        WriteString('Apples are good today')
      ELSIF KindOfFruit=orange THEN
        WriteString('No oranges until Tuesday')
      ELSIF KindOfFruit=banana THEN
        WriteString('Bananas overstocked')
      ELSIF KindOfFruit=pear THEN
        WriteString('out of season')
      ELSIF KindOfFruit=grape THEN
        WriteString('Concord priced to sell')
      ELSE WriteString('try again');
      END;
      WriteLn;

    UNTIL s[0]='q';
  END Fruit.
```

As a note of interest, this program uses a string of type **STRING80** for input to allow entire words to be entered, but it only examines the first character of each word. This further illustrates the fact that strings are simply arrays of characters and can be indexed when necessary.

*Using **ORD** and **VAL** With Enumeration Types*

The standard type conversion functions **ORD** and **VAL** may be applied to enumeration types. As was stated in Chapter 3, **ORD**'s most common use is to return the ASCII character code of a character. However, it can be used to return the position of any value of an enumeration type as well. **VAL** converts a **CARDINAL** number into its corresponding enumeration value.

In enumeration types, the positions are numbered starting at 0. Therefore, given enumeration values *N1* through *Nn*, the following is true.

ORD(N1)=0
ORD(N2)=1
ORD(N3)=3
.
.
.
ORD(Nn) = n−1

For example, using the **FRUIT** type defined earlier, **ORD(apple)** is 0, and **ORD(banana)** is 2.

To use **VAL** with enumerations, use the enumeration type name as the target type and **CARDINAL** value of the enumeration value you wish to convert to. For example,

```
KindOfFruit:=VAL(FRUIT,3);
```

places the value **pear** into **KindOfFruit**.

ORD and **VAL** play very important parts in the use of enumerations because they are often the best way to get information into and out of enumeration type variables. In Modula-2 there is no direct way either to display the value of an enumeration variable on the screen or to enter its value from the keyboard. Because of this, it is very common to convert between enumeration types and **CARDINAL**s. For example, the following program will tell you the days of the month of January if you supply the day of the week the month starts on. To keep the program's code very short, only the number equivalent of the day's name is printed. Notice the use of **ORD** and **VAL**.

```
MODULE DayOfMonth;

  FROM InOut IMPORT WriteLn, WriteString, Write,
                    ReadCard, WriteCard, ReadString;

  TYPE
    DAY = (sun,mon, tue, wed, thu, fri, sat);

  VAR
    DayOfWeek: DAY;
    Jan: ARRAY[1..31] OF DAY;
    i,offset: CARDINAL;

BEGIN
  WriteString("what day of week is Jan 1? ");
  ReadCard(offset);
  WriteLn;

  FOR  i:=1 TO 31 DO
    Jan[i]:=VAL(DAY,(i+offset-1) MOD 7);
  END;
```

```
  REPEAT
    WriteString('Enter day (0 to quit): ');
    ReadCard(i); WriteString('  day is ');
    IF (i>0) AND (i<32) THEN
      WriteCard(ORD(Jan[i]),3);
      WriteLn;
    END;
  UNTIL i=0;
END DayOfMonth.
```

This type of input and output is fine for some situations, especially debugging. However, it takes quite a bit more code to actually display the names of the days, as is shown in this second version of the program.

```
MODULE DayOfMonth2;

  FROM InOut IMPORT WriteLn, WriteString, Write,
                    ReadCard, WriteCard, ReadString;

  TYPE
    DAY = (sun,mon, tue, wed, thu, fri, sat);

  VAR
    DayOfWeek: DAY;
    Jan: ARRAY[1..31] OF DAY;
    i,offset: CARDINAL;

BEGIN
  WriteString("what day of week is Jan 1? ");
  ReadCard(offset);
  WriteLn;

  FOR  i:=1 TO 31 DO
    Jan[i]:=VAL(DAY,(i+offset-1) MOD 7);
  END;

  REPEAT
    WriteString('Enter day (0 to quit): ');
    ReadCard(i);
    IF (i>0) AND (i<32) THEN
      DayOfWeek:=Jan[i];
      WriteString('Jan '); WriteCard(i,2);
      WriteString(' is a ');
      (* use CASE statement to convert enumerations to
         strings  *)
      CASE DayOfWeek OF
        sun: WriteString('Sunday') |
        mon: WriteString('Monday') |
        tue: WriteString('Tuesday') |
        wed: WriteString('Wednesday') |
        thu: WriteString('Thursday') |
        fri: WriteString('Friday') |
        sat: WriteString('Saturday')
      END;
      WriteLn;
    END;
  UNTIL i=0;
END DayOfMonth2.
```

Using INC and DEC

Modula-2 has two special built-in procedures, **INC** and **DEC**, that allow enumeration type variables to be incremented or decremented. These are needed because the standard arithmetic operators cannot be used with enumerations. **INC** and **DEC** have the following general format.

INC(<*var*>,<*amount*>);
DEC(<*var*>,<*amount*>);

Here, ***var*** is an enumeration variable, and ***amount*** is the amount that <*var*> is to be incremented or decremented; ***amount*** is optional. If <*amount*> is missing, then the value is assumed to be 1. In a Modula-2 compiler, **INTEGER**, **CHAR**, and **CARDINAL** essentially are treated as built-in enumerations. Thus, both **INC** and **DEC** can be applied to these types as well. To see how **INC** and **DEC** work, examine the following example.

```
TYPE
  T = (a, b, c, d);

VAR
  e: T;

BEGIN
  e:=a;
  INC(e);          (* e = b *)
  INC(e,2);        (* e = d *)
  DEC(e,3);        (* e = a *)
END
```

The short program shown in the next example gives you a taste of how **INC** and **DEC** are used. You should enter this program in your computer and experiment with it.

```
MODULE IncDec;

  FROM InOut IMPORT WriteLn, WriteString, WriteCard;

  TYPE
    STATES = (IL, FL, GA, AK, ME, CA, NY);

  VAR
    st: STATES;
    i: CARDINAL;

BEGIN
  st:=IL;
  INC(st);
```

```
    IF st=FL THEN WriteString('st now has FL') END;
    WriteLn;
    st:=CA;
    DEC(st,2);
    WriteCard(ORD(st),2);   (* will be AK or 3 *)
    i:=10; INC(i);
    WriteCard(i,2);
  END IncDec.
```

Why Enumerations?

Now that you know what enumeration data types are and how to use them, you may want to know why they exist at all and when it is appropriate to use them. There are two reasons why enumeration data types are supported by Modula-2. The first is that they allow you to give certain kinds of values names. This not only makes your code self-documenting, but it also helps you clearly define the exact data a variable may hold.

The second reason is that they help prevent bugs. By carefully defining and restricting the values of a type of data, you can be sure that only valid data are being operated on by your routines. Enumeration type variables always have valid data because, first, you define all possible values in the **TYPE** definition, and second, range checking in Modula-2 is done at run time, so invalid assignments cause errors to be reported. In essence, enumeration types help verify the accuracy of your code.

In real-world programming, enumeration types find their greatest use in large, complex projects where it is important to be able to prove the correctness of a routine. They are seldom used in one-person projects except in special situations, because as the examples have shown, it can be tedious to do I/O operations on them. However, this should not deter you from using them when the occasion calls.

Subrange Types

Type definitions can be used to restrict the range of a built-in data type or a previously defined enumeration. This capability is particularly useful in testing and verifying the correctness of programs. Because Modula-2 checks both types and ranges at run time, restricting the range of values that a variable can have helps expose bugs by causing run-time error messages when any out-of-range values are found. Also, limiting the contents of a variable to only those values that have meaning in terms of the context of a program helps prevent bugs.

The general form of a *subrange* type is

TYPE
  <Sname> = [*C1*..*Cn*];

where ***<Sname>*** is the name of the subrange type, ***C1*** is a constant with the lowest value in the range, and ***Cn*** is a constant with the highest value in the range. For example, to create a new type called **CLOCK** that can only have values 1 through 24, you would write

```
TYPE
  CLOCK = [1..24];
```

Here are some other examples.

```
TYPE

  LETTER = ["A".."Z"];
  YEAR = [1..365];
  INDEX = [-100..100];
```

The valid values of a subrange take on the type of their *base* type. The base type is simply what makes up the subrange. In the example shown here, **LETTER**'s base type is **CHAR**, **YEAR**'s is **CARDINAL**, and **INDEX**'s is **INTEGER**. Subranges may not be created for type **REAL**. When the lowest value is negative, the base type is assumed to be **INTEGER**; otherwise, it is assumed to be **CARDINAL**.

A critical point about subranges is that they are not, and have nothing to do with, arrays. The subrange only specifies a list of possible values a variable may hold; therefore, variables of subrange types are used just like other variables, except that they have a restricted range. For example, the simple timer program that follows uses subrange variables. Notice the use of the library procedure **KeyPressed**. This function returns **TRUE** if a key has been pressed, and **FALSE** otherwise. This function may be in a different library and called something else, depending on the implementation of Modula-2 you are using.

```
MODULE TIMER;

  FROM InOut IMPORT WriteLn, WriteString, Write,
                    WriteCard, Read;
  FROM Keyboard IMPORT KeyPressed;

  TYPE
    CLOCK = [1..24];
    MINUTE = [1..60];
    SECOND = [1..60];

  VAR
    hr: CLOCK;
    min: MINUTE;
    second: SECOND;
    delay:CARDINAL;
    ch: CHAR;

BEGIN
  WriteString('Press a key to start: ');
  Read(ch);
  LOOP
    (* 24 hour timer *)
    FOR hr:=1 TO 24 DO
      FOR min:=1 TO 60 DO
        FOR second:=1 TO 60 DO
          FOR delay:=1 TO 1000 DO END;
          WriteCard(hr,2);
          Write(':');
          WriteCard(min,2);
          Write(':');
          WriteCard(second,2);
          WriteLn;
          IF KeyPressed() THEN EXIT END
        END
      END
    END
  END
END TIMER.
```

You could use this program to time any event up to 24 hours, 60 minutes, and 60 seconds long. Because all systems differ, the variable **delay** will need to be changed to provide accurate timing. Notice how each of the subrange variables is used in the program in a standard fashion. There is no difference between subrange variables and variables of their base type, except in the range of values they can hold.

As mentioned at the start of this section, subranges of enumeration types can also be declared. For example, you can define a subrange type called **WEEKDAY** that has a range of Monday through Friday as shown here.

```
TYPE
  DAY = (sun,mon, tue, wed, thu, fri, sat);
  WEEKDAY = [mon..fri];
```

You might use these two types to modify the **DayOfMonth** program developed earlier so that it prints a list of the work days in January. Here, a nested **FOR** loop is used to determine whether a day is a weekday or falls on a weekend.

```
MODULE WorkDays;

  FROM InOut IMPORT WriteLn, WriteString,
                    ReadCard, WriteCard;

  TYPE
    DAY = (sun,mon, tue, wed, thu, fri, sat);
    WEEKDAY = [mon..fri];
    MONTH = [1..31];
  VAR
    DayOfWeek: DAY;
    Jan: ARRAY[1..31] OF DAY;
    i,offset: MONTH;
    j: WEEKDAY;

BEGIN

  WriteString("what day of week is Jan 1? ");
  ReadCard(offset);
  WriteLn;

  FOR  i:=1 TO 31 DO
    Jan[i]:=VAL(DAY,(i+offset-1) MOD 7);
  END;

  (* display the dates of the business days only *)

  FOR i:=1 TO 31 DO
    FOR j:=mon TO fri DO
      IF Jan[i]=j THEN WriteCard(i,3) END
    END
  END
END WorkDays.
```

As with enumeration types, subranges find their greatest application in large, complex projects where program readability and verification are important.

Sets

Modula-2, along with its predecessor Pascal, are unique among the mainstream, general-purpose programming languages in that they support the **SET** data type. The use and manipulation of sets in Modula-2 closely mirrors that of mathematics, so a brief review of sets and their operations is in order.

Overview of Set Theory

A *set* is a collection of objects. For example, the set of the major American car manufactures is Chrysler, GM, and Ford. In mathematics, sets are usually specified by placing their contents between curly braces. Therefore, in standard set notation, this set would be notated as

{Chrysler, GM, Ford}

You can symbolically denote a set by assigning it to a variable. Here, **Maker** is assigned the set of major car manufacturers.

Maker = {Chrysler, GM, Ford}

Maker now contains the set {Chrysler, GM, Ford}.

A set is said to be a *subset* of another set if all of its members are also members of the other set. For example,

{GM, Ford}

is a subset of **Maker**. However,

{GM, American Motors, Ford}

is *not* a subset of **Maker**, because American Motors is not a member of **Maker**.

To call a set a *superset* of another set implies that the other set is its subset. For instance,

{Chrysler, GM, Ford, Toyota}

is a superset of **Maker**.

An element (object) is either a member of a set, or it is not—it can't be both at the same time. This is called the *exclusionary principle.*

The order of the elements in a set is irrelevant. This means that

{GM, Ford}

is the same as

{Ford, GM}

A set may not contain duplicate members. Therefore, the following set is simply not defined.

{GM, GM}

Finally, a set may be empty; that is, it may contain no members. The empty, or *null,* set is denoted as {}.

Set Operations

Both in mathematics and in Modula-2, several set operations are defined. The Modula-2 symbols for these operations will be used here instead of the standard mathematical symbols, since you will be using them in your programs. For this discussion, assume the following two sets:

A = {1, 2, 3, 4, 5}
B = {4, 5, 6, 7, 8}

The *union* of two sets is a set that contains all the members found in either. In Modula-2, this operation is denoted by the + sign. For example,

A + B

yields the set

{1, 2, 3, 4, 5, 6, 7, 8}

As stated, duplicate members are not allowed, so even though 4 and 5 occurred in each set, they are only represented once in their union.

The *intersection* of two sets is a set that contains only those objects found in both the sets. This operation is denoted by the * sign. Therefore A*B produces the following.

{4, 5}

The *difference* between two sets is the set that contains only elements found in the first set but not in the second set. This operation is denoted by the − sign. For example, A − B yields

{1, 2, 3}

Finally, the *symmetric difference* between two sets is a set that contains the elements that are unique to both sets. This is denoted by the / sign. For example, A/B produces

{1, 2, 3, 6, 7, 8}

Now that you know the basics of sets and their manipulations, it is time to see how they are implemented in Modula-2.

Declaring a Set

Sets are declared in Modula-2 using the **SET** statement. The general form is shown here.

```
TYPE
   <sname> = SET OF <type>;
```

where <***sname***> is the name of the set, and <***type***> is a type specifier for either an enumeration or subrange type.

Because sets are defined only for enumeration or subrange types, a previously defined subrange or enumeration type is required. Therefore, the actual set definition is a combination of two statements: the subrange or enumeration definition and the **SET** definition. The general form of this sequence is shown here.

```
TYPE
   <SetType> = <enumeration-or-subrange>;
   <sname> = SET OF <SetType>;
```

A set of the octal digits, for example, can be created using this code.

```
TYPE
  OCTAL = [0..7];
  OCTSET = SET OF OCTSET;
```

The only exception to this rule is **BITSET**, which is built into the Modula-2 compiler and need not be defined prior to use.

The type **BITSET** is a set of the numbers between 0 and N−1, where N is the number of bits in a word. For most 16-bit systems, this means the numbers 0 through 15.

Variables of set types are declared like all other variables, as the following examples show.

```
VAR
  LOW, HI: OCTSET;
  FirstByte: OCTSET;
  SecondByte: OCTSET;
  info: BITSET;
```

One point to keep in mind is that generally set definitions are limited to only a few elements. Often this number falls in the range 16 to 32.

Using Sets

Now you can define sets, but there are several rules that you need to know in order to use them. First, a set variable can be assigned a set constant using the general form

<SetVar>:=<SetType>{set};

where ***<SetVar>*** is a variable of ***<SetType>***, and ***set*** is a valid set of ***<SetType>***. Using **OCTSET**, defined earlier, the following statement assigns **LOW** the value **{1,2,3}**.

```
LOW:=OCTSET{1,2,3};
```

As stated, the set type must precede the actual set. This is essentially an explicit type reference and is required. The statement shown here is wrong and will not compile.

```
LOW:={1,2,3};   (* WRONG *)
```

Although assigning set constants can be useful during initialization, generally either set variables are assigned to other set variables, or elements are included or excluded from existing set variables. Modula-2 has two built-in procedures that can be used to include or exclude (remove) an element from a set. **INCL** adds a member to a specified set, and **EXCL** removes a member from a specified set. The general forms of these procedures are

INCL(<*SetVar*>,<*element*>);
EXCL(<*SetVar*>,<*element*>);

where <***SetVar***> is a set variable, and <***element***> is a valid member of its set type. For example, using **OCTSET**,

```
HI:=OCTSET{}; (* empty set *)
INCL(HI,1);   (* HI = {1} *)
INCL(HI,3);   (* HI = {1, 3} *)
INCL(HI,5);   (* HI = {1, 3, 5} *)
EXCL(HI,3);   (* HI = {1, 5} *)
```

the final value of **HI** is {1, 5}.

Modula-2 provides the operator **IN** to determine whether an element is part of a set. The result of the **IN** operation is **BOOLEAN** and can be used in the **IF** statement and the **WHILE/DO** and **REPEAT/UNTIL** loops. The general form of the **IN** operation is

<*element*> IN <*Set*>

where <***element***> is the element being searched for in set <***Set***>. Therefore, this sequence of code will print the message **is in** on the screen.

```
LOW:=OCTSET{1, 2, 3};
IF 2 IN LOW THEN WriteString('is in') END;
```

The following simple program illustrates what you have learned so far. You might want to enter this into your computer and play with it a little before continuing.

```
MODULE SetExample;

  FROM InOut IMPORT WriteLn, WriteString;

  TYPE
    OCTAL = [0..7];
    OCTSET = SET OF OCTAL;
```

```
    VAR
      LOW, HI: OCTSET;

  BEGIN
    LOW:=OCTSET{1,2};
    IF 1 IN LOW THEN WriteString('1 included') END;
    WriteLn;
    INCL(LOW,4);
    IF 4 IN LOW THEN WriteString('4 included') END;
    WriteLn;

    HI:=LOW;
    EXCL(HI,2);
    IF NOT (2 IN HI) THEN WriteString('2 not in HI') END;
    WriteLn;
    IF HI <= LOW THEN WriteString('HI is subset of LOW') END;
  END SetExample.
```

As you learned earlier in this section, Modula-2 supports four set operations:

+ union
− difference
* intersection
/ symmetric difference

These operations allow you to perform complex set manipulations quickly, bypassing a long series of **IF**s, **INCL**s, and **EXCL**s. In fact, **INCL** and **EXCL** are simply special cases of + and −. For example, writing

```
INCL(HI,1);
EXCL(HI,4);
```

is the same as writing

```
HI:=HI+OCTSET{1};
HI:=HI-OCTSET{4};
```

The following program illustrates the use of some of the operations and provides a different example for you to study. This program creates two sets, based on your input, of friends and foes among the superpowers and then determines if any foes are also part of NATO.

```
MODULE FriendFoe;

  FROM InOut IMPORT WriteLn, WriteString, Write,
                    Read;

  TYPE
    COUNTRIES = (France, Germany, England, US, Russia, China);
    MajorPowers = SET OF COUNTRIES;
       VAR
```

```
     friends, foes: MajorPowers;
     NATO: MajorPowers;
     ch: CHAR;

BEGIN   friends:=MajorPowers{};    foes:=MajorPowers{};
NATO:=MajorPowers{US, England, Germany, France};

   (* build sets of both friends and foes.*)    REPEAT
     WriteString('Enter a friend (q to quit): ');
     Read(ch); Write(ch);
     CASE ch OF
       'f': INCL(friends,France) |
       'g':  INCL(friends,Germany)  |
       'e': INCL(friends,England) |
       'u': INCL(friends,US) |
       'r': INCL(friends,Russia) |
       'c': INCL(friends,China)
     ELSE
     END;
     WriteLn;   UNTIL ch='q';    foes:=MajorPowers{France, Germany,
England,
                     US, Russia, China}-friends;    IF Russia IN
foes THEN WriteString('Russia is foe ') END;   IF US IN friends
THEN WriteString(' US is friend') END;  IF
(NATO*foes)<>MajorPowers{} THEN
     WriteString('foes in NATO')   END; END FriendFoe.
```

Notice that the last **IF** statement uses set intersection to determine if there are any foes in NATO.

Although sets are intellectually stimulating and have their place in certain areas of programming—especially programming illustrating set theory—they should not be used when a simpler data type will do. The reason for this is twofold. First, set operations take longer to perform than simple arithmetic; hence, they slow down your program. Second, it is very difficult and tedious to perform input and output operations on set data types, as the examples in this section have shown.

EXERCISES

1. Show the **TYPE** and **VAR** declarations that create three string variables called **S1**, **S2**, and **S3** of type **STRING40**, which is a 40-byte character array.

2. What is the difference between an enumeration and a subrange?

3. What is the difference between an enumeration and a set?

4. Given

$$A = \{a, b, c, d\}$$
$$B = \{d, e, f, g\}$$

show the outcome of A+B, A∗B, A−B, A/B.

5. What is wrong with this code fragment?

```
TYPE
  T = [1..10];
VAR
  X: INTEGER;
  Y: T;

BEGIN
  Y:=8;
  X:=Y;
```

6. Given

```
TYPE
  T: (A, B, C, D, E, F);
```

what is **ORD(C)**? What is **VAL(T,5)**?

ANSWERS

1.
```
TYPE
  STRING40 = ARRAY [0..39] OF CHAR;

VAR
  S1,S2,S3: STRING40;
```

2. An enumeration is a user-defined type in which all possible values are given names and explicitly stated. A subrange is a user-defined type that is a restricted range of a previously defined or standard type.

3. An enumeration is a list of possible values. A set is a grouping of objects.

4. A+B = {a, b, c, d, e, f, g}
   A∗B = {d}
   A−B = {a, b, c}
   A/B = {a, b, c, e, f, g}

5. By default, the base type of **T** is **CARDINAL**; hence, **Y** is essentially of type **CARDINAL**. Therefore assigning the **INTEGER X** to **Y** results in a type mismatch.

6. **ORD(C)** is 2, and **VAL(T,5)** is F.

Procedures

CHAPTER 6

Until now, all the programs that you have seen consisted of declarations and a main body of code. While this is fine for very simple programs and for learning the basics of Modula-2, it is not adequate for any real task. In this chapter you will learn about one of Modula-2's most important constructs, the **PROCEDURE**, and see how it expands its power.

What Are ***PROCEDUREs?***

PROCEDUREs are, in essence, stand-alone subroutines. Recall that a block of code is an indivisible grouping of statements that are logically connected. A **PROCEDURE** extends this concept further by allowing a block of code to be given a name and referenced (executed) simply by using that name. Therefore, a **PROCEDURE** is a block of code that is executed whenever its name is encountered.

PROCEDUREs are building blocks of Modula-2 programs, and virtually all programming takes place within them. Unlike BASIC subroutines (GOSUBs), which are inseparable from the program itself, Modula-2 **PROCEDURE**s are like little programs that can be thought of as separate from the main body of the program. Like all subroutines, they can be called repeatedly from various parts of the main program or from other procedures. They may also take arguments and return values.

Basic Form Of a ***PROCEDURE***

All **PROCEDURE**s in Modula-2 have the following general form.

```
PROCEDURE <ProcName> (parameter-list);
            <constant-declarations>
            <type-declarations>             Declaration section
            <variable-declarations>
            <procedure-declarations>
BEGIN
    <statement-body>                        PROCEDURE code
END <ProcName>;
```

Here, ***ProcName*** is the name of the **PROCEDURE**. If the **PROCEDURE** has parameters, they must be included in the ***parameter-list***; otherwise, the list and the parentheses can be omitted. **PROCEDURE**s must end with the **PROCEDURE** name followed by a semicolon. As you can see, the form of a **PROCEDURE** is very similar to that of a **MODULE** with the single exception that a **PROCEDURE** may not **IMPORT** another **PROCEDURE**; this must be done by the **MODULE**. Note that it is possible to define a **PROCEDURE** inside another **PROCEDURE**.

PROCEDURE names follow the same rules as variable names. They also should not be the same as any of the standard procedures found in the libraries of your compiler.

PROCEDUREs are declared just prior to the main body of code in a **MODULE**, as shown here.

```
MODULE ModName;
      <import-list>
      <constant-declarations>
      <type-declarations>
      <variable-declarations>
      <procedure-declarations>
BEGIN
      <statement-body>
END ModName.
```

There are several types of **PROCEDURE**s: **PROCEDURE**s with no parameters, **PROCEDURE**s with parameters, and **PROCEDURE**s that return a value. Each of these will be examined in turn.

Creating a ***PROCEDURE***

As a first example, you will create three simple **PROCEDURE**s, called **P1**, **P2**, and **P3**, that print their name on the screen when they are executed. They will look like this:

```
PROCEDURE P1;
BEGIN
  WriteString('This is P1');
  WriteLn;
END P1;

PROCEDURE P2;
BEGIN
  WriteString('This is P2');
  WriteLn;
END P2;

PROCEDURE P3;
BEGIN
  WriteString('This is P3');
  WriteLn;
END P3;
```

Now that the **PROCEDURE**s have been defined, put them together with a program that will execute them, such as the one that follows.

```
MODULE ProcTest;
  FROM InOut IMPORT WriteString, WriteLn;

  PROCEDURE P1;
  BEGIN
    WriteString('This is P1');
    WriteLn;
  END P1;

  PROCEDURE P2;
  BEGIN
    WriteString('This is P2');
    WriteLn;
  END P2;

  PROCEDURE P3;
  BEGIN
    WriteString('This is P3');
    WriteLn;
  END P3;

BEGIN  (* MODULE code *)
  P1;  (* execute P1 *)
  P2;  (* execute P2 *)
  P3;  (* execute P3 *)
END ProcTest.
```

Now follow the execution of this program. A **MODULE** (program) begins execution with the first statement of its **MODULE** code; that is, it does not execute any **PROCEDURE**s just because they are declared in the program and appear prior to the main body of code. If you have only programmed in BASIC or another simple language, this may be unsettling. However, remember that a **PROCEDURE** declaration is just that: a declaration and definition of what the **PROCEDURE** will do; it does not cause execution. To reiterate, when the **MODULE** begins execution, it starts with the first statement in its code, not the first **PROCEDURE**. In the example program shown, the first statement is **P1;**. This means that **PROCEDURE P1** will be executed, and the message **This is P1** will be printed on the screen. The process of invoking a **PROCEDURE** is commonly referred to as *calling* the **PROCEDURE**. When the statement **END P1;** is encountered, **P1**'s execution is completed, and execution resumes at the next statement after the call. In this case, the next statement is **P2;**, which means that **P2** will execute. Finally, **P3** will execute, and the program will end. When the program is run, its output will be as follows:

```
This is P1
This is P2
This is P3
```

If **PROCEDURE**s are new to you, you should enter this program and experiment with it until you understand what is happening. (BASIC programmers: Executing a **PROCEDURE** is a little like using GOSUB, except **PROCEDURE**s are much more flexible.)

Now that you have seen how to create and execute a **PROCEDURE**, look at a somewhat more complex example. The program shown here will compute the common living space of a house. In its present form it contains no **PROCEDURE**s.

```
MODULE Area;
  (* compute the common living area of a house *)
  FROM InOut IMPORT ReadCard, WriteCard, WriteString,
                    WriteLn;

   VAR
     l,w,area: CARDINAL;


BEGIN
  area:=0;
  WriteString("enter length and width for living room: ");
  ReadCard(l);
  WriteString(' by ');
  ReadCard(w);
  WriteLn;
  area:=l*w+area;  (* living room *)

  WriteString("enter length and width for dining room: ");
  ReadCard(l);
  WriteString(' by ');
  ReadCard(w);
  WriteLn;
  area:=l*w+area;  (* dining room *)

  WriteString("enter length and width for kitchen: ");
  ReadCard(l);
  WriteString(' by ');
  ReadCard(w);
  WriteLn;
  area:=l*w+area;  (* kitchen *)

  WriteString("enter length and width for recreation room: ");
  ReadCard(l);
  WriteString(' by ');
  ReadCard(w);
  WriteLn;
  area:=l*w+area;  (* recreation room *)

  WriteString('Total common living space of house is: ');
  WriteCard(area,5);
  WriteString(' square feet.');
END Area.
```

As you can see, the code fragment

```
ReadCard(l);
WriteString(' by ');
ReadCard(w);
WriteLn;
area:=l*w+area;
```

is repeated four times in the program. Not only is this wasteful in terms of memory usage, but it makes the program appear more complex than it really is. Since this piece of code is exactly the same each time it is used, it is a prime candidate for transformation into a **PROCEDURE**. Doing this will shorten the program and make it easier to read. The **PROCEDURE FindArea**, shown here, contains the repeated code.

```
PROCEDURE FindArea;
BEGIN
  ReadCard(l);
  WriteString(' by ');
  ReadCard(w);
  WriteLn;
  area:=area+l*w;
END FindArea;
```

Remember, **FindArea** is the **PROCEDURE**'s name and is used to reference the **PROCEDURE** in the main program.

Before **FindArea** can be used, the **MODULE** code must be altered. To do this, the code that has been placed in **FindArea** must be deleted from the program and replaced with a call to **FindArea**. The shorter and more efficient version of the program is shown here.

```
MODULE Area;
  (* compute the common living area of a house *)
  FROM InOut IMPORT ReadCard, WriteCard, WriteString,
                    WriteLn;

  VAR
    l,w,area: CARDINAL;

  PROCEDURE FindArea;
  BEGIN
      ReadCard(l);
      WriteString(' by ');
      ReadCard(w);
      WriteLn;
      area:=area+l*w;
    END FindArea;

  BEGIN
    area:=0;
    WriteString("enter length and width for living room: ");
    FindArea;
```

```
    WriteString("enter length and width for dining room: ");
    FindArea;
    WriteString("enter length and width for kitchen: ");
    FindArea;
    WriteString("enter length and width for recreation room: ");
    FindArea;
    WriteString('Total common living space of house is: ');
    WriteCard(area,5);
    WriteString(' square feet.');
  END Area.
```

Global and Local Variables

As you saw in the general format for **PROCEDURE**s, it is possible to declare variables inside a **PROCEDURE**. As you will see, where a variable is declared has substantial impact on how your programs operate.

There are essentially two kinds of variables: *global* and *local*. A global variable is known throughout the entire **MODULE** and may be used by any **PROCEDURE** inside the same **MODULE** and by the main body of code. This is why the **PROCEDURE FindArea** did not need to declare any variables of its own—it simply used the ones declared by the **MODULE**. By contrast, a local variable is known to and may be used by only the **PROCEDURE** in which it is declared. This means that a variable declared inside a **PROCEDURE** can be used by that **PROCEDURE**, but by no other **PROCEDURE** or **MODULE** code (an exception is nested **PROCEDURE**s, described later in this chapter).

There is another very important difference between local and global variables. A global variable exists the entire time the program is executing, but a local variable exists only while the **PROCEDURE** in which it is declared executes. In fact, local variables go in and out of existence each time their **PROCEDURE** is entered and left. This means that *local variables do not hold their values between* **PROCEDURE** *calls.*

The reason that global variables can stay in existence the entire life of a program is that storage for them is in a special place in memory that is not used for anything else during the execution of a program. However, local variables are stored in the stack space of the computer's memory. As you probably know, the stack is used for a variety of purposes as a program executes, and so storage in it can be only temporary. (A stack is simply a region of memory set aside to hold information related to the execution of a program, such as return addresses, the contents of the registers of the CPU, and in the case of many high-level programming languages, the information related to a subroutine call.)

To see how local variables work, you can rewrite the **Area** program slightly to make the variables **l** and **w** local only to **FindArea**. Because they are no longer needed elsewhere, they need not be declared by the **MODULE** and can be removed from it. The program now looks like this:

```
MODULE Area;
  (* compute the common living area of a house *)
  FROM InOut IMPORT ReadCard, WriteCard, WriteString,
                    WriteLn;

  VAR
    area: CARDINAL;

  PROCEDURE FindArea;
    VAR
      l,w:CARDINAL;     (* used only by FindArea *)
  BEGIN
    ReadCard(l);
    WriteString(' by ');
    ReadCard(w);
    WriteLn;
    area:=area+l*w;
  END FindArea;


BEGIN
  area:=0;
  WriteString("enter length and width for living room: ");
  FindArea;
  WriteString("enter length and width for dining room: ");
  FindArea;
  WriteString("enter length and width for kitchen: ");
  FindArea;
  WriteString("enter length and width for recreation room: ");
  FindArea;
  WriteString('Total common living space of house is: ');
  WriteCard(area,5);
  WriteString(' square feet.');
END Area.
```

Note that it is necessary to leave **area** global; otherwise, **area** would not be available for use by the **MODULE** code. It is important to remember that **l** and **w** now may not be used by the **MODULE** code because they are not known there. Trying to reference them outside of **FindArea** would result in a compile-time error.

Because local variables are known only to the **PROCEDURE**s in which they are declared, it is possible to have global and local variables with the same name without conflicts or side effects. To see how this works, consider the following program.

```
MODULE Scope;
  FROM InOut IMPORT WriteCard, WriteString, WriteLn;

  VAR
    i: CARDINAL;     (* this is global *)

  PROCEDURE A;
    VAR
      i:CARDINAL;      (* this is local to A *)
  BEGIN
    i:=10;           (* this affects only local i *)
    WriteString('i in A: ');
    WriteCard(i,5);
    WriteLn;
  END A;

  PROCEDURE B;
  BEGIN
    i:=100;          (* this affects global i *)
  END B;

BEGIN
  i:=1;
  WriteString('global i: ') ;
  WriteCard(i,3);  (* prints 1 *)
  WriteLn;
  A;
  WriteString('global i after calling A: ');
  WriteCard(i,3);  (* prints 1 *)
  WriteLn;
  B;
  WriteString('global i after calling B: ');
  WriteCard(i,3);  (* prints 100 *)
END Scope.
```

In this program, there are two distinct variables called **i**. The **i** declared inside **PROCEDURE A** has no effect on the global **i**. The output obtained is

```
global i: 1
i in A: 10
global i after calling A: 1
global i after calling B: 100
```

Because the **i** declared in **A** is known only to **A**, it does not affect the global variable of the same name.

When a global and local variable both have the same name, the local variable will be used inside the **PROCEDURE** in which it is declared instead of the global variable. This is because during compilation, each time a variable is encountered inside a **PROCEDURE**, the Modula-2 compiler first checks the variables declared inside that **PROCEDURE** to see if the variable has been declared there. Only if the variable has not been declared in the **PROCEDURE** are the global declarations examined.

It is also possible for more than one **PROCEDURE** to have a variable of the same name without causing any harm or side effects. For example, consider this code:

```
PROCEDURE A;
   VAR
      X: INTEGER;
BEGIN
.
.
.
END A;

PROCEDURE B;
   VAR
      X: INTEGER;
BEGIN
.
.
.
END B;
```

Here, **A**'s **X** has nothing to do with **B**'s **X**. In fact, it is extremely common to use the same variable names for counters, temporary values, and similar elements. Later in this chapter you will learn more about the formal rules that govern what variables are known where.

PROCEDUREs *With Parameters*

In the examples you have seen so far, no information was explicitly passed to a **PROCEDURE**. However, many **PROCEDURE**s require some information from the calling routine in order to be useful. Although this can, in theory, be done using global variables, this is not desirable for two reasons. First, having many global variables in a program invites side effects, such as the accidental changing of the value of a variable. (This side effect is extremely common in BASIC because all variables must be global.) Second, using global variables in **PROCEDURE**s reduces the generality of the routine. The solution to these problems is the *parameter.*

You have already been using procedures with parameters because most of the standard library routines have one or more parameters. For example, **WriteCard** has two parameters: the number to be displayed and the field width. **PROCEDUREs** that you write use parameters in the same way.

A parameter is a special local variable that is used to pass information into a **PROCEDURE**. Parameters are declared in a parenthesized list immediately following the **PROCEDURE** name. The general form of this list is

(*Var1*:<*type*>; *Var2*:<*type*>; ... ; *VarN*:<*type*>)

where ***Var1*** through ***VarN*** are the parameter names, and ***type*** is the type of each parameter. Parameters of the same type may be listed together separated by commas. Parameters of different types are separated by semicolons. ***Var1*** through ***VarN*** are called the *formal parameters* of the **PROCEDURE**. For example, the following **PROCEDURE** has one parameter, **i**. The **PROCEDURE** computes the factorial of this parameter and displays the result on the screen.

```
PROCEDURE  Fact(i:CARDINAL);
(* compute factorial of i *)
  VAR
    x,y:CARDINAL;

  BEGIN
    y:=1;
    FOR x:=1 TO i DO
      y:=y*x;
    END;
    WriteCard(y,5);
    WriteLn;
  END Fact;
```

The following program shows how **Fact** can be used.

```
MODULE Factorial;
  FROM InOut IMPORT ReadCard, WriteCard, WriteString,
                    WriteLn;

   VAR
     f: CARDINAL;
     answer: CARDINAL;

   PROCEDURE  Fact(i:CARDINAL);
   (* compute factorial of i *)
     VAR
       x,y:CARDINAL;
```

```
BEGIN
  y:=1;
  FOR x:=1 TO i DO
    y:=y*x;

  END;
  WriteCard(y,5);
  WriteLn;
END Fact;

BEGIN
  Fact(1);
  Fact(2);
  Fact(3);
  Fact(4);
END Factorial.
```

Because **Fact** has one parameter, you must supply one *argument* when you call **Fact**. An argument is the actual information the **PROCEDURE** uses when it is executed. The value of the argument is copied into parameter **i** each time **Fact** is executed. Thus, **Fact** can be used to compute the factorial of any number. This program will print the numbers 1, 2, 6, and 24 on the screen.

The arguments in a **PROCEDURE** do not need to be constants. They can also be variables, as shown in the following program. Here, the value of the variable **f** is passed to **Fact**.

```
MODULE Factorial;
  FROM InOut IMPORT ReadCard, WriteCard, WriteString,
                    WriteLn;

   VAR
     f: CARDINAL;
     answer: CARDINAL;

   PROCEDURE  Fact(i:CARDINAL);
   (* compute factorial of i *)
     VAR
       x,y:CARDINAL;

     BEGIN
       y:=1;
       FOR x:=1 TO i DO
         y:=y*x;
       END;
       WriteCard(y,5);
       WriteLn;
     END Fact;


BEGIN
  REPEAT
    WriteString("enter number: ");
```

```
      ReadCard(f);
      WriteLn;
      WriteString('Answer is: ');
      Fact(f);  (* compute factorial *)
    UNTIL f=0;
  END Factorial.
```

The important point to remember is that the type of the argument must be the same as the type of the parameter that is to receive it. For example, the following code fragment is incorrect and either will not compile or will produce an error, depending on your compiler, because of the type mismatch.

```
MODULE IncorrectProgram;

  VAR
    X: INTEGER;

  PROCEDURE SQR(NUM:CARDINAL);
  BEGIN
    .
    .
    .
  END SQR;

BEGIN
  X:=-1;
  SQR(X);  (* type mismatch *)
END IncorrectProgram.
```

Storage for parameters, as for other local variables, is on the stack.

Value and Variable Parameters

In Modula-2, there are two ways for parameters to be defined. They can be defined either as *value parameters* or as *variable parameters*. So far, we have been using only value parameters; however, variable parameters can greatly increase the power of **PROCEDUREs**. To understand the difference between the two definitions of parameter, you need to know a little about how arguments are passed to **PROCEDUREs**.

Arguments may be passed to procedures in one of two ways. The first way is *call by value.* This method copies the *value* of the argument into the formal parameter of the **PROCEDURE**. This means that any changes made to the parameter do not affect the actual variable used as the argument because the **PROCEDURE** operates only on a copy of the argument, not on the argument itself. In Modula-2, parameters called in this way are known as *value parameters* because only their values are passed.

Call by reference is the second way arguments can be passed to a **PROCEDURE**. In this method, the actual variable used as an argument is passed to the **PROCEDURE**. This means that changes made to the parameter inside the **PROCEDURE** also affect the variable outside the **PROCEDURE** used to call the **PROCEDURE**. Parameters called in this way are known as *variable parameters* in Modula-2 because, conceptually, the actual variable used in the call is passed to the function. (Technically, it is the *address* of the argument that is passed to the formal parameters, but this distinction is not important to the discussion here.) To specify a variable parameter you must place the reserved word **VAR** in front of the parameter's name.

To understand the difference between value and variable parameters, look at the following incorrect program that attempts to use the **PROCEDURE Swap** to exchange the values of two **INTEGER** variables.

```
MODULE Wrong;
  FROM InOut IMPORT WriteInt;
  VAR
    a,b: INTEGER;


  PROCEDURE Swap(x,y:INTEGER);
    VAR
      t:INTEGER;
  BEGIN
    t:=x;
    x:=y;
    y:=t;
  END Swap;

BEGIN
  a:=10;
  b:=20;
  Swap(a,b);  (* won't do anything *)
  WriteInt(a,5);
  WriteInt(b,5);
END Wrong.
```

This program will compile and run, but the values **a** and **b** will not be exchanged by the **PROCEDURE Swap**. The reason for this is that **Swap** is defined as having value parameters. This means that when **Swap** is called, only the values **a** and **b** are passed to parameters **x** and **y**. Inside **Swap**, the values of **x** and **y** are exchanged, but this exchange has no effect on **a** and **b**. Therefore, the program displays 10 20.

To make **Swap** work, variable parameters must be used. It is very simple to accomplish this because it requires a change only to the parameter list. The reserved word **VAR** is placed as shown here.

```
PROCEDURE Swap(VAR x,y:INTEGER);
```

This change causes the arguments themselves to be used in the **PROCEDURE**. Therefore, when **x** and **y** are exchanged inside **Swap**, **a** and **b** are also exchanged. With this correction, the program now runs properly and displays 20 10.

Another way to remember the difference between value and variable parameters is that a value parameter is unidirectional—information is passed to the **PROCEDURE**, but is not passed back. A variable parameter is bidirectional—information is passed to the **PROCEDURE** and is passed back as well.

When to Use Value And Variable Parameters

The kind of parameter that should be used depends upon whether the calling variable is to be altered. When you need to affect the value of an argument, then you must use a variable parameter. When the argument is not going to be changed, then you should use a value parameter.

You may be wondering why there are two kinds of parameters since, in theory, a variable parameter could be used in place of a value parameter so long as you were careful not to change its value. The answer is bug prevention. Using a value parameter *guarantees* that the argument in a

PROCEDURE call will not be changed. Therefore, there can be no accidental side effects, and anyone reading the program will know that the argument has the same value after the call that it had before the call. A secondary consideration is that some routines are shorter and more efficient when value parameters are used.

In addition to the factors already mentioned, another factor also affects the choice of parameter types. As you will see in the next section, a **PROCEDURE** can explicitly return a value, making it possible to pass information back to the calling routine without using a variable parameter. Of course, only one value can be returned, so in situations like the **Swap PROCEDURE**, where two arguments must be changed, the variable parameter still is necessary.

Function ***PROCEDUREs***

So far, all the **PROCEDURE**s in this chapter have been *proper procedures*. This means that the procedural code is used to perform some sort of task related to the main program. A second kind of **PROCEDURE**, called a *function procedure,* is used to compute and return a result. You have already seen some function procedures, such as **TRUNC**, **ORD**, and **FLOAT**.

A function **PROCEDURE** is the same as a proper **PROCEDURE** except for two elements. First, the type of value to be returned must be declared. This is done by placing a semicolon and a type directly after the parameter list, as shown in the following examples.

```
PROCEDURE SQR(I:REAL): REAL; (* return REAL *)
PROCEDURE IsIn(I,N:INTEGER) : BOOLEAN; (* return BOOLEAN *)
PROCEDURE FindLoc (ZIP:CARDINAL): CARDINAL; (* return CARDINAL *)
```

Second, the **RETURN** statement must be specified. The **RETURN** statement performs two functions. First, it is used to pass the value of the **PROCEDURE** back to the calling routine. Second, it causes the immediate return of the **PROCEDURE**; that is, it terminates the execution of the function **PROCEDURE** at the point of the **RETURN** statement. (Pascal programmers: This is a completely different method of returning a function value than is used by Pascal so pay special attention to the next few examples.)

In this first example, you will rewrite the **Fact PROCEDURE** into a function **PROCEDURE**, as shown here.

```
PROCEDURE  Fact(i:CARDINAL): CARDINAL;
  VAR
    x,y:CARDINAL;

  BEGIN
    y:=1;
    FOR x:=1 TO i DO
      y:=y*x;
    END;
    RETURN y;
  END Fact;
```

As you can see, the function **Fact** is declared to return a **CARDINAL** value, and the **RETURN** statement is added. Remember, the type of the value returned by the **RETURN** statement must agree with the type that the function is declared to return.

Now that **Fact** has been turned into a function **PROCEDURE**, the calling routine must be altered to reflect this, as is shown in the next program.

```
MODULE Factorial;  (* function PROCEDURE version *)
  FROM InOut IMPORT ReadCard, WriteCard, WriteString,
                    WriteLn;

   VAR
     f: CARDINAL;
     answer: CARDINAL;

   PROCEDURE  Fact(i:CARDINAL): CARDINAL;
     VAR
       x,y:CARDINAL;

     BEGIN
       y:=1;
       FOR x:=1 TO i DO
         y:=y*x;
       END;
       RETURN y;
     END Fact;

BEGIN
  REPEAT
    WriteString("enter number: ");
    ReadCard(f);
    WriteLn;
    answer:=Fact(f);  (* here, answer is assigned the value
                         of Fact *)
    WriteString('Answer is: ');
    WriteCard(answer,5);
    WriteLn;
  UNTIL f=0;
END Factorial.
```

Here, the returned value of **Fact** is assigned to the variable **answer** using the standard assignment operator. Remember that the variable receiving the value of a function **PROCEDURE** must have the same type as the return value of the **PROCEDURE**. For this reason, **answer** must be declared as a **CARDINAL** value.

It is important to understand that function procedures, like variables or constants, may be used in expressions. For example, the following are valid Modula-2 statements.

```
X:=Fact(5) div 3;

IF Fact(a) < 100 THEN WriteCard(a,3) END;
```

In fact, the main body of code for the factorial program can be rewritten more efficiently as follows.

```
BEGIN
  REPEAT
    WriteString("enter number: ");
    ReadCard(f);
    WriteLn;
    WriteString('Answer is: ');
    WriteCard(Fact(f),5);
    WriteLn;
  UNTIL f=0;
END Factorial.
```

Here, the variable **answer** is no longer needed, and **Fact** is used directly inside the call to **WriteCard**.

There can be more than one **RETURN** statement inside a function **PROCEDURE**. When this is the case, the first **RETURN** encountered terminates the **PROCEDURE** and passes its value back to the calling routine. For example, the following function returns the value of **x** divided by **y**, unless **y** is zero.

```
PROCEDURE Divide(x,y:INTEGER):INTEGER;
BEGIN
  IF y=0 THEN RETURN -1 END;
  RETURN x DIV y;
END Divide;
```

Notice that no **ELSE** or **ELSIF** is needed because, if **y** is equal to 0, **Divide** terminates—the division does not take place—and returns the value −1 to the calling routine.

If a function **PROCEDURE** is created that has no arguments, the parentheses are still necessary, both in the declaration and each time the **PROCEDURE** is referenced. For example, you might have a **PROCEDURE** that returns **TRUE** if a special device is online, and **FALSE** if the device is offline. In this case, no input parameters are needed. The function could look like this:

```
PROCEDURE OnLine():BOOLEAN;
BEGIN
  IF DeviceOnLine RETURN TRUE END;
  RETURN FALSE;
END OnLine;
```

Each time this function is referenced in a program, parentheses must be used. For example, examine the following code.

```
IF OnLine() THEN ReTry END;
```

and

```
WHILE NOT OnLine() DO
  .
  .
  .
END;
```

The reason you must use parentheses, even if there are no arguments, is to distinguish a function name from a variable name.

Recursion

Recursion is the process of defining something in terms of itself. This is sometimes called *circular definition* and is very common in real life. For example, the English language is recursive because the dictionary definitions of most words are stated in terms of other words, which may themselves be defined in terms of the original words.

In a computer language, recursion means that a subroutine contains a call to itself; that is, the subroutine is defined at least partially in terms of itself. A **PROCEDURE** is said to be *recursive* if one or more of its statements executes a call to itself. Not all languages allow recursion; BASIC and FORTRAN, for example, do not. However, recursion can be a very powerful programming tool if it is used in the right way. Modula-2 allows recursion, as do most other modern programming languages.

Examine the **PROCEDURE** in this first example of recursion.

```
PROCEDURE R(i:INTEGER):INTEGER;
BEGIN
  IF i=0 THEN RETURN i END;
  R(i-1);
  WriteInt(i,5);
END R;
```

This **PROCEDURE** prints the numbers 1 through **i** on the screen. Here is how it works. When **R** is called, the value of **i** is tested against 0. If **i** equals 0, then **R** returns, and nothing else happens. However, if **i** is greater than 0, then **R** is called again with **i−1** . This process continues until **i** has the value 0. Then the whole chain of calls begins to unravel, with each call to **R** returning to the previous one, and the numbers are printed on the screen.

The key point to the operation of recursive routines is this: The second call to **R** does not terminate the first call. Instead, it temporarily suspends its execution. Therefore, the value of the local variable **i** is not lost, but is stored until execution resumes. When the second **R** begins execution, it creates a new **i** for itself. In this way, the two variables do not overwrite each other's values.

Recursion, as it is often applied to programming, is essentially another form of loop control. In fact, many algorithms have both recursive and *iterative* versions. An iterative algorithm uses a built-in loop statement, whereas a recursive algorithm uses repeated calling of the routine to achieve the same end. For example, you can rewrite the previously developed iterative version of **Fact** so that it is a recursion function **PROCEDURE**, as shown here.

```
PROCEDURE  FactR(i:CARDINAL): CARDINAL;
  VAR
    x:CARDINAL;

  BEGIN
    IF i=1 THEN RETURN 1 END;
    x:=FactR(i-1) * i;
    RETURN x;
  END FactR;
```

In this recursive version, there is no **FOR** loop because the factorial of **i** is computed by repeatedly calling **FactR** with one less than **i** . So, if the factorial of 3 were to be computed, the following would take place. First, **FactR** would be called with 3, so **i** would be equal to 3. Since it is not equal to 1, the statement

```
x:=FactR(i-1) * i;
```

would be executed. However, to evaluate the right side of the assignment, the call to **FactR(i−1)** first needs to be performed. Therefore, **FactR** is called a second time with the value 2. At this point it is important to remember that the second call does not destroy the value of the local variables from the first call—the second call's variables are different. Since **i** still is not equal to 1, **FactR** is called again with 1. Now **i** is equal to 1, so the value 1 is returned for the second call, which results in **x** being assigned the value 1*2. This value is returned to the original call, and **x** is assigned the value of 2*3, or 6, which is the answer passed to the calling routine.

Although recursive routines have a very important place in certain algorithms, especially certain sorting routines, they can be difficult to develop and understand. Also, some programmers seem to be able to think recursively more easily than others. Generally speaking, if you feel comfortable with recursive routines, then use them. If you do not, then use iterative methods (although you should understand how recursive routines work).

As you know, storage for parameters and local variables is created dynamically on the stack of the computer. Because recursive routines allocate space for their parameters and variables each time a call is executed, it is possible to have a *stack overrun.* When this occurs the stack has grown so large that it collides with either your program's code, other variables, or operating system code. In correct recursive routines, this situation is extremely unlikely, but when you are developing a recursive routine, it does occasionally happen. The best way to avoid a system crash of this nature is to use many print statements in your routines until they are debugged so that you can cancel execution if your routine begins to run away.

Finally, each recursive routine must have an **IF** statement that, at some point, prevents the recursive call from being made. If this statement is not present, the routine will call itself indefinitely.

Nested ***PROCEDUREs***

As stated earlier in this chapter, a **PROCEDURE** may also contain **PROCEDURE** declarations. When a **PROCEDURE** is defined inside another **PROCEDURE**, it is called a *nested **PROCEDURE***. A simple example of a nested **PROCEDURE** is shown in the following program.

```
MODULE nested;
  FROM InOut IMPORT WriteLn, WriteString, WriteInt;

  PROCEDURE A;
    VAR
      Count:INTEGER;

    PROCEDURE B;   (* inside A *)
      VAR
        I:INTEGER;
    BEGIN   (* B *)
      WriteString('Count is: ');
      WriteInt(Count,3);
      FOR I:=-5 TO 5 DO
        WriteInt(I,3)
      END;
    END B;

  BEGIN (* A *)
    FOR Count:=1 TO 4 DO
      WriteLn;
      WriteString('calling B ');
      B;
      END;
    END A;

BEGIN   (* MODULE code *)
  A;
END nested.
```

Because **B** is declared inside of **A**, **B** knows about both its own variable **I** and **A**'s variable **Count**. However, **A** has no knowledge of **I**, since **A** is outside of **B**. In essence, **Count** is global *within **PROCEDURE A*** and is therefore known to **B**, which is inside **A**, but **I** is local to **B** and is therefore not known to **A**. The output from this program is the following line printed four times.

calling B Count is: N −5 −4 −3 −2 −1 0 1 2 3 4 5

Here, **N** is the value of **Count**.

Because **B** is inside **A**, it is not possible for **B** to be called directly by the **MODULE** code. This is because **B** is shielded by **A** and so is not "visible" to the **MODULE**.

Here is another example of nested procedures. In this case, both **A** and **B** use the variable name **I**.

```
MODULE nested;
  FROM InOut IMPORT WriteLn, WriteString, WriteInt;

  PROCEDURE A;
    VAR
      I:INTEGER;

    PROCEDURE B;  (* inside A *)
      VAR
        I:INTEGER;
    BEGIN  (* B *)
      FOR I:=-5 TO 5 DO
        WriteInt(I,3)
      END;
    END B;

  BEGIN (* A *)
    FOR I:=1 TO 4 DO
      WriteLn;
      WriteString('calling B');
      B;
    END;
  END A;

BEGIN  (* MODULE code *)
  A;
END nested.
```

This program prints the following line four times.

calling B −5 −4 −3 −2 −1 0 1 2 3 4 5

The program works this way. The main **MODULE** code calls **A**. Inside **A** is a loop that calls **B** four times. **A** and **B**'s **I** are completely separate variables; thus, what happens to **I** inside **B** has no effect on the **I** inside **A**. The reason that both **A** and **B** can use the variable name **I** without conflict is that **B**'s **I** is local only to **B** and is not known to **A**.

Scope

It is now time to discuss explicitly the rules that govern what and where variables and procedures are known to other parts of a program. In computer science this is called defining the *scope rules* of the language. In some computer languages, such as C and FORTRAN, the scope rules are very simple because nested **PROCEDURE**s are not supported. Hence, there are only global and local variables, and that's that. However, because Modula-2 is a formally block-structured language that allows the declaration of **PROCEDURE**s inside of **PROCEDURE**s, the rules are more complex.

Let's start with an example.

```
MODULE Scope;

  VAR
    a,b,c: REAL;

PROCEDURE A;
  VAR
    d:INTEGER;
      .
      .
      .
 END A;

PROCEDURE B;
  VAR
    e:INTEGER;
  PROCEDURE C;
    VAR
      f:BOOLEAN;
    BEGIN (* C inside B *)
      .
      .
      .
    END C;
 BEGIN  (* B *)
      .
      .
      .
 END B;

PROCEDURE D;
  VAR
    g:INTEGER;
      .
      .
      .
 END A;

    BEGIN
      .
      .
      .
    END Scope.
```

Table 6-1. Scope of Variables and Procedures

	MODULE	A	B	C	D
PROCEDUREs	ABD	BD	ACD		AB
Variables	abc	abcd	abce	abcef	abcg

The scope of each variable and **PROCEDURE** is shown in Table 6-1. Figure 6-1 diagrammatically shows the scope of the program.

The following scope rules state explicitly what the example implied. Here the term *identifier* is used to stand for a **PROCEDURE**, variable, constant, or type definition.

1. An identifier is known to the **PROCEDURE** in which it is declared and to all **PROCEDURE**s enclosed by that **PROCEDURE**, unless rule 2 applies.

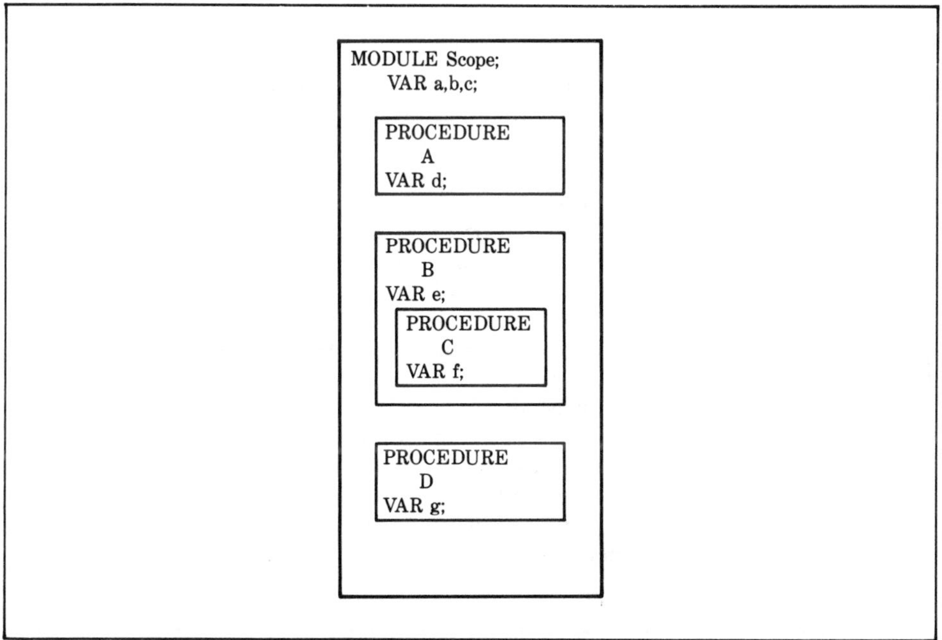

Figure 6-1. Scope of program Scope

2. If an inner **PROCEDURE** uses the same identifier name as an outer **PROCEDURE**, the inner **PROCEDURE** name takes precedence.

Whenever you have any doubts about what is known where, you need only draw a diagram similar to Figure 6-1 to find your answer.

Standard Procedures

Modula-2 has several built-in standard procedures that do not need to be **IMPORT**ed from a library. These procedures are listed in Table 6-2.

You have already learned about most of these procedures in previous chapters. The **PROCEDURE**s **NEW** and **DISPOSE** will be discussed in

Table 6-2. Modula-2 Standard Procedures

Name	Purpose
ABS(n)	Returns the absolute value of *n*
CAP(c)	Returns the uppercase equivalent of *c*
CHR(n)	Returns the character with ASCII code *n*
DISPOSE(p)	Frees a region of memory
FLOAT(n)	Converts CARDINAL *n* into a REAL number
HIGH(a)	Returns the high index boundary of array *a*
NEW(p)	Allocates a region of memory
ODD(n)	Returns TRUE if *n* is odd
ORD(n)	Returns *n*'s ordinal number
TRUNC(n)	Converts REAL *n* into a CARDINAL number
VAL(t,n)	Converts *n* into its equivalent of type *t*
DEC(n)	Returns $n-1$
DEC(n,m)	Returns $n-m$
EXCL(s,e)	Removes *e* from set *s*
HALT	Stops program execution
INC(n)	Returns $n+1$
INC(n,m)	Returns $n+m$
INCL(s,e)	Includes *e* in set *s*

Chapter 9, and **HIGH** will be examined in the next section of this chapter. This leaves only **CAP** and **HALT** to examine here.

CAP

CAP is used to return the uppercase equivalent of a letter. If a letter is already uppercase, then no change occurs. Also, if the character passed to **CAP** is not a letter, then no change occurs. The following program, which reads characters from the keyboard and displays them in uppercase, illustrates **CAP's** use. Execution is terminated by typing the $ character.

```
MODULE CapTest;
  FROM InOut IMPORT Read, Write;

  VAR
    ch: CHAR;

BEGIN

REPEAT
    Read(ch);
    ch:=CAP(ch);
    Write(ch);
  UNTIL ch='$';
END CapTest.
```

HALT

The HALT PROCEDURE is used to cause immediate termination of a program. This is not a "clean" stop because debugging information usually is displayed on the screen. **HALT's** use should be restricted either to debugging or, in rare cases, to where a catastrophic error requires immediate termination of a program.

An example of a program that might use **HALT** is a real-time program that controls external events at, for instance, a power plant or factory. Imagine a situation in which a computerized factory has a broken conveyor belt, and the program running the factory should immediately stop. The following code fragment shows how this could be done.

```
IF ConveyorBroken() THEN HALT END;
```

Arrays as Parameters

A complete discussion of arrays is deferred until Chapter 10, but the simple case of single-dimensional arrays used as parameters to procedures is discussed here. Presenting this topic now will enable you to use strings (arrays of characters) as parameters for **PROCEDURE**s.

As you know, the type of a parameter must match the type of the variable used in the **PROCEDURE** call. In theory, this means that the types of the elements in both the argument and the parameter must be the same and that the range of each also must be the same. For arrays, however, this rule is relaxed slightly. Modula-2 requires any array variable passed to a **PROCEDURE** to have elements of the same types, but the array boundaries may be different. This allows the creation of general-purpose procedures that take array arguments. However, the programmer is responsible for preventing out-of-bounds conditions.

To declare an array parameter, you simply specify the array type without any range. For example, here **str** is an array of characters.

```
PROCEDURE S(str:ARRAY OF CHAR);
```

Any character array could now be passed to **PROCEDURE S**. A declaration of this type is called an **open array** because boundaries are not explicitly defined.

All open arrays assume a lower boundary of 0, even if the array passed to the **PROCEDURE** has a different lower boundary. This does not imply that you cannot access all the elements; it just means that inside the **PROCEDURE**, all arrays are indexed starting from 0. (Formally, all elements of the argument array are mapped onto an array of the same size, but with indexes starting at 0.) The upper boundary of the array can be computed using the **HIGH PROCEDURE**. **HIGH** returns the upper boundary of the array used as its argument. For example, if **A** is declared as

```
A: ARRAY [0..100] OF INTEGER;
```

then **HIGH(A)** will return the value 100.

You can use open arrays to create versatile string handling **PROCEDURE**s to help make programming easier. For example, the following

PROCEDURE essentially combines **WriteString** and **WriteLn**, allowing the output of a string and a carriage return in one step.

```
PROCEDURE Puts(s:ARRAY OF CHAR);
  BEGIN
    WriteString(s);
    WriteLn;
  END Puts;
```

Using **Puts**, you can replace the statements

```
WriteString('hello');
WriteLn;
```

with

```
Puts('hello');
```

Arrays may also be variable parameters, thus allowing **PROCEDUREs** to be written that modify the calling array. A good example of this is the **PROCEDURE Gets**, shown here. It inputs a string of characters entered from the keyboard.

```
PROCEDURE Gets(VAR a:ARRAY OF CHAR);
  CONST
    BS = 8;   (* backspace *)

  VAR
    ch: CHAR;
    i:CARDINAL;
  BEGIN
    i:=0;
    REPEAT
      Read(ch);
      Write(ch);
      IF ORD(ch)=BS THEN i:=i-1;   (* is backspace *)
      ELSIF (ch<>EOL) AND (i<HIGH(a)) THEN
        a[i]:=ch;
        i:=i+1;
      END;
    UNTIL (ch=EOL) OR (i=HIGH(a));
    a[i]:=CHR(0);   (* all strings end in 0 *)
  END Gets;
```

Unlike the library **PROCEDURE ReadString**, which, in most implementations, terminates on spaces, tabs, and carriage returns, **Gets** reads characters until a carriage return is typed. This allows an entire line of text to be read instead of only a word at a time.

There are several points of interest in **Gets**. First, the **IMPORT** list of any listing, which must include the constant **EOL**. **EOL** is defined inside **InOut** and is the character returned when a carriage return is struck. Its actual value may vary among compilers, but since you always can **IMPORT** its value from **InOut**, its actual value is of no interest. Also, **Gets** defines the constant **BS**, which is the ASCII code for a backspace. **Gets** uses the **HIGH PROCEDURE** to prevent an array boundary error. If the last character position of the array is reached, the routine automatically returns.

As you learned earlier, all strings shorter than the maximum size of the array end in a null. A null is an ASCII 0, which can be created using **CHR(0)** and assigned to the array element. This step is necessary to properly terminate strings that are shorter than the supporting array's maximum length. For simplicity, **Gets** ends all strings with a null.

The following short program illustrates a call to **Gets**.

```
MODULE GetStr;
  (* read and write a string using Gets and WriteString *)
  FROM InOut IMPORT Read, Write, WriteString, EOL;

  VAR
    str: ARRAY [0..79] OF CHAR;

  PROCEDURE Gets(VAR a:ARRAY OF CHAR);
    CONST
      BS = 8;  (* backspace *)

    VAR
      ch: CHAR;
      i:CARDINAL;
    BEGIN
      i:=0;
      REPEAT
        Read(ch);
        Write(ch);
        IF ORD(ch)=BS THEN i:=i-1;  (* is backspace *)
        ELSIF (ch<>EOL) AND (i<HIGH(a)) THEN
          a[i]:=ch;
          i:=i+1;
        END;
      UNTIL (ch=EOL) OR (i=HIGH(a));
      a[i]:=CHR(0);  (* all strings end in 0 *)
    END Gets;

BEGIN
  Gets(str);
  WriteString(str);
END GetStr.
```

Writing Your Own ***PROCEDUREs***

Several characteristics separate well-written **PROCEDURE**s from poorly written ones. The ability to write good **PROCEDURE**s is learned largely through experience, but the following rules will help.

First, **PROCEDURE**s should be as general as possible. This means that they should not rely upon global variables but should, instead, be passed what information they need. If information needs to be passed back, it should be passed either through **VAR** parameters or as a function result. There are two reasons for writing routines this way: There will be fewer side effects than when global data are used, and you will be able to use the routines in a variety of situations without rewriting them. For example, two versions of **SwapGreaterThan**, a **PROCEDURE** that exchanges the values of its arguments only if the first value is greater than the second, are shown here. The first version relies on the global variables **X** and **Y**, while the second uses parameters.

```
VAR
  X,Y: INTEGER;   (* used by SwapGreaterThan *)

PROCEDURE SwapGreaterThan;
  (* this version is poor because it can only swap
     globals X and Y *)
  VAR
    T: INTEGER;
BEGIN
  IF X>Y THEN
    T:=X;
    X:=Y;
    Y:=T;
  END
END SwapGreaterThan;

(*

  This version uses parameters and can be used to exchange
  the values of any two INTEGER variables
*)

PROCEDURE SwapGreaterThan(VAR X,Y:INTEGER);
  (* this version is much more general *)
  VAR
    T: INTEGER;
```

```
BEGIN
  IF X>Y THEN
    T:=X;
    X:=Y;
    Y:=T;
  END
END SwapGreaterThan;
```

As you can see, the first version can only be used to exchange the values of the global variables **X** and **Y**, whereas the second version will exchange the values of any two **INTEGER** variables.

Second, make sure that your **PROCEDURE**s represent one and only one indivisible task—they should never be just a place to put code. If you follow this rule, your programs will always be easier to read and modify.

Third, don't overuse **PROCEDURE**s. You should almost never create **PROCEDURE**s with just one line of code in them. This is both inefficient and misleading.

*Program Organization Using **PROCEDURE**s*

Now that you know something about **PROCEDURE**s, it is time to see how to properly use them in your programs. In general, a well-written Modula-2 program will have a very small amount of main **MODULE** code, and this code will be used to call **PROCEDURE**s. The **MODULE** code should read like an outline to your program, with most of the actual work being done in the supporting **PROCEDURE**s.

The program that follows, a final, somewhat longer, example, performs the four basic arithmetic functions based on menu selection. It is a revision, using **PROCEDURE**s, of the program developed in Chapter 3 and is a better way to code the program.

```
MODULE Calc;
  FROM InOut IMPORT ReadCard, WriteCard, WriteString,
                    WriteLn, Read, ReadInt, WriteInt;

   VAR
     choice:CARDINAL;
     x,y: INTEGER;
```

```
PROCEDURE Puts(s:ARRAY OF CHAR);
  BEGIN
    WriteString(s);
    WriteLn;
  END Puts;

PROCEDURE Menu():CARDINAL;
  VAR
    ch:CARDINAL;
  BEGIN
    Puts('     1. Add');
    Puts('     2. Subtract');
    Puts('     3. Multiply');
    Puts('     4. Divide');
    Puts('     5. Quit');
    REPEAT
      WriteString('Enter Choice: ');
      ReadCard(ch);
      WriteLn;
    UNTIL (ch>=1) AND (ch<=5);
    WriteLn;
    RETURN ch;
  END Menu;

PROCEDURE GetNums(VAR x,y:INTEGER);
BEGIN
  WriteString('Enter first number: ');
  ReadInt(x);
  WriteLn;
  WriteString('Enter second number: ');
  ReadInt(y);
  WriteLn;
END GetNums;

BEGIN
  REPEAT
    choice:=Menu();
    IF choice<>5 THEN
      CASE choice OF
        1: GetNums(x,y);
           WriteInt(x+y,5) |
        2: GetNums(x,y);
           WriteInt(x-y,5) |
        3: GetNums(x,y);
           WriteInt(x*y,5) |
        4: GetNums(x,y);
           IF y<>0 THEN WriteInt(x DIV y,5) END;
      END;
    END;
    WriteLn;
  UNTIL choice=5;
END Calc.
```

EXERCISES

1. Is a **PROCEDURE** a program?

2. In the following program, which variables are global and which are local to **PROCEDURE A**?

```
MODULE T;
  VAR
    A,B,C: REAL;

  PROCEDURE A(X:REAL);
    VAR
      COUNT:INTEGER;
  BEGIN
    .
    .
    .
  END A;

BEGIN
  .
  .
  .
END T.
```

3. What is wrong with the following code fragment?

```
PROCEDURE A;
  VAR
    T: CARDINAL;
  BEGIN
    T:=T+1;
    WriteCard(T,5);
    WriteString('calls to A');
  END A;
```

4. Write a **PROCEDURE** that uses a string and an **INTEGER** as parameters to construct a general terminal input routine that uses the string as a prompt and returns the result in **INTEGER I** (this means that **I** must be a variable parameter).

5. What is wrong with the following recursive routine?

```
PROCEDURE A(I:INTEGER):INTEGER;
BEGIN
  RETURN A(I-1);
  WriteInt(I,5);
END A;
```

6. Draw a scope diagram of this program.

```
MODULE Scope;
  VAR
    A,B: INTEGER;

  PROCEDURE P1;
    VAR
      J,K:REAL;
  BEGIN
    .
    .
    .
  END P1;

  PROCEDURE P2(Q:BOOLEAN);

    PROCEDURE P3inP2;
      VAR
      M,N:INTEGER;
  BEGIN
      .
      .
      .
  END P3inP2;

BEGIN
  .
  .
  .
END P2;

BEGIN
  .
  .
  .
END Scope.
```

7. Enter the final program example of this chapter, called **Calc**, and experiment with various modifications and enhancements.

ANSWERS

1. No, they are not programs because they cannot exist outside of a **MODULE**.

2. Global: **A**, **B**, and **C**. Local: **X** and **COUNT**.

3. **T** is a local variable defined in **A**. The code implies that **T** can be used to keep track of how many times the **PROCEDURE** has been executed; however, this is impossible because **T's** value is destroyed each time **A** is exited. Also, **T** is never initialized.

4.
```
PROCEDURE Input(S:ARRAY OF CHAR; VAR I:INTEGER);
BEGIN
  WriteString(S);
  ReadInt(I);
END Input;
```

5. The routine will call itself indefinitely and ultimately crash whatever program it is in.

6.

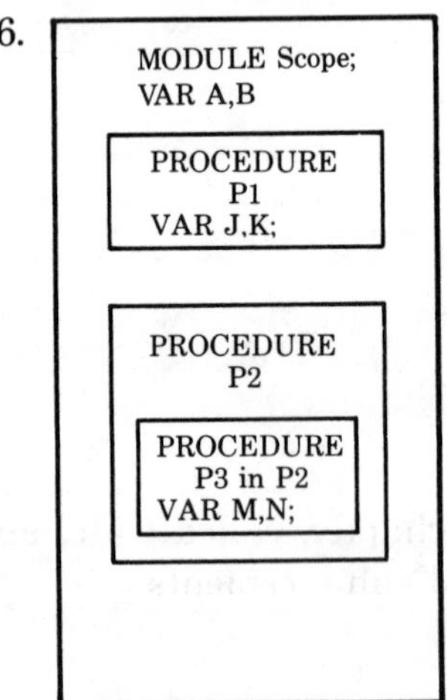

RECORDs

CHAPTER 7

A **RECORD** is a grouping of logically related variables into a conglomerate variable. In a sense, **RECORDs** parallel **PROCEDUREs**; a **PROCEDURE** is a block of logically connected code, and a **RECORD** is a block of logically connected data. Unlike an array in which all the elements of the array must be of the same type, a **RECORD** allows its elements to be of different types. **RECORDs** have several advantages. Because **RECORDs** can be used as parameters of **PROCEDUREs**, large amounts of information can easily be passed without using excessively long parameter lists. A **RECORD** tells anyone reading your program that the variables that form the **RECORD** are related to each other. Arrays of **RECORDs** can greatly simplify certain routines and completely eliminate the necessity of using parallel arrays. You need to understand **RECORDs** in order to use the random file routines discussed in Chapter 8. Finally, as you will see in Chapter 9, **RECORDs** enhance Modula-2's dynamic allocation routines.

Declaring ***A RECORD***

A **RECORD** declaration essentially is a user-defined data type. Therefore, very often a **RECORD** type is created in the **TYPE** definition section of the **MODULE** or **PROCEDURE**. In this case, the general form of the **RECORD** declaration is

```
TYPE
RecName = RECORD
            var1: type;
            var2: type;
            var3: type;
            .
            .
            .
            varN; type;
          END;
```

where ***RecName*** is the name of the **RECORD**, ***var1*** through ***varN*** are the names of the individual variables that form the **RECORD**, and ***type*** is the type of the variables. The variables that comprise a **RECORD** are referred to as *fields* or *elements.*

For example, the following code defines a **RECORD** type called **R** that has three elements.

```
TYPE
  R = RECORD
        A: INTEGER;
        B: BOOLEAN;
        C: REAL;
      END;
```

The scope of the fields defined inside a **RECORD** are local only to that **RECORD**. Because of this, the same names may be used both for fields inside a **RECORD** and for names of other global or local variables.

At this point, no variable has been created; only a template has been defined. To actually create a variable you must declare it in the variable declaration section. For example, to create a **RECORD** variable called **foobar** of **RECORD** type **R**, you would write

```
VAR
  foobar: R;
```

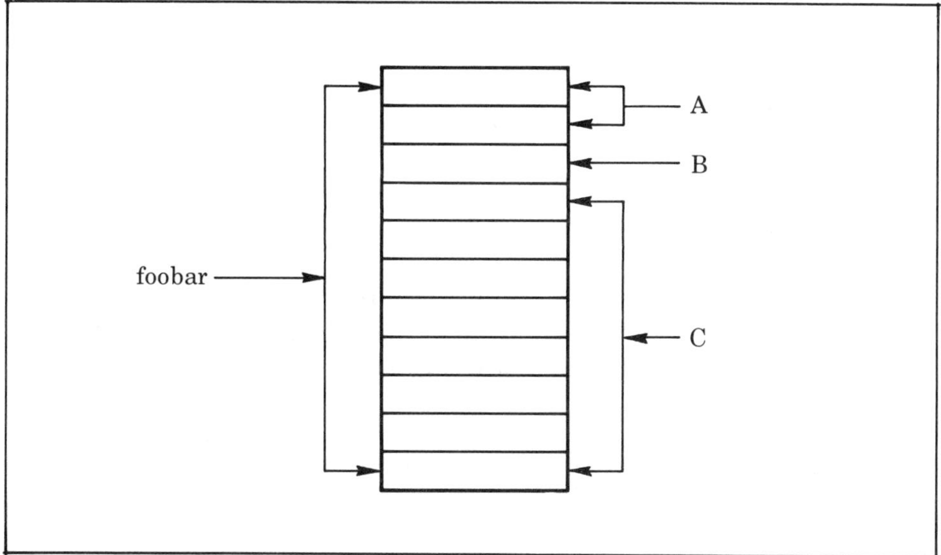

Figure 7-1. Conglomerate variable **foobar** in memory

This declares a conglomerate variable with the name **foobar** that has separate elements. Figure 7-1 shows graphically how **foobar** appears in memory.

Accessing Fields Inside a ***RECORD***

Accessing the individual fields of a **RECORD** requires the use of a *field-selector.* The general form of a field selection is

<RecordName>.<field-name>

where ***<RecordName>*** is the name of the **RECORD** variable, and ***<field-name>*** is the name of the specific field accessed. Sometimes, when discussing field referencing, the period is called the *dot* operator. For example, in the **foobar** variable declared earlier, the following assignment statements place the values 10 into **A**, **TRUE** into **B**, and 10.12 into **C**.

```
foobar.A:=10;
foobar.B:=TRUE;
foobar.C:=10.12;
```

Fields of **RECORDs** can be used wherever any simple variable can be used. For example,

```
WriteInt(foobar.A,5);
```

will output the value of the **A** field of **foobar**.

Enter the short program shown here that illustrates the use of **RECORDs** and tinker with it until you feel comfortable with its operation.

```
MODULE foobar;
  FROM InOut IMPORT ReadInt, WriteInt, WriteString,WriteLn;
  FROM RealInOut IMPORT WriteReal;

  TYPE

    R = RECORD
        A: INTEGER;
        B: BOOLEAN;
        C: REAL;
    END;

  VAR
    foobar: R;

BEGIN

  REPEAT
    WriteLn;
    WriteString('enter a number: ');
    ReadInt(foobar.A); WriteLn;
    WriteInt(foobar.A,5);
    foobar.C:=FLOAT(foobar.A)/2.0;
    foobar.B:=foobar.C<100.0;
  UNTIL foobar.B=FALSE;
END foobar.
```

RECORD *Assignment*

Although each field in a **RECORD** may be used just as any other normal variable, the actual **RECORD** variable itself may not. The only operation for the entire **RECORD** that is valid is assignment. For example, given

```
TYPE
  R = RECORD
        I: INTEGER;
        J: CARDINAL;
        K: CHAR;
  END;

VAR
  rec1, rec2: R;
```

it is possible to write

```
rec1:=rec2;
```

This is equivalent to writing

```
rec1.I:=rec2.I;
rec1.J:=rec2.J;
rec1.K:=rec2.K;
```

One **RECORD** may be assigned to another if and only if the definitions of the **RECORD**s are exactly the same.

Complex ***RECORD*** *Fields*

Until now, all the variables that have comprised a **RECORD** have been simple. However, it is possible for a **RECORD** also to contain complex variables, such as arrays, enumerations, subranges, and even other records.

An example that uses complex field types is a **RECORD** that holds the make, model, year, list, and wholesale price of an automobile, as shown here.

```
TYPE
    CAR = RECORD
        make: (Ford, GM, Chrysler);
        model: ARRAY [0..20] OF CHAR;
        year: [1950..1990];
        cost: RECORD  (* nested record *)
                list: REAL;
                wholesale: REAL;
        END;
    END;
```

Here, **make** is an enumeration, **model** is an array of characters, **year** is a subrange, and **cost** is a **RECORD**. Let's look at each of these separately.

The element **make** is an enumeration that defines who the maker of the car is. There is no difference between the way this and any other enumeration variable works. Assuming that **auto** is a **RECORD** of type **CAR**, then the following assigns the value **GM** to **make**:

```
auto.make:=GM;
```

Subranges, like enumerations, work the same with **RECORDs** as they do with other variables. For example, the following code prints a car's year on the screen.

```
WriteCard(auto.year,5);
```

As with any subrange, it is your responsibility to ensure that the range boundaries are not exceeded during run time.

Arrays as fields in a **RECORD** behave as they do with normal variables, but it is easy to get confused about where to place the array index. You only have to remember that the array index must be placed next to the array variable. Thus, to assign 'F' to the first character position in **model**, you would write

```
auto.model[0]:='F';
```

If the array is suitable for strings, as is **model**, then it may be used wherever any other string or string variable normally could be used. For example, the pair of statements shown here reads and writes the car model to the console.

```
ReadString(auto.model);
WriteString(auto.model);
```

Nested ***RECORDs***

A nested **RECORD**, like **cost**, is referenced in the same way as any other variable. For example, if **auto** is assumed to be of type **CAR**, then to assign **list** of **cost** of **auto** the value $1234.23, you would use the following statement:

```
auto.cost.list:=1234.23;
```

Here, **list** is selected from **cost**, which, in turn, is selected from **auto**.You should remember that the dot operator proceeds left to right, with the leftmost **RECORD** being the outermost, and the rightmost being the innermost. **RECORDs** may be nested to any level, although your compiler may impose restrictions.

Passing ***RECORDs*** *To* ***PROCEDUREs***

In Modula-2 it is very easy to pass a **RECORD** to a **PROCEDURE** because **RECORDs** can be used as parameters. This feature makes it very easy to pass large amounts of information into a **PROCEDURE** while avoiding the overly long list of parameters that would result if each field were specified separately.

To see how a **RECORD** can be passed to a **PROCEDURE**, we will look at a procedure that will display all the information about an automobile that is contained in a **RECORD** of type **CAR**, as developed in the previous section.

```
PROCEDURE DisplayCar(C:CAR);
BEGIN
  CASE C.make OF
    Ford:  WriteString('Ford ') |
    GM: WriteString('GM ') |
    Chrysler: WriteString('Chrysler ')
  END;
  WriteString(C.model);
  WriteCard(C.year,5);
  WriteString(' list $');
  WriteReal(C.cost.list,15);
  WriteString(' wholesale $');
  WriteReal(C.cost.wholesale,15);
END DisplayCar;
```

As you can see, the parameter **C** is declared to be of type **CAR**. When this **PROCEDURE** is called, the argument also must be of type **CAR**. When the call executes, the entire **RECORD** is passed into **DisplayCar**, meaning that the individual fields can be accessed inside the **PROCEDURE**. To see how this works, study the following program, which assigns values to **auto** and uses **DisplayCar**, to display the information on the screen.

```
MODULE CarDealership;
  FROM InOut IMPORT ReadCard, WriteCard, WriteString,WriteLn;
  FROM RealInOut IMPORT WriteReal;

TYPE
    CAR = RECORD
        make: (Ford, GM, Chrysler);
        model: ARRAY [0..20] OF CHAR;
        year: [1950..1990];
        cost: RECORD  (* nested record *)
                list: REAL;
                wholesale: REAL;
        END;
    END;


  VAR
    auto: CAR;

  PROCEDURE DisplayCar(C:CAR);
  BEGIN
    CASE C.make OF
      Ford:  WriteString('Ford ') |
      GM: WriteString('GM ') |
      Chrysler: WriteString('Chrysler ')
    END;
      WriteString(C.model);
      WriteCard(C.year,5);
      WriteString(' list $');
      WriteReal(C.cost.list,15);
      WriteString(' wholesale $');
      WriteReal(C.cost.wholesale,15);
  END DisplayCar;


BEGIN
  (* first put information into the RECORD variable auto *)
  auto.make:=Ford;
  auto.model:='Thunderbird';
  auto.year:=1986;
  auto.cost.list:=14312.78;
  auto.cost.wholesale:=10978.04;
  (* now call DisplayCar to display information on the
     screen *)
  DisplayCar(auto);
END CarDealership.
```

It is also possible to declare variable **RECORD** parameters so that changes inside the **PROCEDURE** will affect the calling argument. This is important, because **RECORD** types may *not* be **RETURN**ed by a function **PROCEDURE**.

Direct Declaration

As you will learn when you begin using **RECORD**s in your programs, the best way to declare a **RECORD** variable is to first define a **RECORD** type and then declare a variable of that type, as was done in the previous examples. However, it is possible to skip explicit type definition and declare **RECORD** variables directly. For example,

```
VAR
  foobar: RECORD
            A: INTEGER;
            B: BOOLEAN;
            C: REAL;
          END;
```

declares **foobar** as a **RECORD** consisting of one **INTEGER**, one **BOOLEAN**, and one **REAL**.

You might be wondering why this approach to declaring a **RECORD** variable is used less often than the other approach, even though the other approach requires two steps. The answer is that it is not possible to use the direct declaration method when declaring a parameter for a **PROCEDURE**. When you want to use a **RECORD** as a parameter, you must first define a **RECORD** type and then use that type in the parameter declaration portion of the **PROCEDURE**. For example, this code fragment is incorrect and will not compile.

```
(* incorrect *)
PROCEDURE WRONG(x:RECORD
                    A:INTEGER;
                    B:REAL;
                END;);
```

In addition to the problem with **PROCEDURE**s, it is also usually easier to define a **RECORD** type that will be used many times rather than retyping its definition each time the **RECORD** variable is needed.

Arrays of ***RECORDs***

Although single **RECORD** variables are helpful in organizing your code and can simplify passing large amounts of information into a **PROCEDURE**, the real utility of **RECORDs** becomes apparent when **RECORDs** are arrayed. To see how powerful arrays of **RECORDs** can be, a simple mailing list program will be developed using an array of **RECORDs** to hold the address information.

A **RECORD** is the perfect data type for a mailing list because each address in the list is comprised of several pieces of related information. We will be using the following **RECORD**:

```
TYPE
  ADDR = RECORD
       name: ARRAY [0..30] OF CHAR;
       street: ARRAY [0..30] OF CHAR;
       city: ARRAY [0..30] OF CHAR;
       state: ARRAY [0..3] OF CHAR;
       zip: CARDINAL;
  END;
```

The mailing list will be stored in an array of **RECORDs** called **mlist**, which is declared as shown here.

```
VAR
  mlist: ARRAY [0..LSIZE] OF ADDR; (* array of addresses *)
```

LSIZE is a constant that determines the size of the list.

Before constructing the mailing list program, look at how individual **RECORDs**, and fields inside those **RECORDs**, are accessed.

Indexing an array of **RECORDs** is no different from indexing an array of any of the elementary data types. For example, to reference the third **RECORD** in **mlist**, you would write

```
mlist[3]
```

Therefore, to assign the ZIP code 61853 to the **zip** field of **RECORD** 10 in **mlist**, you would write

```
mlist[10].zip:=61853;
```

Sometimes beginning Modula-2 programmers are confused when an array variable is used as a field. Remember, you first select the **RECORD**, then the field, and then the element. For example, to compare the first character of the **name** field in the thirtieth **RECORD** of **mlist** to 'A', you would write

```
IF mlist[30].name[0]='A' THEN ...
```

The mailing list program performs five functions. It allows the user to enter an address, delete an address, print the entire list, find a specific address based on the name, and exit. (Later, in Chapter 8, you will learn how to use disk files to save and load the list.)

Before you actually start writing the various **PROCEDURE**s that will form the mailing list program, the following declarations are necessary.

```
FROM InOut IMPORT Read, Write, WriteString, WriteLn,
              WriteCard, ReadCard, EOL;
FROM Strings IMPORT CompareStr;
CONST
  LSIZE = 100;

TYPE
  ADDR = RECORD
      name: ARRAY [0..30] OF CHAR;
      street: ARRAY [0..30] OF CHAR;
      city: ARRAY [0..30] OF CHAR;
      state: ARRAY [0..3] OF CHAR;
      zip: CARDINAL;
  END;

VAR
  mlist: ARRAY [0..LSIZE] OF ADDR; (* array of addresses *)
  choice: CARDINAL;
```

Here, the constant **LSIZE** is arbitrarily given the value 100; however, it could be any value that you choose. The global variable **choice** is used to select various operations performed by the program.

The mailing list program will assume that any **RECORD** that has a zero length entry in the **name** field will be considered empty and available for use. Therefore, before the list can be used, it must be initialized to empty using **Init**, shown here.

```
PROCEDURE Init; (* initialize list *)
  VAR
    t:CARDINAL;
```

```
BEGIN
  (* use a null string in name field to indicate an
     empty RECORD *)
  FOR t:=0 TO LSIZE DO
    mlist[t].name:="";
  END;
END Init;
```

Since the list cannot be used until there is something in it, the **PROCEDURE Enter**, which allows the user to enter addresses in the list, must be developed next. However, before an entry can be made, an empty **RECORD** must be available. This is achieved using **GetEmpty**, which returns either the index of an empty **RECORD** or a −1, which signifies that the list is full. Both of these **PROCEDURE**s are shown here.

```
PROCEDURE GetEmpty(): INTEGER; (* return next empty
                      location in list, -1 if full *)
  VAR
    i:CARDINAL;
BEGIN
  FOR i:=0 TO LSIZE DO
    IF CompareStr(mlist[i].name,"")=0 THEN
      RETURN i;    (* is an empty location *)
    END;
  END;
  RETURN -1; (* list full *)
END GetEmpty;

PROCEDURE Enter; (* enter a name into the list *)
  VAR
    i: INTEGER;

BEGIN
  i:=GetEmpty();
  IF i<>(-1) THEN
    WriteString('Enter name: ');
    Gets(mlist[i].name);
    WriteString('Enter street: ');
    Gets(mlist[i].street);
    WriteString('Enter city: ');
    Gets(mlist[i].city);
    WriteString('Enter state: ');
    Gets(mlist[i].state);
    WriteString('Enter ZIP: ');
    ReadCard(mlist[i].zip); WriteLn; WriteLn;
  END
END Enter;
```

Notice that **Enter** uses the **PROCEDURE Gets**, developed in the last chapter. It must be included in the program prior to its use here. This is an excellent illustration of the advantages of generalized subroutines. Now that **Gets** is written and debugged, it can be used over and over again without having to be rewritten.

GetEmpty introduces a new library routine called **CompareStr**, which is found in the library **MODULE Strings**. **CompareStr** has the following general form:

CompareStr(*s1,s2*);

where ***s1*** and ***s2*** are strings. **CompareStr** returns an **INTEGER** value determined by a comparison of its arguments. If ***s1*** and ***s2*** are equal, 0 is returned. If ***s1*** is less than ***s2***, −1 is returned. If ***s1*** is greater than ***s2***, 1 is returned. There are several other useful string routines in **Strings**; these will be covered in Chapter 10 and as needed.

Examine **Enter** and you will begin to see how powerful arrays of **RECORDs** are. Because an index can be used to select a specific **RECORD**, **Enter** can be used to enter information in any **RECORD** in **mlist**, not just in a specific **RECORD**.

Next we will develop a routine to print the mailing list. Because different compilers on different systems have different methods of routing output to the printer, the mailing list here will simply be displayed on the screen. However, you should easily be able to redirect the list to the printer by reading your user manual.

Two routines are used to display the list. The first one, called **List**, scans the entire array looking for **RECORDs** with entries. Remember: If the **name** field has something in it, it is assumed to be a valid address. Each time an address is found, the **PROCEDURE Display** is called; this prints the address. The **PROCEDUREs List** and **Display** are shown here.

```
PROCEDURE Display(ml: ADDR);
BEGIN
  Puts(ml.name);
  Puts(ml.street);
  Puts(ml.city);
  Puts(ml.state);
  WriteCard(ml.zip,5);
  WriteLn; WriteLn;
END Display;

PROCEDURE List;  (* display the entire list *)
  VAR
    i:CARDINAL;
BEGIN
  FOR i:=0 TO LSIZE DO
    IF CompareStr(mlist[i].name,"")<>0 THEN
      Display(mlist[i]);
    END
  END
END List;
```

Very often you will want to search a mailing list using a person's name to find an address. To accommodate this type of inquiry, the **Find PROCEDURE** was developed. It first asks the user for the name of the person sought; it then sequentially searches the list, using **CompareStr**, looking for a match. If a match is found, the index is returned; otherwise, −1 is returned. **Find** is called using **Locate**, which, upon finding a match, calls **Display** using the **RECORD** of the address, as shown here.

```
PROCEDURE Find():INTEGER;  (* return the index of a name *)
  VAR
    f: CARDINAL;
    s: ARRAY [0..30] OF CHAR;
BEGIN
  WriteString('Enter name to find: ');
  Gets(s);
  FOR f:=0 TO LSIZE DO
    IF CompareStr(s,mlist[f].name)=0 THEN RETURN f END;
  END;
  RETURN -1;  (* not found *)
END Find;

PROCEDURE Locate;  (* display an address based
                      on the name field *)
  VAR
    i: INTEGER;
BEGIN
  i:=Find(); (* find the name *)
  IF i<>(-1) THEN Display(mlist[i]); END;
END Locate;
```

The routine **Delete** is used to remove an address from the list. **Delete** works just like **Locate**, except that instead of displaying the entry, it marks the entry empty, thereby freeing the space for another address.

```
PROCEDURE Delete; (* remove an address based
                     on the name field *)
  VAR
    i: INTEGER;
BEGIN
  i:=Find(); (* find the name *)
  IF i<>(-1) THEN
    mlist[i].name:=""; (* mark as empty *)
  END;
END Delete;
```

The final routine that we need to develop is the menu driver, which is used to prompt the user. It is shown here.

```
PROCEDURE Menu():CARDINAL;
  VAR
    ch:CARDINAL;
  BEGIN
    Puts('     1. Enter an address');
    Puts('     2. Delete an address');
    Puts('     3. Find an address');
    Puts('     4. List all addresses');
    Puts('     5. Quit');
    REPEAT
      WriteString('Enter Choice: ');
      ReadCard(ch);
      WriteLn;
    UNTIL (ch>=1) AND (ch<=5);
    WriteLn;
    RETURN ch;
  END Menu;
```

Note that **Puts**, developed in the last chapter, is used in **Menu** and must be included in the program prior to its use here.

The entire mailing list program is shown here. Enter this program and play with it until you are sure that you understand how it works.

```
MODULE Mlist;  (* a simple in-RAM mailing list program
                  that uses an array of RECORDS *)

  FROM InOut IMPORT Read, Write, WriteString, WriteLn,
                    WriteCard, ReadCard, EOL;
  FROM Strings IMPORT CompareStr;

  CONST
    LSIZE = 100;

  TYPE
    ADDR = RECORD
        name: ARRAY [0..30] OF CHAR;
        street: ARRAY [0..30] OF CHAR;
        city: ARRAY [0..30] OF CHAR;
        state: ARRAY [0..3] OF CHAR;
        zip: CARDINAL;
    END;

  VAR
    mlist: ARRAY [0..LSIZE] OF ADDR; (* array of addresses *)
    choice: CARDINAL;

  PROCEDURE Gets(VAR a:ARRAY OF CHAR);
    CONST
      BS = 8;  (* backspace *)

    VAR
      ch: CHAR;
      i:CARDINAL;
```

```
 BEGIN
   i:=0;
   REPEAT
     Read(ch);
     Write(ch);
     IF ORD(ch)=BS THEN i:=i-1;  (* is backspace *)
     ELSIF (ch<>EOL) AND (i<HIGH(a)) THEN
       a[i]:=ch;
       i:=i+1;
     END;
   UNTIL (ch=EOL) OR (i=HIGH(a));
   a[i]:=CHR(0);  (* all strings end in 0 *)
 END Gets;

PROCEDURE Puts(s:ARRAY OF CHAR);
BEGIN
  WriteString(s);
  WriteLn;
END Puts;

PROCEDURE Menu():CARDINAL;
  VAR
    ch:CARDINAL;
  BEGIN
    Puts('    1. Enter an address');
    Puts('    2. Delete an address');
    Puts('    3. Find an address');
    Puts('    4. List all addresses');
    Puts('    5. Quit');
    REPEAT
      WriteString('Enter Choice: ');
      ReadCard(ch);
      WriteLn;
    UNTIL (ch>=1) AND (ch<=5);
    WriteLn;
    RETURN ch;
  END Menu;

PROCEDURE GetEmpty(): INTEGER; (* return next empty
                      location in list, -1 if full *)
  VAR
    i:CARDINAL;
BEGIN
  FOR i:=0 TO LSIZE DO
    IF CompareStr(mlist[i].name,"")=0 THEN
      RETURN i;   (* is an empty location *)
    END;
  END;
  RETURN -1; (* list full *)
END GetEmpty;

PROCEDURE Enter; (* enter a name into the list *)
  VAR
    i: INTEGER;
BEGIN
  i:=GetEmpty();
  IF i<>(-1) THEN
    WriteString('Enter name: ');
    Gets(mlist[i].name);
    WriteString('Enter street: ');
```

```
    Gets(mlist[i].street);
    WriteString('Enter city: ');
    Gets(mlist[i].city);
    WriteString('Enter state: ');
    Gets(mlist[i].state);
    WriteString('Enter ZIP: ');
    ReadCard(mlist[i].zip); WriteLn; WriteLn;
  END
END Enter;

PROCEDURE Display(ml: ADDR);
BEGIN
  Puts(ml.name);
  Puts(ml.street);
  Puts(ml.city);
  Puts(ml.state);
  WriteCard(ml.zip,5);
  WriteLn; WriteLn;
END Display;

PROCEDURE List;  (* display the entire list *)
  VAR
    i:CARDINAL;
BEGIN
  FOR i:=0 TO LSIZE DO
    IF CompareStr(mlist[i].name,"")<>0 THEN
      Display(mlist[i]);
    END
  END
END List;

PROCEDURE Find():INTEGER;  (* return the index of a name *)
  VAR
    f: CARDINAL;
    s: ARRAY [0..30] OF CHAR;
BEGIN
  WriteString('Enter name to find: ');
  Gets(s);
  FOR f:=0 TO LSIZE DO
    IF CompareStr(s,mlist[f].name)=0 THEN RETURN f END;
  END;
  RETURN -1;  (* not found *)
END Find;

PROCEDURE Locate;  (* display an address based
                      on the name field *)
  VAR
    i: INTEGER;
BEGIN
  i:=Find(); (* find the name *)
  IF i<>(-1) THEN Display(mlist[i]); END;
END Locate;

PROCEDURE Delete; (* remove an address based
                     on the name field *)
  VAR
    i: INTEGER;
BEGIN
  i:=Find(); (* find the name *)
  IF i<>(-1) THEN
```

```
      mlist[i].name:=""; (* mark as empty *)
    END;
  END Delete;

  PROCEDURE Init; (* initialize list *)
    VAR
      t:CARDINAL;
  BEGIN
    (* use a null string in name field to indicate an
       empty RECORD *)
    FOR t:=0 TO LSIZE DO
      mlist[t].name:="";
    END;
  END Init;

  BEGIN
    Init;  (* prepare the list *)
    REPEAT
      choice:=Menu();
      CASE choice OF
        1: Enter |
        2: Delete |
        3: Locate |
        4: List |
        5: Puts('program completed');
      END;
    UNTIL choice=5;
  END Mlist.
```

Variant ***RECORDs***

In Modula-2 it is possible to define a **RECORD** that can take on different forms at different points in your program. **RECORDs** of this type are called *variant* ***RECORDs***. The **RECORDs** used so far in this chapter have all had fixed fields. However, it is possible to make the elements change dynamically to accommodate different needs.

Let's begin with an example. Suppose that you are designing a program that will print payroll checks for a factory that employs both salaried and hourly workers. You decide to use the following **RECORD** to hold the necessary information about each employee.

```
EMP = RECORD
    name: ARRAY[0..20] OF CHAR;
    hourly: BOOLEAN;
    NumHoursWorked: CARDINAL; (* for hourly *)
    wage: CARDINAL;          (* workers only *)
    salary: CARDINAL;        (* salaried workers only *)
END;  (* RECORD *)
```

Here, the **BOOLEAN** value **hourly** is used to determine whether the worker is an hourly employee (**TRUE**) or a salaried employee (**FALSE**). For salaried workers, the fields **NumHoursWorked** and **wage** are not needed, and for hourly employees, **salary** is not used. In both cases, there is wasted space in the **RECORD**, which is inefficient.

By using Modula-2's variant **RECORD** capability, this inefficiency can be eliminated by using **hourly** to select either **salary** or **NumHoursWorked** and **wage**, as shown here.

```
EMP = RECORD
    name: ARRAY[0..20] OF CHAR;

    (* variant portion of RECORD *)
    CASE hourly: BOOLEAN OF
      TRUE: NumHoursWorked: CARDINAL;
            wage: CARDINAL |
      FALSE: salary: CARDINAL;
    END;  (* CASE *)
    END;  (* RECORD *)
```

Here, a variation on the **CASE** statement is used to determine which field will be in use for each employee. If **hourly** is **TRUE**, then **NumHoursWorked** and **wage** will be selected; otherwise, **salary** will be active. Note that the field not selected is not defined and should not be used.

The general form of the variant portion of a **RECORD** is

CASE <*selector*>:<*type*> OF
    <*const1*>: <*var-list*>
    <*const2*>: <*var-list*>
    <*const3*>: <*var-list*>
    .
    .
    .
    <*constN*>: <*var-list*>;
END;

where ***<selector>*** is the variable used to determine which of the fields will be selected. In Modula-2 literature this is called either the *discriminator* or the *tag field.* Because you are also declaring the discriminator in the **CASE** statement, you must remember to include the discriminator type. You may use only simple types or previously defined types; enumerations, subranges, and other complex types are not allowed.

The following **PROCEDURE**, which prints employees' names and pay for both salaried and hourly workers, illustrates how variant **RECORDs** can be used.

```
PROCEDURE PrintPay(E:EMP);
BEGIN
  WriteString(E.name);
  IF E.hourly THEN
    WriteCard(E.NumHoursWorked*E.wage,5);
  ELSE
    WriteCard(E.salary,10);
  END;
END PrintPay;
```

Here, if **hourly** is **TRUE**, then **wage** is multiplied by **NumHoursWorked** to compute the pay; otherwise, the **salary** value is printed.

The key point to remember about variant **RECORDs** is that their exact form is determined at run time and is changeable. This means that the same **RECORD** can actually have different forms at different times in the program. This can make variant **RECORDs** very powerful, but it also makes them very susceptible to errors. Every routine that uses a variant always must check the state of the discriminator before accessing one of the variant fields; otherwise, run-time errors will result.

To see another example of variant **RECORDs**, we can rewrite portions of the mailing list program developed earlier so that it can accommodate both U.S. and foreign postal codes. Many countries use both numbers and letters in their postal codes; therefore, a string of characters instead of a number must be used. The first step is to change the declaration of **ADDR**, as shown here.

```
ADDR = RECORD
    name: ARRAY [0..30] OF CHAR;
    street: ARRAY [0..30] OF CHAR;
    city: ARRAY [0..30] OF CHAR;
    state: ARRAY [0..3] OF CHAR;
    CASE  US: BOOLEAN OF
      TRUE: zip: CARDINAL |
      FALSE: PostalCode: ARRAY[0..10] OF CHAR
    END;
END;
```

Now, if the address is foreign, then **PostalCode** is selected; otherwise **zip** is used.

With this change we need to alter the routines that do input and output. Here is the modified **Enter PROCEDURE**.

```
PROCEDURE Enter; (* enter a name into the list *)
  VAR
    i: INTEGER;
    US: CHAR;
```

```
BEGIN
  i:=GetEmpty();
  IF i<>(-1) THEN
    WriteString('Enter name: ');
    Gets(mlist[i].name);
    WriteString('Enter street: ');
    Gets(mlist[i].street);
    WriteString('Enter city: ');
    Gets(mlist[i].city);
    WriteString('Enter state: ');
    Gets(mlist[i].state);

    (* zip or PostalCode *)
    WriteString("US citizen? (Y/N): ");
    Read(US);
    IF US='Y' THEN mlist[i].US:=TRUE
    ELSE mlist[i].US:=FALSE;
    END;
    IF mlist[i].US THEN
      WriteString('Enter ZIP: ');
      ReadCard(mlist[i].zip); WriteLn;
    ELSE
      WriteString('Enter PostalCode: ');
      Gets(mlist[i].PostalCode);
    END;
      WriteLn;
  END
END Enter;
```

As you can see, the input routine must first assign a value to **US** before it can assign a value to either **zip** or **PostalCode**.

The **Display** routine must also be changed, as shown here, so that it will display the proper output based on the state of **US**.

```
PROCEDURE Display(ml: ADDR);
BEGIN
  Puts(ml.name);
  Puts(ml.street);
  Puts(ml.city);
  Puts(ml.state);
  IF ml.US THEN
    WriteCard(ml.zip,5);
    WriteLn;
  ELSE
    Puts(ml.PostalCode);
  END;
  WriteLn;
END Display;
```

One final note: You must always remember to set and check the value of the discriminator before accessing any variant field.

WITH

As you can imagine, typing the **RECORD** name and the dot operator over and over again can sometimes become tedious. To help ease this problem, Modula-2 offers the **WITH** statement, which specifies the **RECORD** that you are working with. The general form is

WITH <*record-name*> DO
<*body-of-code*>
END;

where ***<record-name>*** is the specific **RECORD** in use. Once **WITH** is implemented, the code inside the **WITH** will not need to use **RECORD** name or the dot operator. Look, for example, at the following code.

```
MODULE WithExample;

TYPE
  R= RECORD
        A: INTEGER;
        B: CARDINAL;

  END;

VAR
  REC: R;

BEGIN
  WITH REC DO
    A:=-10;
    B:=100;
  END;
END WithExample.
```

The assignments inside the **WITH** statement are equivalent to these without a **WITH** statement:

```
REC.A:=-10;
REC.B:=100;
```

As another example, the routine **PrintPay** is shown here using a **WITH** statement.

```
PROCEDURE PrintPay(E:EMP);
BEGIN
  WITH E DO
    WriteString(name);
```

```
    IF hourly THEN
      WriteCard(NumHoursWorked*wage,5);
    ELSE
      WriteCard(salary,10);
    END;
  END; (* WITH *)
END PrintPay;
```

WITH statements can be nested so that two or more different **RECORD**s can easily be used at the same time, but this requires that there be no common field names among them.

Remember that the **WITH** statement can lead to conflicts between the names of global variables and the names of the fields of the **RECORD**. There may be times when you will have to change the name of one or the other if you use **WITH**.

EXERCISES

1. Define a **RECORD** called **Airplane** that has fields for the number of engines, the number of passengers, the range, and the name.

2. Using **Airplane**, defined in exercise 1, write a short **PROCEDURE** that displays the contents of the **RECORD** on the screen.

3. What is the difference between a **RECORD** and an array?

4. Modify **Airplane** in exercise 1 so that it is a variant **RECORD** using the **BOOLEAN** discriminator **CARGO** to select between cargo load capacity and number of passengers.

5. Change the following code so that it makes use of the **WITH** statement.

```
state.state:='Texas';
state.county:='Pacos';
state.capital:='Austin';
```

ANSWERS

1.
```
TYPE
   Airplane = RECORD
                  engines: CARDINAL;
                  NumPas: CARDINAL;
                  range: CARDINAL;
                  name: ARRAY [0..30] OF CHAR;
   END;
```

2.
```
PROCEDURE Display(A: Airplane);
BEGIN
  WITH A DO
    WriteCard(engines,5);
    WriteCard(NumPas,5);
    WriteCard(range,5);
    WriteString(name);
  END; (* WITH *)
END Display;
```

3. An array must be comprised of like elements, whereas a **RECORD** can be made up of several different types of variables.

4.
```
TYPE
   Airplane = RECORD
                  engines: CARDINAL;
                  range: CARDINAL;
                  name: ARRAY [0..30] OF CHAR;
                  CASE Cargo: BOOLEAN OF
                    TRUE: capacity: CARDINAL |
                    FALSE: NumPas: CARDINAL;
                  END;
   END;
```

5.
```
WITH state DO
  state:='Texas';
  county:='Pacos';
  capital:='Austin';
END:
```

Input, Output, And Disk Files

CHAPTER 8

Most useful programs utilize disk files either for data storage or for temporary work areas, and every computer language provides some method of creating and maintaining disk files. Modula-2 essentially provides two ways to access disk files—sequentially and randomly—with each method supported by its own distinct set of routines.

In Modula-2, sequential file access is surprisingly simple: It uses the same routines that provide console I/O. Unlike many other languages, Modula-2's general purpose I/O routines, such as **Read**, **Write**, and **WriteString**, are not restricted to use only with the console, but can also be applied to other sequential devices and disk files. Therefore, sequential file access is achieved with the same routines you have already been using, except that the routines have been instructed to direct their input and output elsewhere. These routines are sometimes called *high-level* or *formatted* I/O routines. They are called *high level* because they present a logical view of the input/output hardware to the programmer (low-level routines present a more physical view). They are called *formatted* routines because procedures can be used to write and read various data types, such as **REAL**s, strings, and **INTEGER**s, directly, without the need for manual conversions.

On the other hand, Modula-2's random-access routines are often referred to as *low-level* or *unformatted* because they relate closely to the operating system, and they can only read and write characters, bytes, and words directly, meaning that special methods must be employed to write other data types. Although the routines that form this file system are not technically specified as part of the Modula-2 language, they were created by Wirth as part of the original Modula-2 implementation and have become standard.

Because high-level sequential file access functions require the use of the basic I/O routines, we will begin our dicussion with a quick review.

High-Level I/O Routines

Modula-2's *high-level formatted* I/O routines are found in the files **InOut**, for all nonfloating-point data, and **RealInOut**, for floating-point information. Table 8-1 lists these routines.

You are already familiar with most of these routines from the previous chapters. The two routines **ReadWrd** and **WriteWrd** cannot be used with the console and apply only to disk files. They will be studied later, in Chapter 13, when system-dependent issues are discussed.

WriteOct is used to write a **CARDINAL** in octal format. The basic form is

WriteOct(<*num*>,<*width*>);

where ***num*** is a **CARDINAL**, and ***width*** is the minimum field width. **WriteHex** writes a **CARDINAL** number in hexadecimal format and has the same general form as **WriteOct**.

As you know, the procedure **ReadString** terminates on any ASCII character that is equal to or less than a space. The character that caused termination is found in the variable **termCH**, which must be **IMPORT**ed from **InOut**. Therefore, the following loop can be used to read an entire line of text up to a carriage return.

```
    i:=0;
    REPEAT  (* read it one character at a time *)
      Read(str[i]);
      i:=i+1;
    UNTIL NOT Done;

    CloseInput;  (* reset input to console *)
    WriteString(str);

  END SeqFile.
```

This program contains some very important elements. First, notice the loop used to redirect output.

```
REPEAT
  OpenOutput("")
UNTIL Done;  (* request filename until valid *)
```

The loop will repeat until **Done** is **TRUE**, indicating that the user has actually specified a valid device or file name. The same type of loop is used when opening input. You should always use a piece of code like this to make sure the user has not made a mistake.

Notice also that once the program is finished with the redirected output, the output destination is reset to the console. It is good programming practice to do this immediately after the redirection is finished to avoid accidentally writing additional, unwanted output.

The code used to read a file, shown here, is perhaps the most important element of the program.

```
i:=0;
REPEAT  (* read it one character at a time *)
  Read(str[i]);
  i:=i+1;
UNTIL NOT Done;
```

Notice that a **REPEAT/UNTIL** loop is used to guarantee that at least one iteration will occur. **Done** is checked at the bottom of the loop and, if the value is **FALSE**, the loop terminates. Remember, a **FALSE** value for **Done** indicates that the end of the file has been reached.

Finally, the **IMPORT** list must include **Done** from **InOut**.

The following program, which copies one file to another, provides another example of the redirected sequential I/O facility.

```
MODULE Copy;
  FROM InOut IMPORT OpenOutput, CloseOutput, Done, Write,
                   WriteString, OpenInput, Read, CloseInput;

  VAR
    ch: CHAR;

BEGIN
  (* open input file *)
  WriteString("Enter input file: ");
  REPEAT
    OpenInput("")
  UNTIL Done; (* request filename until valid *)

  (* open output file *)
  WriteString("enter output file name: ");
  REPEAT
    OpenOutput("")
  UNTIL Done;  (* request filename until valid *)

  (* copy the file *)
  REPEAT
    Read(ch);
    Write(ch);
  UNTIL NOT Done;  (* Done is FALSE when EOF is reached *)

  CloseInput;  (* reset input to console *)
  CloseOutput; (* reset output to console *)
END Copy.
```

Redirecting I/O to Other Devices

I/O redirection can be used to access devices other than disk drives. This is accomplished through the use of special names, which stand for these devices. For example, the copy program can be used to print a file on the printer. This is done by specifying the printer device code when prompted for output. The device code for the printer varies among Modula-2 compilers and operating systems. However, for most MS-DOS/PC-DOS versions the code is **PRN:**. The special device codes recognized by your Modula-2 compiler can be found in your user manual.

Limitations of Redirected Sequential I/O

There are two main reasons that few commercial programs use Modula-2's built-in I/O redirection facility. The first is that prompt messages cannot be controlled. The prompts **in**> and **out**>, although adequate for debugging or for programmer utilities, are not sufficient for the average end user; commercial-quality software always controls the screen and the environment.

Second, sequentially accessed files are useful for only a limited number of tasks because, for information in the middle of the file to be read, all prior information must be read first. Commercial programs that use files often deal with several thousand bytes of information, and access time would simply be too great if the entire file had to read each time a selected piece of information was required. This is why randomly accessed files—the subject of the rest of this chapter—are so important.

Random-Access Files

Random-access file routines are found in a library module called **FileSystem**. (Remember that some implementations may call this library and the routines by slightly different names.) **FileSystem** contains routines to open, close, read, and write files. Table 8-2 lists the random-access file procedures. Keep in mind that these routines have nothing to do with those found in **InOut**.

As you can see, the routines found in **FileSystem** essentially are divided into three groups, based on the type of file they will be accessing. In this chapter, we are only concerned with *text* files. Text files contain only printable ASCII characters. The other type of file is called a *binary file*, and it may contain nonprintable information. You will learn about these routines in Chapter 13.

Also found in **FileSystem** is the **RECORD** of type **File**, which is used to hold information about a file. **File** is used to create file descriptors. A file descriptor is a variable of type **File** used to hold all necessary information about the file. Most of the fields in the file descriptor are used only by the file-handling procedures found in **FileSystem** and are not relevant to the code you develop. However, two fields are needed to write proper applications. The first field is the **BOOLEAN eof**, which is used to indicate that the end of the file has been reached. The second is the enumeration **res**, which shows the results of various operations. Table 8-3 shows the possible values for **res** and their meanings.

Table 8-2. Random-Access File Routines

Name	Function
Text and binary files	
Name	**Function**
Create	Creates a temporary file
Close	Closes a file
Lookup	Opens or creates a permanent file
Rename	Renames a file
Delete	Removes a file
SetRead	Sets a file's status to read-only
SetWrite	Sets a file's status to write-only
SetModify	Sets a file's status to read/write
SetOpen	Sets file to open but idle
Reset	Positions file pointer at top of file
SetPos	Puts file pointer at specified location
GetPos	Gets current position of file pointer
Length	Gets length, in bytes, of file
Text files only	
Name	**Function**
ReadChar	Reads a character from a file
WriteChar	Writes a character to a file
Binary files only	
Name	**Function**
ReadWord	Reads a word from a file
WriteWord	Writes a word to a file
ReadByte	Reads a byte from a file
WriteByte	Writes a byte to a file

How to Find, Open, and Close A File

To open a file using Modula-2's disk file routines requires a two-step process. First the file must be located (or created), and then it must be set to one of the various open states: read, write, modify, or idle.

To locate a file requires the use of **Lookup**, which has the general form

Lookup(<*filevar*>, <*filename*>, <*create*>);

Table 8-3. Values for **res**

Value	Meaning
done	Successful termination of routine
notdone	Unsuccessful termination of routine
notsupported	For internal use of FileSystem routines
callerror	Improper file access attempted (e.g., trying to read from a file that is opened for write operations)
unknownmedium	Specified drive does not exist
unknownfile	File specified for Delete routine is nonexistent
paramerror	Parameter error (e.g., invalid file name)
toomanyfile	Built-in file limit exceeded
eom	End of medium; disk out of space

where ***filevar*** is the variable of type ***File*** (file descriptor) that will be assigned to the disk file when a successful lookup occurs, ***filename*** is a string that must contain a valid filename, and ***create*** is a **BOOLEAN** that determines whether a nonexistent file should be created. A successful lookup is indicated when the **res** field of **filevar** is set equal to **done**.

The following code fragment shows the proper way to look up a file for input.

```
REPEAT
  WriteString('Enter input filename: ');
  ReadString(fname);  WriteLn;
  Lookup(F,fname ,FALSE); (* must be there *)
UNTIL F1.res = done;
```

The code works like this. First, the user enters a file name, and **Lookup** searches the disk directory for a file with that name. If one is found, then **F** is assigned to that file, and **F.res** will equal **done**. Because the create flag is **FALSE**, the file must be found for the operation to succeed. If the file is not found, the loop repeats. Using this routine guarantees that you have a valid file. Keep in mind that in some situations, output files are created as needed, so the value of the **create** parameter may be **TRUE**.

Once a file has been found and a **File** variable assigned to it, the file can be opened for access using **SetRead**, **SetWrite**, or **SetModify**, whose general forms are

```
SetRead(<filevar>);

SetWrite(<filevar>);

SetModify(<filevar>);
```

where ***filevar*** is the file descriptor assigned to the disk file you wish to open. **SetRead** opens a file for input, or *read-only,* operations—it may not be written to. **SetWrite** opens a file for output, or *write-only* operations—it cannot be read. **SetModify** opens a file for input and output, or *read-write,* operations.

It is also possible to idle a file; that is, to have a file open but not active. This is done using **SetOpen**, which has the general form

SetOpen(<*filevar*>);

After a call to **SetOpen**, the file may not be accessed until it is set to one of the other open states.

The success of these operations is indicated when the **res** field of the file variable is set to **done**.

A file is closed with a call to **Close**. Close performs an orderly shutdown of the file. This includes writing any information held in a temporary disk buffer to the disk file. (This is sometimes referred to as *flushing* the buffer.) You may not be aware of it, but all disk file routines use a small portion of memory to hold information written to or read from a disk file. This temporary storage is typically a few hundred bytes long and is used to increase the efficiency of disk operations. If your program does not call **Close** prior to exit, then any information left in this buffer will not be written to disk and will be lost. Therefore, always close files when you are done with them. The general form of **Close** is

Close(<*filevar*>);

Reading and Writing

Unlike high-level sequential file routines, which let you read and write data of all types fairly easily, random-access routines operate only on characters, bytes, and words. (In this chapter we will not worry about byte and word data or the routines that support them, since they depend upon system-dependent information found in the **SYSTEM** library. These and other features are the subject of Chapter 13.) This means that while you can read and write characters, you cannot read or write **REAL**s, for example. For other types of data to be used with low-level file routines you must write your own special conversion functions. (In Chapter 13 you will learn that it is possible to read and write blocks of memory, which eases this problem to some extent.)

Internal to the file system is the *file pointer.* The file pointer is an internal variable that keeps track of the current position of your routines in a file. You can think of a file pointer as an arrow that points to the current character. Each read and write operation moves the pointer forward one position.

WriteChar is used to write a character to a file. Its general form is

WriteChar(<*filevar*>,<*ch*>);

where ***filevar*** is the file descriptor, and ***ch*** is the character to be written. A successful write operation sets the **res** field to **done**. If no space is left on the disk drive, then **res** will be set to **eom** (end of medium).

Each call to **WriteChar** writes the character at the current file pointer position and then increments that pointer by one. Therefore, the following code fragment will write an array of ten characters from the string **name** to a file.

```
t:=0;
REPEAT
  WriteChar(F,name[t]);
  t:=t+1;
UNTIL (t=10) OR F.res<>done;
```

ReadChar is used to read characters from a file. It has the general form

ReadChar(<*filevar*>,<*ch*>);

Each time **ReadChar** is called, a character is read from the current file pointer and the pointer is incremented. If an attempt is made to read past the end of the file, the **eof** field of **filevar** is set to **TRUE**. A successful read sets **res** to **done**. Reading the end-of-file character places a null (ASCII 0) into the character. The following routine shows how to properly read characters from a file and display them on the screen.

```
REPEAT
  ReadChar(F1,ch);
  IF ch<>CHR(0) THEN Write(ch);   (* don't print EOF *)
UNTIL F1.eof;
```

A Simple Example

To gain an understanding of how to use these routines, start with a new version of the file copy program, as shown here.

```
MODULE RandCopy;
  FROM InOut IMPORT ReadString, WriteString, WriteLn, EOL,
              OpenOutput, CloseOutput, Done, Write;

  FROM FileSystem IMPORT File, Response, Lookup, SetWrite,
        SetRead, Close, ReadChar, WriteChar;

  VAR
    ch: CHAR;
    F1, F2: File;
    fname: ARRAY[0..30] OF CHAR;
    h,l: CARDINAL;
BEGIN
  REPEAT
    WriteString('Enter input filename: ');
    ReadString(fname);  WriteLn;
    Lookup(F1,fname ,FALSE); (* must be there *)
  UNTIL F1.res = done;

  REPEAT
    WriteString('Enter output filename: ');
    ReadString(fname);  WriteLn;
    Lookup(F2,fname ,TRUE); (* create if not there *)
  UNTIL F2.res = done;

  SetRead(F1);
  SetWrite(F2);

  REPEAT
    ReadChar(F1,ch);
    IF ch<>CHR(0) THEN WriteChar(F2,ch); END;
  UNTIL F1.eof OR (F2.res=eom);

  Close(F1); Close(F2);
END RandCopy.
```

Look first at the **IMPORT** list. Notice that the **RECORD File** and the enumeration **Response** are imported along with the various file-handling routines from **FileSystem**. In general, all **MODULEs** that use the low-level, random-access procedures will need to use **File** and **Response**, so you should plan on including them in the **IMPORT** list.

The files are located using the standard **lookup** loops discussed earlier. Once the files have been located and assigned to the file descriptors **F1** and **F2**, the files are set to read and write status by the lines

```
SetRead(F1);
SetWrite(F2);
```

The actual copy operation takes place in this loop:

```
REPEAT
  ReadChar(F1,ch);
  IF ch<>CHR(0) THEN WriteChar(F2,ch); END;
UNTIL F1.eof OR (F2.res=eom);
```

Notice that when the end-of-file character is read, it is not written to the output file. The end-of-file character will be written to the output file when the file is closed; it should not be written manually by your routines. In addition, the loop checks not only for the end of the input file, but also for room on the disk medium for the output file.

The program ends by closing the files. Once again, this is necessary to ensure that the internal buffers used by the file routines are written to disk and that an end-of-file mark is placed at the end of the output file.

*Using **SetPos***

In the preceding example, both the input and output files were read in strictly sequential order. Because of the added flexibility and control you, the programmer, have over low-level random-access routines, it is not uncommon for such routines to be used with sequential operations or for the same program to access a file both sequentially and randomly at different times. However, the true power of low-level routines is in their random access.

The routine **SetPos** is used to position the file pointer anywhere in the file. **SetPos** uses as its argument the absolute byte position at the start of the file. Its general form is

SetPos(<*filevar*>,<*high*>,<*low*>);

where ***high*** is the high-order word of the position, and ***low*** is the low-order word of the position. Both must be **CARDINAL**s. Because files often contain more than 65,535 bytes (one word) and Modula-2 does not support long **CARDINALs**, two numbers must be used to represent the file position. You can think of these numbers as forming a 32-bit **CARDINAL**. The final file pointer position is computed according to the following formula:

$$pos = high * (2^{16}) + low$$

If you are willing to restrict your files to 65,535 bytes or less, then you can simply set ***high*** to zero. For simplicity, the programs in this chapter make that restriction.

Hence, to move the file pointer to the 465th byte of **F1**, you would write

```
SetPos(F1,0,465);
```

If the operation succeeds, **F1.res** equals **done**.

It is important to remember that the first byte in a file is byte zero. Therefore,

```
SetPos(F1,0,0);
```

will position the file pointer to the top of the file.

The following program illustrates how **SetPos** works. It allows you to specify any byte in a text file and then displays the character in that location.

```
MODULE SetPosExample;
  FROM InOut IMPORT ReadString, WriteString, WriteLn,
                    ReadCard, Write;

  FROM FileSystem IMPORT File, Response, Lookup, SetRead, SetPos,
        Close, ReadChar;

  VAR
    F1: File;  (* variable of type File *)
    ch: CHAR;
    fname: ARRAY [0..20] OF CHAR;
     i: CARDINAL;

BEGIN
  REPEAT
    WriteString('Enter Filename: ');
    ReadString(fname);
    Lookup(F1,fname ,FALSE);
  UNTIL F1.res = done;

  SetRead(F1);
```

```
    REPEAT
      WriteString('Enter character to read: ');
      ReadCard(i); WriteLn;
      SetPos(F1, 0, i);  (* go to ith byte in file *)
      IF F1.res <> done THEN
        WriteString('Out of bounds');
        WriteLn;
      ELSE
        ReadChar(F1,ch);  (* read and *)
        Write(ch);     (* display char at position i *)
      END;
    UNTIL F1.eof;
    Close(F1);
  END SetPosExample.
```

Enter this program and try it to fully appreciate its random-access nature.

A Second Example

Another very useful routine found in **FileSystem**, **Length**, returns the length of a file in bytes. The general form of **Length** is

Length(<*filevar*>, <*high*>, <*low*>);

where ***high*** is the high-order part of the file's length, and ***low*** is the low-order part. These two values form the 32-bit value that is the length of the file. They work just like those of **SetPos**, with the actual length being computed using the following formula:

$$pos = high * (2^{16}) + low$$

If you restrict your files to less than or equal to 65,535, then ***high*** will always be zero. For simplicity, this restriction is assumed for the examples in this chapter.

You can use a combination of **Length** and **SetPos** to create a reverse-copy program. In this program the contents of the input file are copied in reverse order to the output file; that is, if the input file contains

this is a test

then the output file will contain

tset a si siht

after the reverse copy.

Look at the following program.

```
MODULE ReverseCopy;  (* copy in reverse *)

  FROM InOut IMPORT ReadString, WriteString, WriteLn, EOL,
               OpenOutput, CloseOutput, Done, Write;

  FROM FileSystem IMPORT File, Response, Lookup, SetWrite, SetPos,
        SetRead, Close, ReadChar, WriteChar, Length;

  VAR
    ch: CHAR;
     F1, F2: File;
     fname: ARRAY[0..30] OF CHAR;
     h,l: CARDINAL;
BEGIN
  REPEAT
    WriteString('Enter input filename: ');
    ReadString(fname);  WriteLn;
    Lookup(F1,fname ,FALSE); (* must be there *)
  UNTIL F1.res = done;

  REPEAT
    WriteString('Enter output filename: ');
    ReadString(fname);  WriteLn;
    Lookup(F2,fname ,TRUE); (* create if not there *)
  UNTIL F2.res = done;

  SetRead(F1);
  SetWrite(F2);

  Length(F1,h,l);  (* assume length less than 64K *)
  l:=l+1;  (* set up for algorithm *)
  REPEAT
    l:=l-1;
    SetPos(F1, 0, l);
    ReadChar(F1,ch);
    IF ch<>CHR(0) THEN WriteChar(F2,ch); END;
  UNTIL (l=0) OR (F2.res=eom);

  Close(F1); Close(F2);
END ReverseCopy.
```

The program works as follows. The length of the input file is determined with a call to **Length**, and this value is used to control the loop. The first pass through the loop causes the last character in the file to be read from the input file and written as the first character to the output file. The next iteration reads the next-to-last character from the input file and writes it as the second character to the output file. The process continues until the first character of the input file is written as the last character of the output file.

Using Random Access With Arrays

Until now, the examples have used random access only with character data. However, most real-world applications use complex data types such as arrays. The methods used to store and access these types of data are essentially the same except that your program must perform some additional bookkeeping functions.

Consider, for example, a program that looks up a part's name and price using a special part number that is also that part's index number in a disk file. In this system, a user could look up any part in the database of parts if the part number is known. Assume that each entry in the parts database is organized as shown here.

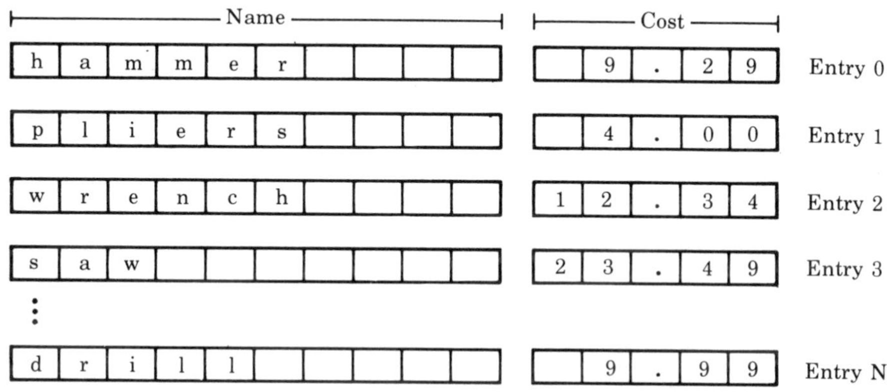

In the file, each part is allocated ten characters and each price is allocated five characters. Therefore, the program that uses this file needs the following variables:

```
name: ARRAY[0..9] OF CHAR;
cost: ARRAY[0..4] OF CHAR;
```

Assuming that the parts database is called *Parts*, the following program can be used to look up the name and price of any part number.

```
MODULE Parts;
  FROM InOut IMPORT ReadString, WriteString, WriteLn,
                    ReadCard, Write;

  FROM FileSystem IMPORT File, Response, Lookup, SetRead, SetPos,
        Close, ReadChar;
  CONST
    EntrySize = 15;

  VAR
    F1: File;  (* variable of type File *)
    ch: CHAR;
    fname: ARRAY [0..20] OF CHAR;
    name: ARRAY[0..9] OF CHAR;
    cost: ARRAY[0..4] OF CHAR;
    i,t: CARDINAL;

BEGIN
  Lookup(F1,'parts' ,FALSE);
  IF F1.res = done THEN SetRead(F1); END;

  REPEAT
    WriteString('Enter part number ');
    ReadCard(i); WriteLn;
    SetPos(F1, 0, i*EntrySize);
    IF F1.res = paramerror THEN
      WriteString('Out of bounds');
      WriteLn;
    ELSE
      FOR t:=0 TO 9 DO
        ReadChar(F1,name[t]);
      END;

      FOR t:=0 TO 4 DO
        ReadChar(F1,cost[t]);
      END;
      WriteString(name);
      WriteString(': $');
      WriteString(cost);
    END;
  UNTIL F1.eof;
  Close(F1);
END Parts.
```

In this program, the constant **EntrySize** is used in conjunction with the part number to determine the proper place to position the file pointer. The value of **EntrySize** is determined by adding the number of characters in **name** and the number of characters in **cost**, which is 10+5, or 15.

Each time the user enters a part number, **SetPos** moves the file pointer to the correct part using

```
SetPos(F1, 0, i*EntrySize);
```

Therefore, part 0 is located at byte 0 in the file, part 1 at byte 15, part 2 at byte 30, and so forth. So, if part number 2 is entered, then

wrench $12.34

is displayed.

The key point here is that your program must use a multiplier to determine the next position in a file that uses a complex data type.

In Chapter 13, which deals with system-dependent functions, you will learn another way to read and write complex data types directly.

Writing Numbers to Files

The high-level I/O system allowed you simply to redirect the standard console routines, but the low-level random-access file system does not. As you have probably noticed, using the character-oriented system there is no way to directly read or write **INTEGERs**, **CARDINALs**, or **REALs**. To do this, you must manually convert data of these types into strings and vice versa.

As discussed earlier, the **RealConversions** library is used to convert **REALs** into strings and strings into **REALs**. All other number conversion routines are found in the **NumberConversion** library. (Remember: The actual names of these libraries may vary slightly among implementations.) **NumberConversion** contains the procedures shown in Table 8-4.

Table 8-4. **Number Conversion** Procedures

Name	**Function**
StringToCard	Converts a string into a CARDINAL
CardToString	Converts a CARDINAL into a string
StringToInt	Converts a string into an INTEGER
IntToString	Converts an INTEGER into a string

You can use these routines to help you read and write numbers to and from a disk file. For example, the short program shown here will first convert a **REAL** and then a **CARDINAL** and write the values to a disk file in string form.

```
MODULE NumOutput;
  FROM InOut IMPORT ReadString, WriteString, WriteLn;

  FROM FileSystem IMPORT File, Response, Lookup, SetWrite,
                  Close, WriteChar;
  FROM NumberConversion IMPORT CardToString;

  FROM RealConversions IMPORT RealToString;

  VAR
     okay: BOOLEAN;
     F1: File;
     fname: ARRAY[0..30] OF CHAR;
     str: ARRAY[0..30] OF CHAR;
     i,j: CARDINAL;
     r: REAL;

BEGIN

  REPEAT
    WriteString('Enter output filename: ');
    ReadString(fname);  WriteLn;
    Lookup(F1,fname ,TRUE); (* create if not there *)
  UNTIL F1.res = done;

  SetWrite(F1);

  i:=1234;
  r:= 123.34;

  (* convert a REAL into a string and write it out *)
  RealToString(r,3,10,str,okay);
  FOR j:=0 TO 9 DO WriteChar(F1,str[j]); END;

  (* convert a CARDINAL to a string and write it out *)
  CardToString(i,str,5);
  FOR j:=0 TO 4 DO WriteChar(F1,str[j]); END;

  Close(F1);
END NumOutput.
```

For input operations, you will need to read in a string and convert it back into a number using one of the standard conversion procedures.

Using **Delete**

The last disk procedure that we will look at in this chapter is **Delete**, which is used to remove a disk file. The general form of this routine is

Delete (<filename>,<filevar>);

where ***filename*** is a string that contains the name of the file to erase, and ***filevar*** is a variable of type **File** that uses the **res** field to indicate the success or failure of the operation.

The use of **Delete** is illustrated by the following simple program that deletes a user-specified disk file.

```
MODULE DelFile;
  FROM InOut IMPORT ReadString, WriteString, WriteLn;

  FROM FileSystem IMPORT File, Response, Delete;


  VAR
     F1: File;
     fname: ARRAY[0..30] OF CHAR;

BEGIN
  REPEAT
    WriteString('Enter filename to delete: ');
    ReadString(fname);  WriteLn;
    Delete(fname ,F1); (* delete file *)
  UNTIL F1.res = done;

END DelFile.
```

As you can see, unlike all the other disk file routines, it is not necessary to perform a **Lookup** on a file prior to deleting it. If the file is not found, or if the disk is write-protected, then the **res** field will be set to **notdone**; otherwise, it will be set to **done**.

EXERCISES

1. Explain the essential difference between a sequential-access routine and a random-access routine.

2. Write a short program, using high-level sequential I/O routines, that replaces one user-specified word with another (that is, execute a global search and replace).

3. What is wrong with the following program fragment?

```
MODULE wrong;
.
.
.
BEGIN
    WriteString("enter output filename: ");
    OpenOutput(" ");
    WriteString("Enter input file name: "); OpenInput(" ");
.
.
.
END wrong.
```

4. Explain what a file descriptor is and how one is created. Give an example.

5. What is the **res** field of a file descriptor used for?

6. A mailing list program was developed in Chapter 7. However, this program was severely limited because it could not store addresses. Using low-level file routines, create two procedures, called **Save** and **Load**, that will save and load the mailing list. Also, rewrite portions of the program as necessary to integrate these routines.

ANSWERS

1. In a sequential access routine, information can be read or written only in ascending order. In a random-access routine, information can be read or written in any order.

2.
```
MODULE SearchandReplace;
  FROM InOut IMPORT OpenOutput, CloseOutput, Done, Write,
                    WriteLn, ReadString, WriteString, OpenInput,
                    Read, CloseInput, termCH;

  FROM Strings IMPORT CompareStr;

  VAR
    w1,w2,w3: ARRAY[0..79] OF CHAR;

BEGIN
  WriteString("enter word to replace: ");
  ReadString(w1);
  WriteLn;
  WriteString("enter word to substitute: ");
  ReadString(w2);
  WriteLn;

  (* open input file *)
  WriteString("Enter input file: ");
  REPEAT
    OpenInput("")
  UNTIL Done; (* request filename until valid *)

  (* open output file *)

  WriteString("enter output file name: ");
  REPEAT
    OpenOutput("")
  UNTIL Done;  (* request filename until valid *)

  (* copy the file *)
  REPEAT
    ReadString(w3);
    IF NOT Done THEN WriteString("not done"); END;
    IF CompareStr(w3,w1)=0 THEN WriteString(w2)
    ELSE WriteString(w3);
    END;
    Write(termCH);
  UNTIL termCH = CHR(0);  (* until EOF is reached *)

  CloseInput;  (* reset input to console *)
  CloseOutput; (* reset output to console *)
END SearchandReplace.
```

3. **OpenOutput** will redirect the output, so the user never will see the second prompt.

4. A file descriptor is a record variable of type **File** that is used to hold information about a file. For example, the following fragment declares **F** to be a file descriptor.

```
VAR
  F: File;
```

5. The **res** field holds the results of an operation, including **done**, **not-done**, and other conditions.

6. The routines **Save** and **Load** are as follows.

```
PROCEDURE Save;  (* save the mailing list *)
  VAR
    t,i:CARDINAL;
    f: File;
    fname: ARRAY[0..30] OF CHAR;
BEGIN
  REPEAT
    WriteString('Enter Filename: ');
    ReadString(fname);  WriteLn;
    Lookup(f,fname ,TRUE); (* create if not there *)
  UNTIL f.res = done;

  Reset(f);  (* re-write from the beginning *)
  SetWrite(f);  (* enable write *)

  FOR i:=0 TO LSIZE DO
    IF CompareStr(mlist[i].name,"")<>0 THEN
    (* Write the record *)
       FOR t:=0 TO HIGH(mlist[i].name) DO
       WriteChar(f,mlist[i].name[t]);
     END;
     FOR t:=0 TO HIGH(mlist[i].street) DO
       WriteChar(f,mlist[i].street[t]);
     END;
     FOR t:=0 TO HIGH(mlist[i].city) DO
       WriteChar(f,mlist[i].city[t]);
     END;
     FOR t:=0 TO HIGH(mlist[i].state) DO
       WriteChar(f,mlist[i].state[t]);
     END;
     FOR t:=0 TO HIGH(mlist[i].zip) DO
       WriteChar(f,mlist[i].zip[t]);
     END;
     END; (* if *)
   END; (* for *)
   Close(f);
END Save;
```

```
PROCEDURE Load;  (* read in the list *)
  VAR
    t,i:CARDINAL;
    f: File;
    fname: ARRAY[0..30] OF CHAR;
BEGIN
  REPEAT
    WriteString('Enter Filename: ');
    ReadString(fname);  WriteLn;
    Lookup(f,fname ,FALSE); (* do not create if not there *)
  UNTIL f.res = done;

  Reset(f);  (* read from the beginning *)
  SetRead(f);  (* enable read *)

  i:=0;
  REPEAT
    (* Read the record *)
     FOR t:=0 TO HIGH(mlist[i].name) DO
       ReadChar(f,mlist[i].name[t]);
     END;
     FOR t:=0 TO HIGH(mlist[i].street) DO
       ReadChar(f,mlist[i].street[t]);
     END;
     FOR t:=0 TO HIGH(mlist[i].city) DO
       ReadChar(f,mlist[i].city[t]);
     END;
     FOR t:=0 TO HIGH(mlist[i].state) DO
       ReadChar(f,mlist[i].state[t]);
     END;
     FOR t:=0 TO HIGH(mlist[i].zip) DO
       ReadChar(f,mlist[i].zip[t]);
     END;
     i:=i+1;
   UNTIL f.eof AND (i<LSIZE);  (* until end-of-file *)
   Close(f);
END Load;
```

The entire mailing list program, including all changes necessary to include the **Save** and **Load** procedures, is as follows.

```
MODULE Mlist;  (* a simple mailing list program
                  that uses an array of RECORDS and can
                  save and load addresses *)

  FROM InOut IMPORT Read, Write, WriteString, WriteLn,
                  WriteCard, ReadCard, ReadString, EOL;
  FROM Strings IMPORT CompareStr;

  FROM FileSystem IMPORT Lookup, Close, WriteChar, ReadChar,
                         SetRead, SetWrite, SetModify, File,
                         Response, SetPos, Reset;

  FROM SYSTEM IMPORT TSIZE;

  CONST
    LSIZE = 100;
```

```
TYPE
  ADDR = RECORD
      name: ARRAY [0..30] OF CHAR;
      street: ARRAY [0..30] OF CHAR;
      city: ARRAY [0..30] OF CHAR;
      state: ARRAY [0..3] OF CHAR;
      zip: ARRAY [0..10] OF CHAR;
  END;

VAR
  mlist: ARRAY [0..LSIZE] OF ADDR; (* array of addresses *)
  choice: CARDINAL;

PROCEDURE Gets(VAR a:ARRAY OF CHAR);
  CONST
    BS = 8;  (* backspace *)

  VAR
    ch: CHAR;
    i:CARDINAL;
  BEGIN
    i:=0;
    REPEAT
      Read(ch);
      Write(ch);
      IF ORD(ch)=BS THEN i:=i-1;  (* is backspace *)
      ELSIF (ch<>EOL) AND (i<HIGH(a)) THEN
        a[i]:=ch;
        i:=i+1;
      END;
      UNTIL (ch=EOL) OR (i=HIGH(a));
      a[i]:=CHR(0);  (* all strings end in 0 *)
    END Gets;

PROCEDURE Puts(s:ARRAY OF CHAR);
  BEGIN
    WriteString(s);
    WriteLn;
  END Puts;

PROCEDURE Menu():CARDINAL;
  VAR
    ch:CARDINAL;
  BEGIN
    Puts('    1. Enter an address');
    Puts('    2. Delete an address');
    Puts('    3. Find an address');
    Puts('    4. List all addresses');
    Puts('    5. Save list');
    Puts('    6. Load list');
    Puts('    7. Quit');
    REPEAT
      WriteString('Enter Choice: ');
      ReadCard(ch);
      WriteLn;
    UNTIL (ch>=1) AND (ch<=7);
    WriteLn;
    RETURN ch;
  END Menu;
```

```
PROCEDURE GetEmpty(): INTEGER; (* return next empty
                      location in list, -1 if full *)
  VAR
    i:CARDINAL;
BEGIN
  FOR i:=0 TO LSIZE DO
    IF CompareStr(mlist[i].name,"")=0 THEN
      RETURN i;   (* is an empty location *)
    END;
  END;
  RETURN -1; (* list full *)
END GetEmpty;

PROCEDURE Enter(i: INTEGER); (* enter a name into the list *)
BEGIN
  (* if i= -1 then find new slot; otherwise modify
     existing entry *)

  IF i=(-1) THEN i:=GetEmpty(); END;
  IF i<>(-1) THEN
    WriteString('Enter name: ');
    Gets(mlist[i].name);
    WriteString('Enter street: ');
    Gets(mlist[i].street);
    WriteString('Enter city: ');
    Gets(mlist[i].city);
    WriteString('Enter state: ');
    Gets(mlist[i].state);
    WriteString('Enter ZIP: ');
    Gets(mlist[i].zip); WriteLn; WriteLn;
  END
END Enter;

PROCEDURE Display(ml: ADDR);
BEGIN
  Puts(ml.name);
  Puts(ml.street);
  Puts(ml.city);
  Puts(ml.state);
  Puts(ml.zip);
  WriteLn; WriteLn;
END Display;

PROCEDURE List;  (* display the entire list *)
  VAR
    i:CARDINAL;
BEGIN
  FOR i:=0 TO LSIZE DO
    IF CompareStr(mlist[i].name,"")<>0 THEN
      Display(mlist[i]);
    END
  END
END List;

PROCEDURE Find():INTEGER;  (* return the index of a name *)
  VAR
    f: CARDINAL;
    s: ARRAY [0..30] OF CHAR;
BEGIN
```

```
    WriteString('Enter name to find: ');
    Gets(s);
    FOR f:=0 TO LSIZE DO
      IF CompareStr(s,mlist[f].name)=0 THEN RETURN f END;
    END;
    RETURN -1;  (* not found *)
  END Find;

  PROCEDURE Locate;  (* display an address based
                        on the name field *)
    VAR
      i: INTEGER;
  BEGIN
    i:=Find(); (* find the name *)
    IF i<>(-1) THEN Display(mlist[i]); END;
  END Locate;

  PROCEDURE Delete; (* remove an address based
                       on the name field *)
    VAR
      i: INTEGER;

  BEGIN
    i:=Find(); (* find the name *)
    IF i<>(-1) THEN
      mlist[i].name:=""; (* mark as empty *)
    END;
  END Delete;

  PROCEDURE Save;  (* save the mailing list *)
    VAR
      t,i:CARDINAL;
      f: File;
      fname: ARRAY[0..30] OF CHAR;
  BEGIN
    REPEAT
      WriteString('Enter Filename: ');
      ReadString(fname);  WriteLn;
      Lookup(f,fname ,TRUE); (* create if not there *)
    UNTIL f.res = done;

    Reset(f);  (* re-write from the beginning *)
    SetWrite(f);  (* enable write *)

    FOR i:=0 TO LSIZE DO
      IF CompareStr(mlist[i].name,"")<>0 THEN
      (* Write the record *)
         FOR t:=0 TO HIGH(mlist[i].name) DO
           WriteChar(f,mlist[i].name[t]);
         END;
         FOR t:=0 TO HIGH(mlist[i].street) DO
           WriteChar(f,mlist[i].street[t]);
         END;
         FOR t:=0 TO HIGH(mlist[i].city) DO
           WriteChar(f,mlist[i].city[t]);
         END;
         FOR t:=0 TO HIGH(mlist[i].state) DO
           WriteChar(f,mlist[i].state[t]);
         END;
```

```
          FOR t:=0 TO HIGH(mlist[i].zip) DO
            WriteChar(f,mlist[i].zip[t]);
          END;
        END; (* if *)
      END; (* for *)
      Close(f);
  END Save;

  PROCEDURE Load;  (* read in the list *)
    VAR
      t,i:CARDINAL;
      f: File;
      fname: ARRAY[0..30] OF CHAR;
  BEGIN
    REPEAT
      WriteString('Enter Filename: ');
      ReadString(fname);  WriteLn;
      Lookup(f,fname ,FALSE); (* do not create if not there *)

  UNTIL f.res = done;

  Reset(f);  (* read from the beginning *)
  SetRead(f);  (* enable read *)

  i:=0;
  REPEAT
    (* Read the record *)
     FOR t:=0 TO HIGH(mlist[i].name) DO
       ReadChar(f,mlist[i].name[t]);
     END;
     FOR t:=0 TO HIGH(mlist[i].street) DO
       ReadChar(f,mlist[i].street[t]);
     END;
     FOR t:=0 TO HIGH(mlist[i].city) DO
       ReadChar(f,mlist[i].city[t]);
     END;
     FOR t:=0 TO HIGH(mlist[i].state) DO
       ReadChar(f,mlist[i].state[t]);
     END;
     FOR t:=0 TO HIGH(mlist[i].zip) DO
       ReadChar(f,mlist[i].zip[t]);
     END;
     i:=i+1;
   UNTIL f.eof AND (i<LSIZE);  (* until end-of-file *)
   Close(f);
END Load;


PROCEDURE Init; (* initialize list *)
  VAR
    t:CARDINAL;
BEGIN
  (* use a null string in name field to indicate an
     empty RECORD *)
  FOR t:=0 TO LSIZE DO
    mlist[t].name:="";
  END;

END Init;
```

```
BEGIN
  Init;  (* prepare the list *)
  REPEAT
   choice:=Menu();
    CASE choice OF
      1: Enter(-1) |  (* new entry *)
      2: Delete |
      3: Locate |
      4: List |
      5: Save() |
      6: Load() |
      7: Puts('program completed');
    END;
  UNTIL choice=7;
END Mlist.
```

Pointers and Dynamic Memory Allocation

CHAPTER 9

All of the program examples that you have seen and been working with have had a fixed number of variables. While this is fine for many applications, it can be a serious limitation to programs that need to make the best use of an unknown amount of memory or that process differing amounts of information.

The Unknown Memory Dilemma

In several common types of programs, including databases, text editors, and compilers, the data operated on by the program shrinks or grows as the program executes. Also, certain programs cannot know in advance how much room for storage is needed. For example, consider the mailing list example used in the previous two chapters. How big should the array that holds the address records be? Should its size be determined with a large computer, full of memory, in mind, or should it be geared for a minimal configuration?

If you are a professional programmer, you almost certainly have faced the "unknown memory dilemma." This problem occurs when you write a program that has some aspect of its performance based on the amount of memory inside the computer that executes it, as with the mailing list program. For example, a program for an in-memory sort that can handle 10,000 addresses in a 256K machine may only be able to sort 5,000 addresses in a 128K computer. If this program is to be used on computers of unknown memory sizes, then you cannot use a fixed-size array to hold the sort information. Either the program will not work on machines with small memories because the array will not fit, or you will have to create an array that will work with the smallest amount of memory and not allow users with more memory to use the full capabilities of their computers. It is this type of dilemma that leads us to dynamic memory allocation and pointers.

Dynamic Memory Allocation

Dynamic memory allocation is the process of acquiring storage for information during the execution of a program instead of using fixed variables. This storage is allocated from a region of free memory called the *heap* that, conceptually, lies between your program and the stack. Figure 9-1 shows how memory is organized in a Modula-2 program. (This organization varies somewhat, depending upon the implementation.)

As your program executes, the program code and global variables and constants areas of your program are fixed, but since the stack is used to store both local variables and return addresses from procedure calls, the stack changes size as the program executes. As the stack gets larger, it moves toward the heap. As memory is allocated from the heap, the heap approaches the stack. As you can see, both the heap and the stack have a finite (but generally unknowable) size. In some implementations of Modula-2 it is possible for the stack to overrun the heap, which probably would cause a run-time error, but this situation is very rare.

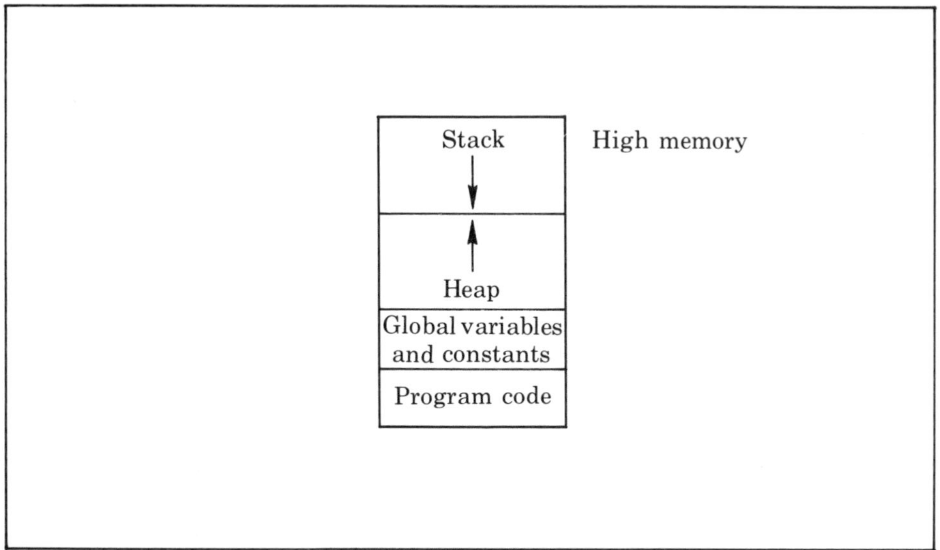

Figure 9-1. Memory organization in a Modula-2 program

The heap is organized by Modula-2 into a list of free memory. As a piece of memory is allocated, it is taken off the free list. When memory is deallocated, it is placed back on the free list. Once a piece of memory has been obtained, it can be used to hold information in much the same way that a normal variable can through the use of pointers.

Pointers

Key to the way Modula-2 handles dynamic allocation is the *pointer*. Simply stated, a pointer is a variable that holds the address of a region of allocated memory. That is, the pointer variable has, as its value, the address of a piece of memory that is used to actually hold some information.

To declare a pointer variable requires that you first define a pointer type in the **TYPE** declaration portion of your program. The general form is

TYPE
<*PointerType*>=POINTER TO <*type*>;

where ***PointerType*** is the name of the new pointer type, and ***type*** is either one of the built-in data types or a user-defined data type that defines the kind of data *PointerType* can point to.

For example, the following defines a pointer type called **Ptype** and declares a variable **p** of that type.

```
TYPE
  Ptype = POINTER TO CARDINAL;

VAR
  p: Ptype;
```

Now **p** can be used to point to a **CARDINAL** value. Remember that the variable **p** does not itself hold a **CARDINAL** value, but rather the address of a region of memory that can hold a **CARDINAL** value.

The type of data that a pointer variable can point to is called its *bound type*. In the example, **p**'s bound type is **CARDINAL**.

NEW and DISPOSE

The only way a pointer variable can be assigned a value is through the use of the built-in procedure **NEW** or one of its support procedures. Because you may wish to return memory back to the heap for reallocation later, Modula-2 includes the built-in procedure **DISPOSE**.

NEW is used to allocate sufficient memory from the heap to accommodate data of its bound type. The general form of **NEW** is

NEW(<*pointer*>);

where ***pointer*** is a valid pointer variable. After the call, ***pointer*** will contain the address of a region of memory large enough to hold its bound type. Therefore, the following fragment will allocate one byte of memory from the heap.

```
TYPE
  Ptype = POINTER TO CHAR;

VAR
  p: Ptype;

BEGIN
  NEW(p);
```

When you wish to release memory previously allocated using **NEW**, you must call **DISPOSE** with the pointer that points to it. The general form is

DISPOSE(<*pointer*>);

where ***pointer*** must be a previously allocated pointer variable. After a call to **DISPOSE**, the memory is available for reallocation. Therefore, the following fragment frees the pointer **p** after its use.

```
TYPE
  Ptype = POINTER TO CHAR;

VAR
  p: Ptype;

BEGIN
  NEW(p);  (* allocate for use *)
.
.
.
  DISPOSE(p);  (* return to the heap for reuse *)
```

It is very important that you never try to **DISPOSE** of either a **NIL** pointer or an invalid pointer because doing so will most likely destroy the heap's list and eventually cause your program to crash.

Keep in mind that the heap is finite, and it is possible to run out of free memory; therefore, **DISPOSE** is very important in many applications.

Before continuing, there is something about **NEW** and **DISPOSE** that you must know. Both are built-in procedures, but they rely on the library procedures **ALLOCATE** and **DEALLOCATE** that are found in **Storage**. Therefore, the following **IMPORT** line must always be included in any program that uses **NEW** and **DISPOSE**.

```
FROM Storage IMPORT ALLOCATE, DEALLOCATE;
```

Assigning Values Using a Pointer

After a valid address has been assigned to a pointer, you can assign a value to the memory location that the pointer points to by using the *dereferencing operator* ^ (sometimes called the *arrow* operator). For example, the following assigns the value 'A' to the memory location pointed to by **p**.

```
TYPE
  Ptype = POINTER TO CHAR;

VAR
  p: Ptype;

BEGIN
  NEW(p);
  p^:='A';
```

As you can see, the ^ follows the pointer variable. To remember what is happening, you could read this line of code as "at the address pointed to by **p**, assign the value 'A'." For example, assume that after the call to **NEW**, **p** contains the address 2000, meaning that the allocated memory is located at 2000. The situation is as shown in Figure 9-2.

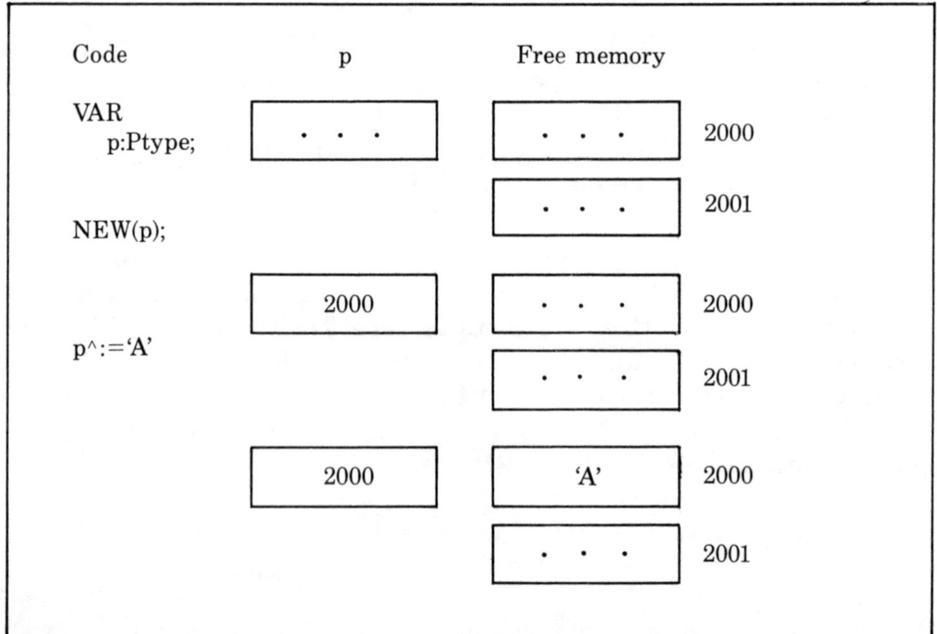

Figure 9-2. Allocation and assignment of a pointer

As is indicated by the diagram, when **p** is declared, its value is undefined; that is, it does not point anywhere. After the call to **NEW**, **p** contains the value 2000 and therefore points to that address. After the assignment, the value of 'A' is placed into the address pointed to by **p**, or 2000.

At this point, you should understand that the statement

```
p:='A';   (* wrong *)
```

has no meaning and will not compile because only addresses may be assigned to a pointer; you must use the dereferencing operator to assign a value to the memory location the pointer points

It is possible to assign one pointer of the same type to another. For example, the following code fragment is perfectly valid.

```
TYPE
  Ptype = POINTER TO REAL;

VAR
  p1, p2: Ptype;

BEGIN
  NEW(p1);
  p2:=p1;
.
.
.
```

However, assignment of a pointer of one type to a pointer of another is not allowed. Therefore, the following fragment will not even compile.

```
(* this example is wrong *)
TYPE
  Ptype = POINTER TO REAL;
  Ptype2 = POINTER TO INTEGER;
VAR
  p1: Ptype;
  p2: Ptype2;

BEGIN
  NEW(p1);
  p2:=p1;   (* wrong, pointers of different types! *)
.
.
.
```

The following simple program declares a pointer variable, allocates memory, assigns that memory the value 10, and prints the value on the screen. Finally, memory is released, and the program terminates.

```
MODULE PointerExample;

  FROM InOut IMPORT WriteCard;

  FROM Storage IMPORT ALLOCATE, DEALLOCATE;

  TYPE
    Ptype = POINTER TO CARDINAL;

  VAR
    p: Ptype;

BEGIN
  NEW(p);   (* allocate storage *)
  p^:=10;   (* assign that memory the value 10 using p *)
  WriteCard(p^,5); (* display on the screen *)
  DISPOSE(p);   (* free the memory *)
END PointerExample.
```

Pointer Comparisons and NIL

Two pointers of the same type can be compared. The only comparison that is useful in most circumstances is equality. It generally does not matter whether one pointer's value is greater or less than another's, since there is no guarantee that memory from the heap will be allocated sequentially. It is not possible to compare pointers of different types.

The most common use for pointer comparisons—indeed probably the reason that they are allowed at all—is to determine whether a pointer variable holds a valid pointer. Before a pointer is given a value through a call to **NEW**, its value is undefined. However, in Modula-2 a special pointer value called **NIL** can be assigned to any type of pointer variable. A **NIL** pointer is a pointer that points nowhere. The exact value of **NIL** is determined by both the compiler you are using and the computer that is executing it, but you need not worry about this because you will simply use the keyword **NIL**. **NIL** is important because it is used to indicate an unassigned pointer. As you will see later in this chapter, **NIL** pointers are used to act as terminators for linked lists.

You must *never* (never ever!) attempt to use a **NIL** pointer unless it is to assign it an actual memory address. Attempting to dereference a **NIL** pointer will cause a run-time error, and execution of your program will stop. (Actually, this is the best that could happen. Depending upon the actual situation, other, more damaging events could occur.)

Uninitialized Pointers

Before a pointer has been assigned a value, either through a call to **NEW** or through an assignment statement, its value is unknown and is whatever value happens to be in that memory location. Actually, then, the pointer does point somewhere, but you do not know where. Therefore, the following code will actually compile and run, but it is disastrously wrong and could cause the computer it was run on to crash.

```
(* This is a dangerously wrong program fragment!!! *)

TYPE
  Ptype = POINTER TO CARDINAL;

VAR
  p: Ptype;

BEGIN
  p^:=100;   (* where is this placed in memory??? *)
.
.
.
```

Since **p** has not been given a valid address, the value 100 will be written to some unknown part of memory. It could be overwriting some of the program's code or data area, the operating system, or the stack, or it could actually go into the heap. This type of an error must be avoided at all cost. However, only you, the programmer, can prevent such an error because the Modula-2 compiler will not be able to find it for you.

This problem leads us to a cardinal rule of programming: Always make sure that you have a valid pointer before using it.

Pointers That Point to Complex Types

In the introductory examples, you have seen how to allocate and assign values to parts of the heap using pointers to the built-in data types. However, in real programs this is very seldom done because there is little or no advantage to be gained. Generally, pointers and dynamic allocation are used on complex data structures such as strings, arrays, and records where an unknown number of these complex types are needed by the program.

For the most part, declaring a pointer to a complex type requires two steps: First, the type must be defined; and second, a pointer type to that type must be defined. For example, the following code defines a string pointer type called **Str79** and declares a variable of that type.

```
TYPE
  Str79 = ARRAY[0..79] of CHAR;

  StrPtr = POINTER TO Str79;

VAR
  S: StrPtr;
```

It is important to note that after a **NEW(S)**, **S** will be pointing to a region of memory that is 80 bytes long, because a call to **NEW** will always allocate sufficient memory for the bound type of whatever pointer it is called with.

To declare a pointer that points to a **RECORD** involves the same process, as the following example shows.

```
TYPE
  REC = RECORD
        C: CARDINAL;
        S: ARRAY[0..10] OF CHAR;
  END;

  RPtr = POINTER TO REC;
```

Now we come to one of the most interesting situations using pointers—and a small exception in the Modula-2 declaration rules. Suppose that you want to define a record that contains, as a field, a pointer that points to another similar type of record. This poses a "chicken before the egg" type of problem. If you define the record first, then how can a pointer that points to that record be a field since the pointer hasn't yet been defined; yet if you define the pointer first, then the record has not yet been defined! You could expect to get compiler error messages indicating you are using an undefined type if you tried to use either approach. The answer is that Modula-2 allows a pointer type to be defined that points to a type that has yet to be defined—this is sort of an implicit **FORWARD** reference. For example, the following **TYPE** declarations define both a record pointer and a record that has a pointer to itself as a field.

```
TYPE
  RecPtr = POINTER TO REC;  (* define record pointer first *)

  REC = RECORD
        C: CARDINAL;
        S: ARRAY[0..10] OF CHAR;
        P: RecPtr;  (* pointer to data of type REC *)
  END;
```

The important point here is that you may declare the pointer prior to declaring the object that it will point to. However, you should only do this in the case of records, like the one shown in the example, when it is necessary; otherwise, it is better to make your declarations in the standard top-down fashion.

Using Pointers

The real power and purpose of pointers and dynamic allocation is for the support of various data structures, such as trees, stacks, queues, and linked lists, which grow or shrink during the execution of a program. Although most of these data structures are beyond the scope of this book, the linked list, which is easy to understand and use, can illustrate the general approach.

A *linked list* is simply a chain of related information in which each item in the chain contains a *link* to the next item in the list. Because a linked list may change in length during the execution of a program, storage for each element must be allocated, which requires the use of pointers.

To implement a linked list requires the use of a complex data structure that includes fields not only for the information, but also for the pointer that provides the link to the next item. The simplest kind of linked list is the *singly linked* list. A singly linked list contains a link to the following (next) element in the list. A *doubly linked* list provides both a link to the following and previous elements in the list. Figure 9-3 illustrates both types of lists.

As the diagram illustrates, the last link in a singly linked list must be **NIL**, indicating that it is the last element in the list. In a doubly linked

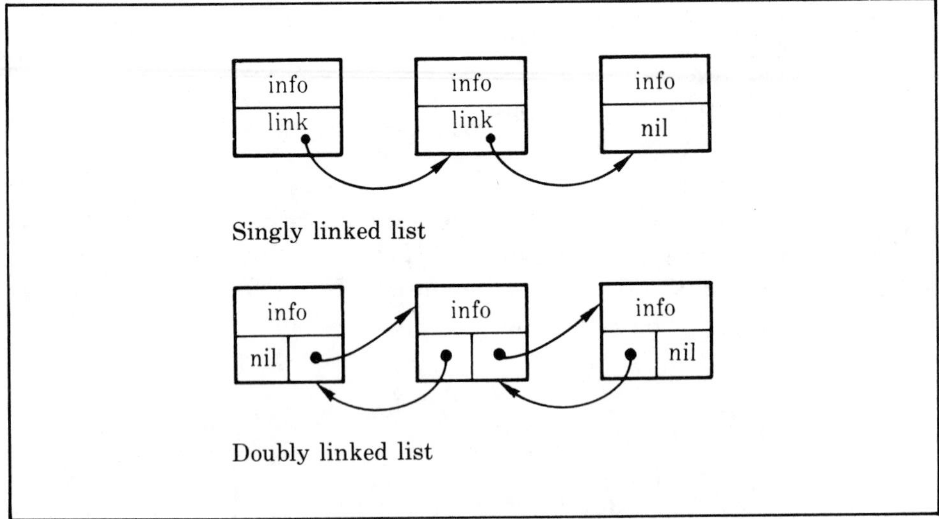

Figure 9-3. Singly and doubly linked lists

list, both the last and first elements must have **NIL** pointers in the appropriate links to signal the beginning and end of the list.

For a simple example of a singly linked list, consider a customer database that is used to relate a customer's name to a unique customer number. The code shown here will create a pointer that points to a **RECORD** that holds both the customer name and number. The program also has a field that is used to hold the address of the next **RECORD** in memory.

```
TYPE
  Ptype = POINTER TO REC;

  REC = RECORD
      CustNumber: INTEGER;
      name: ARRAY[0..79] OF CHAR;
      next: Ptype;
  END;
```

The following short program illustrates how a singly linked customer list can be built and then followed.

```
MODULE PointerExample;

  FROM InOut IMPORT WriteInt, ReadString, WriteString, WriteLn;

  FROM Strings IMPORT CompareStr;
```

```
  FROM Storage IMPORT ALLOCATE, DEALLOCATE;

  TYPE
    Ptype = POINTER TO REC;

    REC = RECORD
        CustNumber: INTEGER;
        name: ARRAY[0..79] OF CHAR;
        next: Ptype;
    END;

  VAR
    p,p2: Ptype;
    start: Ptype;  (* holds the first RECORD *)
    t:INTEGER;

BEGIN
  NEW(p);  (* allocate storage for first *)
  start:=p; (* save starting position *)

  t:=0;
  REPEAT
    WriteString("enter name: ");
    ReadString(p^.name); WriteLn;
    p^.CustNumber:=t;
    t:=t+1;
    p2:=p;
    NEW(p);
    p2^.next:=p;
  UNTIL (CompareStr(p2^.name,"")=0)
  (* stop input if no name is entered *)

  p2^.next:=NIL;  (* terminate list with NIL value for next *)

  (* display list from start *)
  p:=start;
  REPEAT
    WriteString(p^.name);
    WriteInt(p^.CustNumber,5);
    WriteLn;
    p:=p^.next;
  UNTIL p=NIL;

END PointerExample.
```

Notice that not only are the temporary pointers **p** and **p2** needed, but a special pointer called **start**, which is used to store the address of the first **RECORD** in the list, also is required. This brings up a very important aspect of dynamic storage: If you do not manually keep track of where each item is stored (that is, the address of each item), then you will not be able to find the item again. Therefore, it is very important to know where the list begins.

As the list is built, the address of each new **RECORD** is placed in the **next** field of its predecessor. In this way each entry holds a pointer that points to the next entry. When the last entry is made, the **next** field is assigned the **NIL** value, which indicates that there are no further elements in the list.

Once all the names have been entered, the list can be traversed by beginning with the first entry, pointed to by **start**, and simply following the links until a **NIL** value is encountered.

The advantage that has been gained by using a dynamically allocated linked list instead of an array of **RECORD**s is that arbitrarily long lists of customers may be built—up to the available memory in the heap. This differs from an array, in which a fixed list size must be determined at compile time.

A Doubly Linked List Example

Although the singly linked list is adequate for many situations, it has one major drawback: it can only be read in one direction, which can complicate certain searching and sorting routines. For this reason doubly linked lists often are used. As Figure 9-3 shows, a doubly linked list has pointers to both the next and previous elements in the list. This makes it possible to read the list in either direction. Also, if equipment failure should cause one pointer to be destroyed, the list can be reconstructed using the other set of pointers.

A good example of using pointers to make a doubly linked list is a reworking of the mailing list program developed in Chapters 7 and 8. The major advantage the linked-list version will have over its predecessors is that you can enter as many names as you like, up to the limit of your computer's memory, because a fixed size array no longer is used.

Before any routines can be modified, two pointer fields must be added to the record used to hold the address information, as shown here.

```
TYPE
  Ptype = POINTER TO ADDR;

  ADDR = RECORD
      name: ARRAY [0..30] OF CHAR;
      street: ARRAY [0..30] OF CHAR;
      city: ARRAY [0..30] OF CHAR;
      state: ARRAY [0..3] OF CHAR;
      zip: ARRAY [0..10] OF CHAR;
      next: Ptype; (* next address *)
      prior: Ptype;  (* previous address *)
  END;
```

To make the routines work properly and efficiently, you need two pointer variables, called **first** and **last**, which are used to hold pointers that point to the first and last elements in the list. A working pointer, called **p**, also is needed.

Each time an address is entered, a new pointer is passed into the **Enter** procedure. Once the information has been entered, the pointer is linked to the end of the list, and the **last** pointer is updated. **Enter** is shown here.

```
PROCEDURE Enter(p: Ptype); (* enter a name into the list *)
BEGIN
  WriteString('Enter name: ');
  Gets(p^.name);
  WriteString('Enter street: ');
  Gets(p^.street);
  WriteString('Enter city: ');
  Gets(p^.city);
  WriteString('Enter state: ');
  Gets(p^.state);
  WriteString('Enter ZIP: ');
  Gets(p^.zip); WriteLn; WriteLn;
  IF last<>NIL THEN
    last^.next:=p;    (* link into list *)
    p^.prior:=last;
  END;
  p^.next:=NIL;
  last:=p;  (* update last *)
END Enter;
```

The pointer passed to **Enter** is allocated in the main body of the code. Notice that the pointer **first** is assigned the address of the first element in the list.

```
BEGIN
  first:=NIL;
  last:=NIL;
  REPEAT
   choice:=Menu();
    CASE choice OF
      1: IF first=NIL THEN (* first address to be entered *)
           NEW(first);
           p:=first;
           p^.next:=NIL;
           p^.prior:=NIL;
         ELSE NEW(p);
         END;
         Enter(p)  (* new entry *) |
      2: Delete |
      3: Locate |
      4: List |
      5: Save |
      6: Load |
      7: Puts('program completed');
    END;
  UNTIL choice=7;
```

Because the program is no longer using an array, there is no need to initialize it, and so the procedure **Init** is not included.

Finding an address in the list is a simple matter of following the links in the chain until either the proper element is located, or a **NIL** pointer is reached. The **Find** and **Locate** procedures are shown here.

```
PROCEDURE Find():Ptype;   (* return the pointer to the address *)
  VAR
    p:Ptype;
    s: ARRAY [0..30] OF CHAR;
BEGIN
  WriteString('Enter name to find: ');
  Gets(s);
  p:=first;
  WHILE p<> NIL DO
    IF CompareStr(s,p^.name)=0 THEN RETURN p END;
    p:=p^.next;
  END;
  RETURN NIL;   (* not found *)
END Find;

PROCEDURE Locate;   (* display an address based
                       on the name field *)
  VAR
    p: Ptype;
BEGIN
  p:=Find(); (* find the name *)
  IF p<>NIL THEN Display(p); END;
END Locate;
```

Notice that **Find** is a function procedure and returns a pointer that either points to the correct element or is **NIL** if the entry is not found.

It is interesting that it no longer is necessary to mark a record as empty when an address is deleted, as it was in the previous versions, because the address simply is removed from the list and its memory released. In this way, linked-list dynamic allocation routines can actually simplify certain aspects of a program. In the **Delete** procedure, shown here, notice how the links are rearranged, and the pointer is **DISPOSE**d. Sequence is extremely important because once a pointer has been **DISPOSE**d you can make no further use of it.

```
PROCEDURE Delete; (* remove an address based
                     on the name field *)
  VAR
    p: Ptype;
BEGIN
```

```
    p:=Find(); (* find the name *)
    IF p<>NIL THEN  (* remove from list *)
      IF p^.prior <> NIL THEN
        p^.prior^.next:=p^.next;
      ELSE  (* is first element in list *)
        first:=p^.next;
        IF first<>NIL THEN first^.prior:=NIL; END;
      END;
      IF p^.next <> NIL THEN
        p^.next^.prior:=p^.prior;
      ELSE  (* last element in list *)
        last:=p^.prior;
        IF last<>NIL THEN last^.next:=NIL; END;
      END;
      DISPOSE(p); (* release memory *)
    END;
  END Delete;
```

As Figure 9-4 shows, there are three approaches to deleting items from doubly linked lists. A careful reading of the **Delete** code will convince you that all three situations will be handled correctly.

The entire mailing list program using dynamic allocation is shown here.

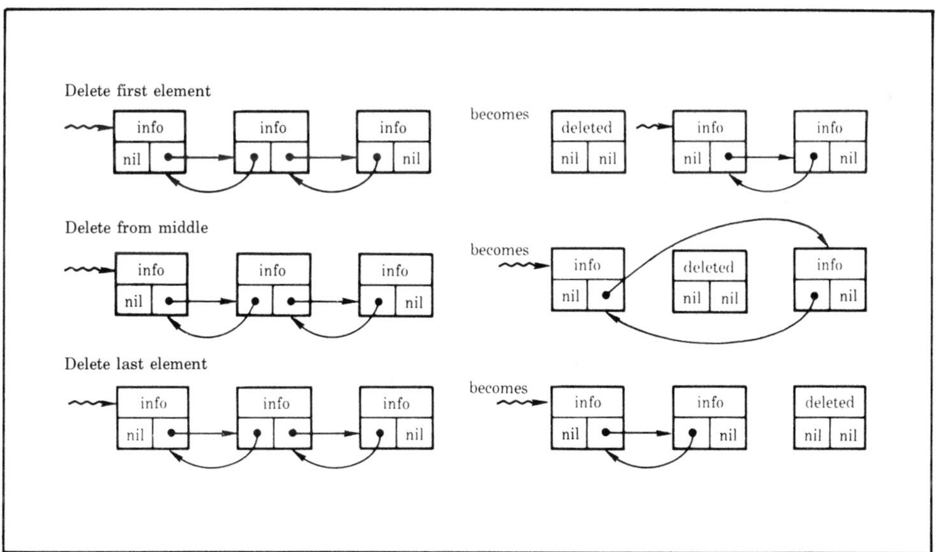

Figure 9-4. Deleting an item from a doubly linked list

```
MODULE MlistPoint;  (* a simple mailing list program
                 that uses dynamic allocation  *)

  FROM InOut IMPORT Read, Write, WriteString, WriteLn,
                 WriteCard, ReadCard, ReadString, EOL;

  FROM Strings IMPORT CompareStr;

  FROM FileSystem IMPORT Lookup, Close, WriteChar, ReadChar,
                        SetRead, SetWrite, SetModify, File,
                        Response, SetPos, Reset;

  FROM Storage IMPORT ALLOCATE, DEALLOCATE;

  TYPE
    Ptype = POINTER TO ADDR;

    ADDR = RECORD
        name: ARRAY [0..30] OF CHAR;
        street: ARRAY [0..30] OF CHAR;
        city: ARRAY [0..30] OF CHAR;
        state: ARRAY [0..3] OF CHAR;
        zip: ARRAY [0..10] OF CHAR;
        next: Ptype; (* next address *)
        prior: Ptype;  (* previous address *)
    END;

  VAR
    p: Ptype;
    first: Ptype; (* first entry in list *)
    last: Ptype;  (* last entry in list *)
    choice: CARDINAL;

  PROCEDURE Gets(VAR a:ARRAY OF CHAR);
    CONST
      BS = 8;  (* backspace *)

    VAR
      ch: CHAR;
      i:CARDINAL;
    BEGIN
      i:=0;
      REPEAT
        Read(ch);
        Write(ch);
        IF ORD(ch)=BS THEN i:=i-1;  (* is backspace *)
        ELSIF (ch<>EOL) AND (i<HIGH(a)) THEN
          a[i]:=ch;
          i:=i+1;
        END;
      UNTIL (ch=EOL) OR (i=HIGH(a));
      a[i]:=CHR(0);  (* all strings end in 0 *)
    END Gets;

   PROCEDURE Puts(s:ARRAY OF CHAR);
     BEGIN
       WriteString(s);
       WriteLn;
     END Puts;
```

```
  PROCEDURE Menu():CARDINAL;
    VAR
      ch:CARDINAL;
    BEGIN
      Puts('     1. Enter an address');
      Puts('     2. Delete an address');
      Puts('     3. Find an address');
      Puts('     4. List all addresses');
      Puts('     5. Save list');
      Puts('     6. Load list');
      Puts('     7. Quit');
      REPEAT
        WriteString('Enter Choice: ');
        ReadCard(ch);
        WriteLn;
      UNTIL (ch>=1) AND (ch<=7);
      WriteLn;
      RETURN ch;
    END Menu;

PROCEDURE Enter(p: Ptype); (* enter a name into the list *)
BEGIN
  WriteString('Enter name: ');
  Gets(p^.name);
  WriteString('Enter street: ');
  Gets(p^.street);
  WriteString('Enter city: ');
  Gets(p^.city);
  WriteString('Enter state: ');
  Gets(p^.state);
  WriteString('Enter ZIP: ');
  Gets(p^.zip); WriteLn; WriteLn;
  IF last<>NIL THEN
    last^.next:=p;   (* link into list *)
    p^.prior:=last;
  END;
  p^.next:=NIL;
  last:=p;  (* update last *)
END Enter;

PROCEDURE Display(p: Ptype);
BEGIN
  Puts(p^.name);
  Puts(p^.street);
  Puts(p^.city);
  Puts(p^.state);
  Puts(p^.zip);
  WriteLn; WriteLn;
END Display;

PROCEDURE List;  (* display the entire list *)
  VAR
    p: Ptype;
BEGIN
  p:=first;
  WHILE p<>NIL DO
    Display(p);
    p:=p^.next;
  END
END List;
```

```
PROCEDURE Find():Ptype;  (* return the pointer to the address *)
  VAR
    p:Ptype;
    s: ARRAY [0..30] OF CHAR;
BEGIN
  WriteString('Enter name to find: ');
  Gets(s);
  p:=first;
  WHILE p<> NIL DO
    IF CompareStr(s,p^.name)=0 THEN RETURN p END;
    p:=p^.next;
  END;
  RETURN NIL;  (* not found *)
END Find;

PROCEDURE Locate;  (* display an address based
                      on the name field *)
  VAR
    p: Ptype;
BEGIN
  p:=Find(); (* find the name *)
  IF p<>NIL THEN Display(p); END;
END Locate;

PROCEDURE Delete; (* remove an address based
                     on the name field *)
  VAR
    p: Ptype;
BEGIN
  p:=Find(); (* find the name *)
  IF p<>NIL THEN  (* remove from list *)
    IF p^.prior <> NIL THEN
      p^.prior^.next:=p^.next;
    ELSE  (* is first element in list *)
      first:=p^.next;
      IF first<>NIL THEN first^.prior:=NIL; END;
    END;
    IF p^.next <> NIL THEN
      p^.next^.prior:=p^.prior;
    ELSE  (* last element in list *)
      last:=p^.prior;
      IF last<>NIL THEN last^.next:=NIL; END;
    END;
    DISPOSE(p); (* release memory *)
  END;
END Delete;

PROCEDURE Save ;  (* save the mailing list *)
  VAR
    t:CARDINAL;
    f: File;
    fname: ARRAY[0..30] OF CHAR;
    p: Ptype;
BEGIN
  REPEAT
    WriteString('Enter Filename: ');
    ReadString(fname);  WriteLn;
    Lookup(f,fname ,TRUE); (* create if not there *)
  UNTIL f.res = done;
```

```
  Reset(f);  (* re-write from the beginning *)
  SetWrite(f);  (* enable write *)

  p:=first;
  WHILE p<>NIL DO
    (* Write the record *)
     FOR t:=0 TO HIGH(p^.name) DO
       WriteChar(f,p^.name[t]);
     END;
     FOR t:=0 TO HIGH(p^.street) DO
       WriteChar(f,p^.street[t]);
     END;
     FOR t:=0 TO HIGH(p^.city) DO
       WriteChar(f,p^.city[t]);
     END;
     FOR t:=0 TO HIGH(p^.state) DO
       WriteChar(f,p^.state[t]);
     END;
     FOR t:=0 TO HIGH(p^.zip) DO
       WriteChar(f,p^.zip[t]);
     END;
     p:=p^.next;
   END; (* while *)
   Close(f);
END Save;

PROCEDURE Load;  (* read in the list *)
  VAR
    t:CARDINAL;
    f: File;
    fname: ARRAY[0..30] OF CHAR;
    p, p2: Ptype;
BEGIN
  REPEAT
    WriteString('Enter Filename: ');
    ReadString(fname);  WriteLn;
    Lookup(f,fname ,FALSE); (* do not create if not there *)
  UNTIL f.res = done;

  Reset(f);  (* read from the beginning *)
  SetRead(f);  (* enable read *)

  (* first free memory *)
  p:=first;
  WHILE p<>NIL DO
    p2:=p^.next;
    DISPOSE(p);
    p:=p2;
  END;

  NEW(first); (* start fresh *)
  p:=first;
  first^.prior:=NIL;
  REPEAT
    (* Read the record *)
    FOR t:=0 TO HIGH(p^.name) DO
      ReadChar(f,p^.name[t]);
    END;
    FOR t:=0 TO HIGH(p^.street) DO
```

```
          ReadChar(f,p^.street[t]);
        END;
        FOR t:=0 TO HIGH(p^.city) DO
          ReadChar(f,p^.city[t]);
        END;
        FOR t:=0 TO HIGH(p^.state) DO
          ReadChar(f,p^.state[t]);
        END;
        FOR t:=0 TO HIGH(p^.zip) DO
          ReadChar(f,p^.zip[t]);
        END;
        IF NOT f.eof THEN (* allocate only if not end of file *)
          NEW(p2);
          p^.next:=p2;
          p2^.prior:=p;
          p:=p2;
        END;
      UNTIL (p=NIL) OR (f.eof);
      last:=p^.prior;
      p^.prior^.next:=NIL;
      Close(f);
    END Load;

  BEGIN
    first:=NIL;
    last:=NIL;
    REPEAT
     choice:=Menu();
      CASE choice OF
        1: IF first=NIL THEN (* first address to be entered *)
              NEW(first);
              p:=first;
              p^.next:=NIL;
              p^.prior:=NIL;
           ELSE NEW(p);
           END;
           Enter(p); |  (* new entry *)
        2: Delete |
        3: Locate |
        4: List |
        5: Save |
        6: Load |
        7: Puts('program completed');
      END;
    UNTIL choice=7;
  END MListPoint.
```

Fragmentation

Fragmentation essentially is a situation that occurs when free memory lies between allocated memory. Although this is often fine when the amount of free memory is large enough to continue to fill allocation requests, it becomes a problem when the pieces of memory are too little by themselves to fill a request, even though, if they were added together, sufficient

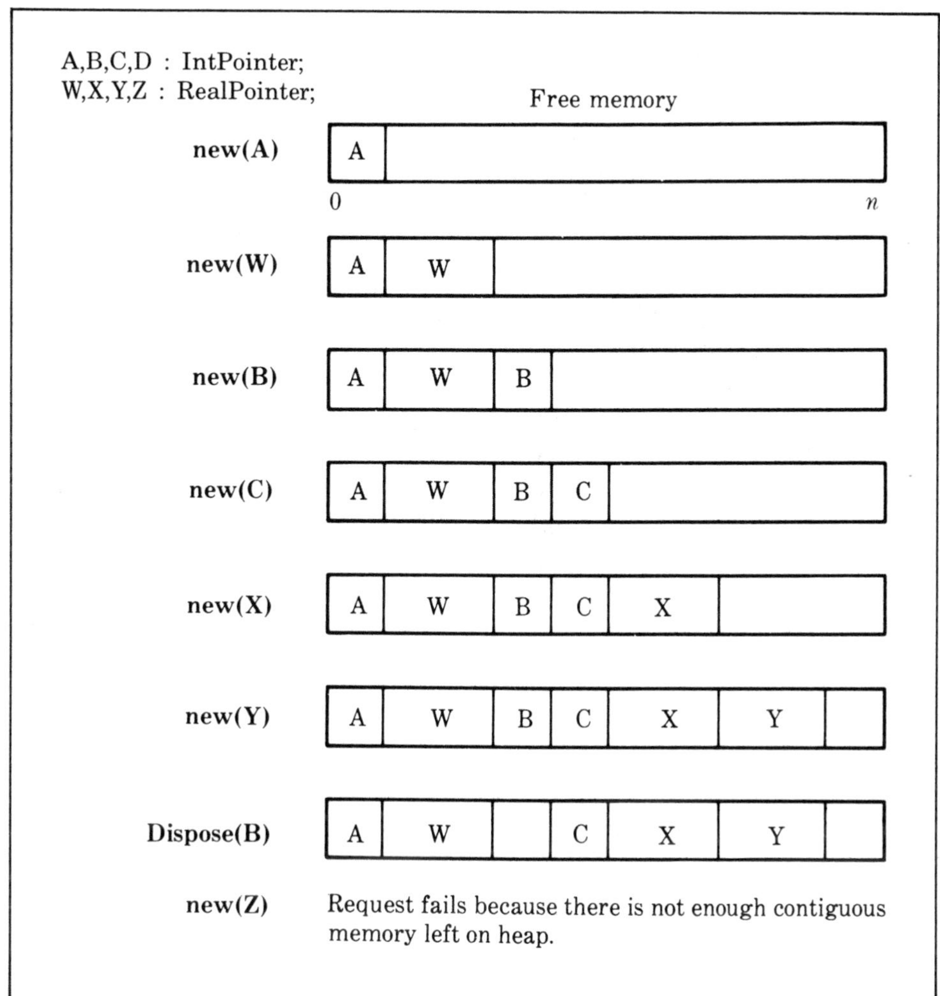

Figure 9-5. Fragmentation in dynamic allocation

memory would be available. Figure 9-5 shows how a sequence of calls to **New** and **Dispose** can produce such a situation.

Some types of fragmentation can be avoided if the dynamic allocation functions combine adjacent regions of memory. For example, if memory regions A, B, C, D in the following sketch were allocated, and then regions B and C were freed, in theory B and C could be combined because they are next to each other. However, if B and D were freed, these could not be combined because C lies between them and is still in use.

A	B	C	D

At first, you might be inclined to suggest that, if B and D were free while C was allocated, why not just move C's contents to D and combine B and C. The trouble with this is that your program would have not known that what was in C had been moved to D.

The only way to avoid excess fragmentation is always to allocate equal amounts of memory. Then all deallocated regions can be reallocated to subsequent requests, and all free memory can be used. If this is not possible, then try to limit the sizes of regions to just a few different amounts. This can sometimes be accomplished by compacting several small requests into a large request. Of course, you never should allocate a lot more memory than you need just to avoid fragmentation because the amount of wasted memory will far outweigh any gains you will receive from avoiding fragmentation. Another solution is, from time to time as a program runs, to write all the program's information in a temporary disk file, free all memory, and read the information back in. When the information is read back in, gaps will be eliminated.

Heap Overflows

What happens if you call **NEW**, and no memory is left in the heap to allocate? The answer is that a *heap overflow* run-time error will occur—a very bad thing. A heap overflow means that there is not enough memory to fulfill the request by **NEW** and, in some systems, the heap has collided with the stack. Although the simple examples given in this chapter have not done so, any real program always must verify that memory is available prior to a call to **NEW**. To do this requires the use of one final routine, called **Available**, from the library **Storage**. **Available** is used to determine whether sufficient storage space is available on the heap prior to an attempt to allocate the storage space. It has the general form

Available(<*NumBytes*>);

where ***NumBytes*** is the number of bytes you would like to allocate. The procedure **Available** returns a **BOOLEAN** value that is **TRUE** if the specified number of bytes can be allocated and **FALSE** otherwise. Therefore, before allocating a pointer to a two-byte **INTEGER**, you should write

```
IF Available(2) THEN NEW(P); END;
```

In this way you can avoid a run-time error.

Very often you will not know exactly how big a variable is, especially with items like **RECORD**s. In this case, you will need to use a special, system-dependent procedure called **TSIZE** to determine the actual size of a type. **TSIZE** is found in the library **SYSTEM**. (We will discuss **SYSTEM** in Chapter 13, where system-dependent routines are covered in detail.) The following program example will work properly, even if the **RECORD VarType** changes in size.

```
MODULE CheckMemory;

  FROM InOut IMPORT WriteString;

  FROM Storage IMPORT ALLOCATE, DEALLOCATE;

  FROM SYSTEM IMPORT TSIZE;

TYPE
  Ptype = POINTER TO VarType;
  VarType = RECORD
        I:INTEGER;
        J:BOOLEAN;
  END;

VAR
  P:Ptype;

BEGIN
  (* use TSIZE to find size of Ptype *)
  IF Available(TSIZE(Ptype)) THEN
    NEW(P);
    (* process normally *)
  ELSE
    WriteString("OUT OF MEMORY");
    P:=NIL;  (* Assign NIL so that it can be checked for later *)
  END;
END CheckMemory.
```

The library routine **TSIZE**, **IMPORT**ed from **SYSTEM**, will return the number of bytes needed to hold a variable of a certain type. Remember: You do not need to use **TSIZE**; however, it makes your code much more portable.

A Few Words About ***ALLOCATE** and **DEALLOCATE***

Recall that **NEW** and **DISPOSE** rely on the routines **ALLOCATE** and **DEALLOCATE**. These routines are system dependent in nature. It is possible to skip **NEW** and **DISPOSE** and use **ALLOCATE** and **DEALLOCATE** directly. However, doing so decreases the portability of your programs and generally should not be done.

Another point of interest is that, although **ALLOCATE** and **DEALLOCATE** are supplied with your compiler, it is not necessary to use them because you can write your own routines. This is seldom done unless a programmer has a very special programming problem. It also decreases the portability of any program that relies on such routines.

EXERCISES

1. What routines are needed to support **NEW** and **DISPOSE** and where are they found?

2. What is wrong with this code?

```
TYPE
  Ptype = POINTER TO REAL;

VAR
  p: Ptype;

BEGIN
  p^:=100.23;
.
.
.
```

3. Write a code fragment that will allocate an **INTEGER** pointer and assign it the value 10.

4. If **REAL**s are eight bytes long, how many bytes of memory will the following routine allocate from the heap? (Assume that **p** is a **REAL** pointer.)

```
FOR T=1 TO 100 DO
  NEW(p);
  .
  .
  .
END;
```

5. Enter the mailing list program and write a routine that displays the list in reverse order by following the **prior** link.

ANSWERS

1. **ALLOCATE** and **DEALLOCATE**, which are found in **Storage**.

2. The pointer **p** has never been assigned a valid address.

3.
```
TYPE
  IPTR = POINTER TO INTEGER;

VAR
  i: IPTR;

BEGIN
  NEW(i);
  i^:=10;
.
.
.
```

4. 800 bytes.

Arrays

CHAPTER 10

Although some array concepts were presented early in this book to enable the use of strings, here they will be discussed in detail. Arrays are very important in computer programming because they allow the easy manipulation of many variables of the same type. In Modula-2 arrays also are used as support for character strings, which makes arrays even more important.

Basic Concepts

An *array* is a group of like variables that are accessed using an index. In Modula-2, arrays may be of one or more dimensions, up to the maximum supported by the compiler. A one-dimensional array can be thought of as a list, a two-dimensional array as a list of lists, a three-dimensional array as a list of a list of lists, and so on. Figure 10-1 shows conceptually how arrays of one through three dimensions appear in memory.

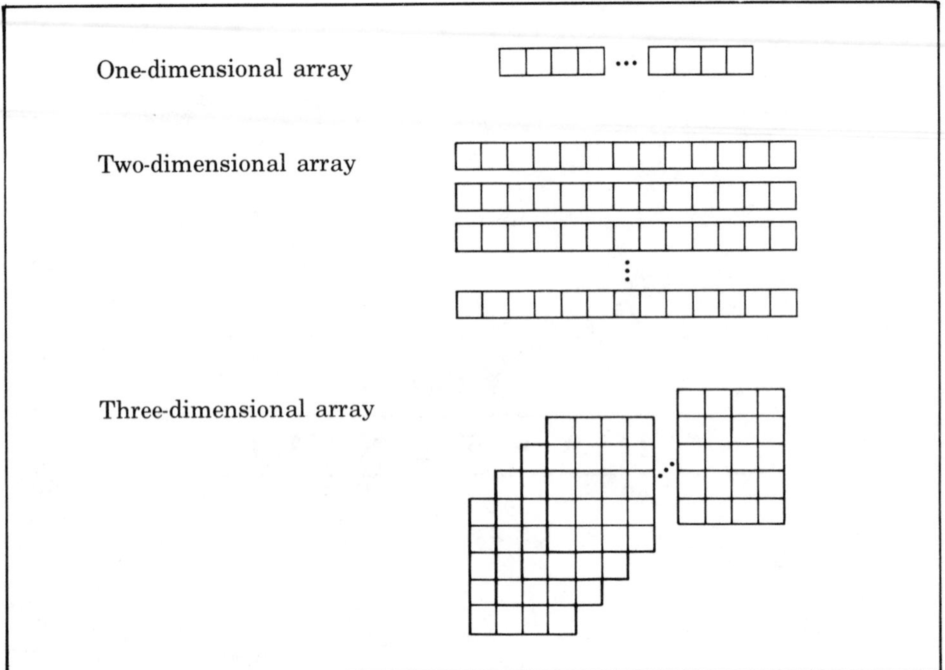

Figure 10-1. One-, two-, and three-dimensional arrays in memory

As you have seen in previous chapters, the general form of a singly dimensioned array declaration is

<*name*>:ARRAY [*start*..*end*] OF <*type*>;

where ***start*** is the index of the first element, and ***end*** is the index of the last element. Therefore, the length of the array is ***end−start+1***.

The maximum size of an array of any given type is governed by many factors, such as the computer being used, the implementation of Modula-2, and the size of each element. However, it is safe to assume that most MS-DOS/PC-DOS implementations do not support an array with a total size of more than 64K bytes.

The size of a one-dimensional array is computed as

length*SizeOfDataType

Therefore, an array declared as

```
a:ARRAY[0..10] OF CHAR;
```

requires 11*1, or 11 bytes of storage.

Declaring Multidimensioned Arrays

Modula-2 supports two declaration methods for multidimensioned arrays: a long form and a shorthand form. We will look at the long form first because it best describes what is actually happening.

The general format of the long-form declaration method for a two-dimensional array is

```
<name>: ARRAY [start1..end1] OF
  ARRAY[start2..end2] OF <type>;
```

where ***start1*** and ***end1*** are the first and last indexes of the first dimension, and ***start2*** and ***end2*** are the first and last indexes of the second dimension.

A three-dimensional array declaration would look like this:

```
<name>: ARRAY [start1..end1] OF
          ARRAY[start2..end2] OF
            ARRAY[start3..end3] OF <type>;
```

Notice that only one data type is specified because all array elements must be the same. The extra dimensions only expand the array; they cannot be used to mix data types. (A mixed data-type array can be formed by using an array of records, however.)

Finally, the general form of an N-dimensional array declaration is

```
<name>: ARRAY [start1..end1] OF
          ARRAY[start2..end2] OF
            ARRAY[start3..end3] OF
                   .
                   .
                   .
                   ARRAY[startN..endN] OF <type>;
```

The amount of storage needed for a multidimensional array is computed as shown, where L represents the length of the various dimensions.

L1*L2*L3 ... *ln*SizeOfData

Therefore,

```
a:ARRAY[1..10] OF
    ARRAY[1..10] OF
      ARRAY[1..5] OF INTEGER;
```

requires 10*10*5*2, or 1000, bytes of storage, assuming that integers are two bytes.

As may be evident, a two-dimensional array is a squared dimension, a three-dimensional array is a cubed dimension, and so forth. Therefore, arrays of dimensions greater than three are seldom used because the amount of storage needed soon exceeds that which is commonly available in computers.

Shorthand Declaration The shorthand multidimensional array declaration essentially does away with the repeated keywords **ARRAY** and **OF** and substitutes commas instead. For example,

```
a: ARRAY[1..10] OF
     ARRAY [3..12] OF REAL;
```

can be shortened to

```
a: ARRAY[1..10], [3..12] OF REAL;
```

This form will be used throughout the remainder of this book because it is the form used by most Modula-2 programmers. Also, it more closely resembles the form generally found in other programming languages and so may seem more natural. However, you may use the long form if you are more comfortable with it.

Accessing Elements In a Multidimensional Array

Given

```
cube: ARRAY [0..4], [1..3], [0..4] OF CARDINAL;
```

the following code accesses element 3,2,2.

```
cube[3,2,2];
```

Figure 10-2 shows graphically where cube [3,2,2] is located.

As you probably surmise from this example, the following is the general form for accessing a specific array element in a multidimensional array called A:

A[first, second, third,. . .,Nth]

That is, each index, in order of declaration, is placed between opening and closing square brackets in a comma-separated list. For example, the following code fragment will load a two-dimensional array with the numbers 1 to 10 and their squares.

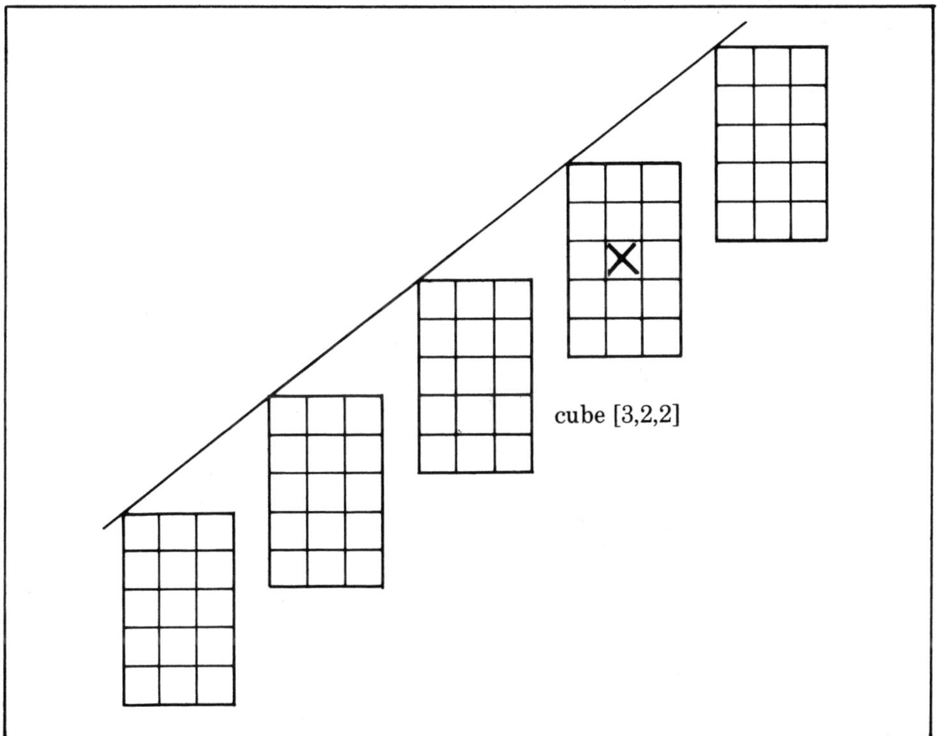

Figure 10-2. Location of cube [3,2,2]

```
VAR
  NumSqr: ARRAY[1..10], [1,2] OF CARDINAL;
  i: CARDINAL;

BEGIN
  FOR i:=1 TO 10 DO
    NumSqr[i,1]:=i;   (* number *)
    NumSqr[i,2]:=i*i;  (* square *)
  END;
```

A Simple Example

To see how a two-dimensional array might be used, consider a program to compute the average grade of each student in a class. In this situation, you will want to have an array that has as its first dimension the number of students in the class and as its second dimension the number of grades per semester. Such an array could be declared as shown here, assuming that there are ten students in the class and eight grades per semester.

```
CONST
  ClassSize = 10;
  GradesPerSemester = 8;

VAR
  grades: ARRAY [1..ClassSize],[1..GradesPerSemester] OF CARDINAL;
```

The use of the **CONST** declarations allows both the size of the class and the number of grades per semester to be changed easily and is generally a good idea when working with arrays.

A second, single-dimension array is used to hold the average for each student and is declared as follows.

```
average: ARRAY [1..ClassSize] OF REAL;
```

To compute the average grades for the class, the procedure **Enter** is called. This routine not only enters the individual grades, but also keeps a running total in a variable called **sum**. This variable is then divided by the number of grades per semester to compute the average.

```
PROCEDURE EnterGrades;
  VAR
  i,j,sum: CARDINAL;
BEGIN
  FOR i:=1 TO ClassSize DO
    WriteString("enter grades for student number");
```

```
    WriteCard(i,3); WriteLn;
    sum:=0;  (* initialize each time through the loop *)
    FOR j:=1 TO GradesPerSemester DO
      WriteString('grade number ');
      WriteCard(j,3); WriteString(': ');
      ReadCard(grades[i,j]);
      WriteLn;
      sum:=sum+grades[i,j];
    END;
    average[i]:=FLOAT(sum)/FLOAT(GradesPerSemester);
  END;
END EnterGrades;
```

Once the grades have been entered, the procedure called **Display-Grades** is used to display the grades and averages for the class.

```
PROCEDURE DisplayGrades;  (* with average *)
   VAR
    i,j: CARDINAL;
    str: ARRAY [0..30] OF CHAR;
    result: BOOLEAN;
BEGIN
  FOR i:=1 TO ClassSize DO
    WriteString("grades for student number");
    WriteCard(i,3); WriteLn;
    FOR j:=1 TO GradesPerSemester DO
      WriteCard(j,3);
      WriteCard(grades[i,j],3);
    END;
    WriteString(' average; ');
    (* standard notation *)
    RealToString(average[i], 3, 10, str, result);
    IF result THEN WriteString(str) END;
    WriteLn;
  END;
END DisplayGrades;
```

Study the way the two-dimensional array accesses are handled and enter these routines and play around with them to better understand array indexing. The entire Grades program is shown here.

```
MODULE Grades;

  FROM InOut IMPORT ReadString, WriteString, ReadCard,
        WriteLn, WriteCard;
  FROM RealConversions IMPORT RealToString;

  CONST
    ClassSize = 10;
    GradesPerSemester = 8;

  VAR
    grades: ARRAY [1..ClassSize],[1..GradesPerSemester] OF CARDINAL;
    i: CARDINAL;
    average: ARRAY [1..ClassSize] OF REAL;
```

```
  PROCEDURE EnterGrades;
    VAR
      i,j,sum: CARDINAL;
  BEGIN
    FOR i:=1 TO ClassSize DO
      WriteString("enter grades for student number");
      WriteCard(i,3); WriteLn;
      sum:=0;  (* initialize each time through the loop *)
      FOR j:=1 TO GradesPerSemester DO
        WriteString('grade number ');
        WriteCard(j,3); WriteString(': ');
        ReadCard(grades[i,j]);
        WriteLn;
        sum:=sum+grades[i,j];
      END;
      average[i]:=FLOAT(sum)/FLOAT(GradesPerSemester);
    END;
  END EnterGrades;

  PROCEDURE DisplayGrades;  (* with average *)
     VAR
      i,j: CARDINAL;
      str: ARRAY [0..30] OF CHAR;
      result: BOOLEAN;
  BEGIN
    FOR i:=1 TO ClassSize DO
      WriteString("grades for student number");
      WriteCard(i,3); WriteLn;
      FOR j:=1 TO GradesPerSemester DO
        WriteCard(j,3);
        WriteCard(grades[i,j],3);
      END;
      WriteString(' average; ');
      (* standard notation *)
      RealToString(average[i], 3, 10, str, result);
      IF result THEN WriteString(str) END;
      WriteLn;
    END;
  END DisplayGrades;

BEGIN
  EnterGrades;
  DisplayGrades;
END Grades.
```

Array Assignments

When two arrays are of the same type, all the values of the elements of one array may be assigned to the other array without each element being assigned individually. For example, given

```
VAR
  A,B: ARRAY [1..10] OF CHAR;
```

after the following statement both **A** and **B** will have elements of the same value.

```
A:=B;
```

This basic concept can be expanded to allow one or more dimensions from a multidimensional array to be copied. For example, given

```
VAR
  A,B: ARRAY [1..10],[1..5] OF CHAR;
```

then

```
B[1]:=A[1];
```

copies the five elements **A[1,1]** through **A[1,5]** to array **B**.

Although these types of array assignments can be very useful for initializing arrays—especially strings—they are not generally helpful because few algorithms perform block transfers of arrays.

Using Arrays for Sorting And Searching

Among the most common uses for arrays is to support sorting and searching algorithms. In this section we will develop both a sort and a search that will illustrate the role arrays play in these routines. For simplicity, only **INTEGER** values will be used; however, you can use whatever types you like.

The Bubble Sort

The *bubble sort* is notorious for being one of the worst sorting algorithms ever invented. However, because of its clear logic and ease of implementation, it is still frequently used to sort small sets of data. We will implement it here because its transparent operation provides an excellent example of array usage.

The bubble sort operates by repeatedly comparing adjacent elements in an array and exchanging values that are out of order. It reads the array N times, where N is the number of elements in the array. After the last pass, the array will be sorted. The bubble sort shown here has only one parameter, **a**, which must be **VAR** and holds the array to be sorted. The size of the array is determined by the **HIGH** function, allowing **BubbleSort** to operate on arrays of various sizes.

```
PROCEDURE BubbleSort(VAR a:ARRAY OF INTEGER);
  VAR
    i,j,k,n: INTEGER;
BEGIN
  n:=HIGH(a);
  FOR i:=1 TO n DO
    FOR j:=n TO i BY -1 DO
      IF a[j-1]>a[j] THEN  (* swap elements *)
        k:=a[j-1];
        a[j-1]:=a[j];
        a[j]:=k;
      END; (* if *)
    END;
  END;
END BubbleSort;
```

The Binary Search

Given a sorted array, a highly efficient searching procedure, called the *binary search*, can be used to locate any specific element. This method uses the "divide and conquer" approach. It first tests the middle element of the array. If this element is larger than the key, the procedure then tests the middle element of the first half; otherwise, it tests the middle element of the second half. This process is repeated until either a match is found, or there are no more elements to test.

For example, given the array

1 2 3 4 5 6 7 8 9

to find the number 4 the binary search would first test the middle, which is 5. Since this is greater than 4, the search would continue with the first half, or

1 2 3 4 5

Here the middle element is 3. This is greater than 4, so the first half is discarded, and the search continues with

4 5

This time a match is found.

The procedure **BinarySearch**, shown here, can be used to determine if an element is part of an array, and if it is, what its index is. Once again, **HIGH** is used to determine the length of the array being searched.

```
PROCEDURE BinarySearch(a:ARRAY OF INTEGER;
                       key:INTEGER;
                       VAR pos: INTEGER): BOOLEAN;
                      (* return TRUE if found *)
  VAR
    n,i,j,middle:INTEGER;

BEGIN
  i:=0; j:=HIGH(a);
  REPEAT
    middle:=(i+j) DIV 2;  (* find middle element *)
    IF key<a[middle] THEN j:=middle-1;
    ELSIF key>a[middle] THEN i:=middle+1;
    ELSE
      pos:=middle;  (* location in array *)
      RETURN TRUE;
    END; (* if *)
  UNTIL i>j;
  RETURN FALSE;
END BinarySearch;
```

Remember that the binary search can only be used on sorted arrays; it will not work on unsorted data.

To see how to use these two procedures, enter the following sample program, which allows you to enter 10 numbers in any order. The program will then sort the numbers and report the array index of each.

```
MODULE SortAndSearch;  (* sorting and searching an array *)

  FROM InOut IMPORT ReadString, WriteString, ReadInt,
        WriteLn, WriteInt;

  VAR
    list: ARRAY[0..9] OF INTEGER;
    i,pos:INTEGER;

  PROCEDURE BubbleSort(VAR a:ARRAY OF INTEGER);
    VAR
      i,j,k,n: INTEGER;
  BEGIN
    n:=HIGH(a);
    FOR i:=1 TO n DO
```

```
      FOR j:=n TO i BY -1 DO
        IF a[j-1]>a[j] THEN  (* swap elements *)
          k:=a[j-1];
          a[j-1]:=a[j];
          a[j]:=k;
        END; (* if *)
      END;
    END;
  END BubbleSort;

  PROCEDURE BinarySearch(a:ARRAY OF INTEGER;
                         key:INTEGER;
                         VAR pos: INTEGER): BOOLEAN;
                        (* return TRUE if found *)
    VAR
      n,i,j,middle:INTEGER;

  BEGIN
    i:=0; j:=HIGH(a);
    REPEAT
      middle:=(i+j) DIV 2;  (* find middle element *)
      IF key<a[middle] THEN j:=middle-1;
      ELSIF key>a[middle] THEN i:=middle+1;
      ELSE
        pos:=middle;  (* location in array *)
        RETURN TRUE;
      END; (* if *)
    UNTIL i>j;
    RETURN FALSE;
  END BinarySearch;

BEGIN
  FOR i:=0 TO 9 DO
    WriteString('Enter an integer: ');
    ReadInt(list[i]);
    WriteLn;
  END;

  BubbleSort(list);

  FOR i:=0 TO 9 DO
    WriteInt(list[i],5);
  END;
  WriteLn;

  REPEAT
    WriteString('Enter value to find: ');
    ReadInt(i);
    IF BinarySearch(list,i,pos) THEN
      WriteString(' found, location is ');
      WriteInt(pos,5);
    ELSE
      WriteString(' not found');
    END;
    WriteLn;
  UNTIL i=0;
END SortAndSearch.
```

Strings

As you know, strings are simply arrays of **CHAR**. This means that they follow the same rules as any other array. However, you should know a few points about their usage and some special string functions that make using them a lot easier.

All strings must be arrays of characters that have their beginning index at zero. Thus, the following array can be used to hold a string of 80 characters.

```
VAR
  str80: ARRAY[0..79] OF CHAR;
```

In Modula-2, all strings end in a *null* (usually ASCII 0), unless they occupy the entire length of the array designated to hold them. For example, given

```
str10: ARRAY[0..9] OF CHAR;
```

after the assignment

```
str10:="Hi there!";
```

Str10 would look like this:

0	1	2	3	4	5	6	7	8	9
H	i		T	h	e	r	e	!	null

Here, the null is used to terminate the string. However, after this assignment statement

```
str10:="Hi there!!";
```

all the character positions would be in use, and no null terminator would be needed. The array **str10** would then become

H	i		T	h	e	r	e	!	!

String Functions

In the library module **Strings** are several useful string functions that perform various string manipulations. We will now examine the most important of these.

CompareStr **CompareStr** is used to compare two strings lexicographically. Its general form is

CompareStr(*s1*, *s2*);

where ***s1*** and ***s2*** are string variables.

CompareStr returns an **INTEGER** value based on the comparison. If the strings are exactly the same, then **CompareStr** returns 0. If *s1* is less than *s2*, then −1 is returned. If *s1* is greater than *s2*, then 1 is returned.

For example,

```
CompareStr("hi","hi");
```

will return 0 because the strings are equal.

Concat **Concat** is used to join two strings together, an operation sometimes called string addition. The general form is

Concat(*s1*, *s2*, *s3*);

where ***s1***, ***s2***, and ***s3*** are strings.

Concat operates by placing ***s1*** followed by ***s2*** into ***s3***. Therefore this procedure leaves ***s1*** and ***s2*** unchanged. For example,

```
Concat("hi ", "there", s3);
```

gives **s3** the value “hi there”.

Copy **Copy** is used to copy a substring from one string variable into another. It has the general form

Copy(*s1, index, length, s2*);

where ***s1*** and ***s2*** are strings, and ***index*** and ***length*** are **CARDINALs.**

Copy works like this: Beginning at the position ***index***, ***length*** characters are copied into *s2*. For example, if **s1** has the value "this is a test", then

```
Copy(s1,5,2,s2);
```

will place the value "is" into **s2**.

Delete **Delete** is used to remove a substring from a string. Its general form is

Delete(s1, index, length);

where ***s1*** is a string, and ***index*** and ***length*** are **CARDINALs.**

Delete works by removing ***length*** characters from ***s1*** starting at ***index***. For example,

```
s1:="this is a test";
Delete(s1,5,3);
```

leaves **s1** with the value "this a test".

Insert **Insert** is basically the opposite of **Delete** and is used to insert a substring into a string. Its general form is

Insert(*substr, str, index*);

where both ***substr*** and ***str*** are strings, and ***index*** is a **CARDINAL.**

Insert works by inserting ***substr*** into ***str*** starting at ***index***. Remember that *str* must be large enough to hold the result, or truncation or a run-time error will occur.

If **str** has the value "abcd" and **substr** has the value "OK", then after

```
Insert(substr, str, 1);
```

str has the value "aOkbcd".

Length **Length** returns the length of a string. Its general form is

Length(*s1*);

For example,

```
Length("hi");
```

is 2.

Pos **Pos** returns the index of the first occurrence of a substring. Its general form is

Pos(*substr, str*)

where both ***substr*** and ***str*** are strings. Its return type is **CARDINAL**.

For example, this code will display the number 5 on the screen.

```
substr:="cat";
str:="horsecatmouse";
WriteCard(Pos(substr,str),5);
```

A Longer Example

Two-dimensional arrays are commonly used to simulate board game matrices, such as those used in chess and checkers. Although it is beyond the scope of this book to present a chess or checkers program, we can develop a very simple version of tic-tac-toe.

The tic-tac-toe matrix will be represented using a 3-by-3 character array. Therefore, the array **matrix** is declared as

```
matrix: ARRAY[1..3],[1..3] OF CHAR;
```

The array **matrix** must be initialized to contain all spaces at the start of the game.

In the version of tic-tac-toe used here, the player will always be X, and the computer will always be O. The player will always go first. When the game starts, the empty matrix will appear like this:

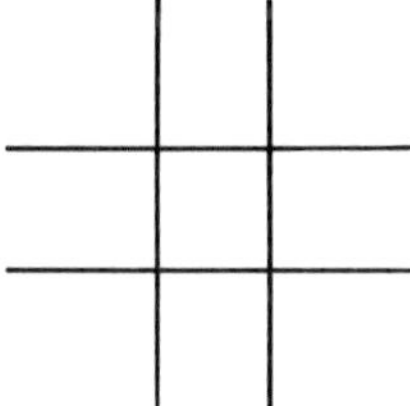

The matrix is printed by the procedure **DisplayMatrix**.

The procedure **GetPlayerMove**, shown here, is used to enter the player's X's. The player enters the position using coordinates, with 1,1 being the upper left-hand corner and 3,3 the lower right-hand corner. The procedure then places the character 'X' in the proper location in the **matrix** array.

```
PROCEDURE GetPlayerMove;
  VAR
    x,y: CARDINAL;
BEGIN
  WriteString('Enter coordinates for your X: ');
  ReadCard(x);
  WriteString('-');
  ReadCard(y);
  IF matrix[x,y]<>' ' THEN
    WriteLn;
    WriteString('Invalid move, try again');
    WriteLn;
    GetPlayerMove;  (* recursive call *)
  ELSE
    matrix[x,y]:='X';
  END;
  WriteLn;
END GetPlayerMove;
```

An interesting aspect of this procedure is that it is recursive when invalid input is used. Although this is not always a good way to reprompt, it can be useful at times.

The computer plays a very simple game. When it is the computer's turn to move, it scans the matrix and puts its 'O' in the first empty location. If it cannot find an empty location, it does nothing. The procedure **GetComputerMove** is shown here.

```
PROCEDURE GetComputerMove;
  VAR
    x,y,i,j: CARDINAL;
BEGIN
```

```
    i:=0; j:=0;  (* initialize to impossible values *)
    FOR x:=1 TO 3 DO
    FOR y:=1 TO 3 DO
      IF matrix[x,y]=' ' THEN
        i:=x;
        j:=y;
      END;
    END;
  END;
  IF i<>0 THEN  (* found a place to move *)
    matrix[i,j]:='O';
  END;
END GetComputerMove;
```

The procedure **Check( )** is used to determine the winner, if any. **Check( )** simply checks all possible ways that either the player or the computer could have won and if it finds three identical marks in a row, it reports the winner. **Check( )** will return an 'X' if the player has won or an 'O' if the computer has won. If there is no winner and all the **matrix** locations are filled, then a draw game is declared, and a 'D' is returned.

```
PROCEDURE Check(): CHAR;  (* see if anyone has won *)
  VAR
    i,j: CARDINAL;
    draw: BOOLEAN;
BEGIN
  FOR i:=1 TO 3 DO  (* check rows *)
    IF (matrix[i,1]=matrix[i,2]) AND (matrix[i,2]=matrix[i,3])
    THEN RETURN matrix[i,1];
    END;
  END;

  FOR i:=1 TO 3 DO  (* check columns *)
    IF (matrix[1,i]=matrix[2,i]) AND (matrix[2,i]=matrix[3,i])
    THEN RETURN matrix[1,i];
    END;
  END;
  (* now check for diagonals *)
  IF (matrix[1,1]=matrix[2,2]) AND (matrix[2,2]=matrix[3,3])
  THEN RETURN matrix[1,1]; END;

  IF (matrix[1,3]=matrix[2,2]) AND (matrix[2,2]=matrix[3,1])
  THEN RETURN matrix[1,3]; END;

  draw:=TRUE;   (* check for draw game *)
  FOR i:=1 TO 3 DO
    FOR j:=1 TO 3 DO
      IF matrix[i,j]=' ' THEN draw:=FALSE; END;
    END;
  END;
  IF draw THEN RETURN 'D'; END;

  RETURN ' ';  (* no match *)
END Check;
```

The routines in this example all access the array **matrix** in different ways. Study them to make sure that you understand each array operation. The entire program, including some additional support procedures, is shown here.

```
MODULE TicTacToe;

  FROM InOut IMPORT ReadString, WriteString, ReadCard,
        WriteLn, WriteCard, Write;

  FROM RealConversions IMPORT RealToString;

  CONST

  VAR
    matrix: ARRAY[1..3],[1..3] OF CHAR;
    done: CHAR;

  PROCEDURE InitMatrix; (* initialize with spaces *)
    VAR
      i,j: CARDINAL;
  BEGIN
    FOR i:=1 TO 3 DO
      FOR j:=1 TO 3 DO
        matrix[i,j]:=' ';
      END;
    END;
  END InitMatrix;

  PROCEDURE GetPlayerMove;
    VAR
      x,y: CARDINAL;
  BEGIN
    WriteString('Enter coordinates for your X: ');
    ReadCard(x);
    WriteString('-');
    ReadCard(y);
    IF matrix[x,y]<>' ' THEN
      WriteLn;
      WriteString('Invalid move, try again');
      WriteLn;
      GetPlayerMove;  (* recursive call *)
    ELSE
      matrix[x,y]:='X';
    END;
    WriteLn;
  END GetPlayerMove;

  PROCEDURE GetComputerMove;
    VAR
      x,y,i,j: CARDINAL;
  BEGIN
    i:=0; j:=0;  (* initialize to impossible values *)
    FOR x:=1 TO 3 DO
      FOR y:=1 TO 3 DO
        IF matrix[x,y]=' ' THEN
```

```
          i:=x;
          j:=y;
        END;
      END;
    END;
    IF i<>0 THEN  (* found a place to move *)
      matrix[i,j]:='0';
    END;
  END GetComputerMove;

  PROCEDURE DisplayMatrix;
     VAR
      i,j: CARDINAL;
  BEGIN
    FOR i:=1 TO 3 DO
      FOR j:=1 TO 3 DO
        Write(' ');
        Write(matrix[i,j]);
        IF j<>3 THEN WriteString(' |'); END;
      END;
      WriteLn;
      IF i<>3 THEN
        WriteString('---|---|---');
        WriteLn;
      END;
    END;
    WriteLn;
  END DisplayMatrix;

  PROCEDURE Check(): CHAR;  (* see if anyone has won *)
    VAR
      i,j: CARDINAL;
      draw: BOOLEAN;
  BEGIN
    FOR i:=1 TO 3 DO  (* check rows *)
      IF (matrix[i,1]=matrix[i,2]) AND (matrix[i,2]=matrix[i,3])
      THEN RETURN matrix[i,1];
      END;
    END;

    FOR i:=1 TO 3 DO  (* check columns *)
      IF (matrix[1,i]=matrix[2,i]) AND (matrix[2,i]=matrix[3,i])
      THEN RETURN matrix[1,i];
      END;
    END;
    (* now check for diagonals *)
    IF (matrix[1,1]=matrix[2,2]) AND (matrix[2,2]=matrix[3,3])
    THEN RETURN matrix[1,1]; END;

    IF (matrix[1,3]=matrix[2,2]) AND (matrix[2,2]=matrix[3,1])
    THEN RETURN matrix[1,3]; END;

    draw:=TRUE;   (* check for draw game *)
    FOR i:=1 TO 3 DO
      FOR j:=1 TO 3 DO
      IF matrix[i,j]=' ' THEN draw:=FALSE; END;
    END;
  END;
  IF draw THEN RETURN 'D'; END;
```

```
  RETURN ' ';  (* no match *)
END Check;

BEGIN
  InitMatrix;
  LOOP
    DisplayMatrix;
    GetPlayerMove;
    done:=Check();  (* see if winner *)
    IF done<>' ' THEN EXIT; END;  (* is winner *)
    GetComputerMove;
    done:=Check();  (* see if winner *)
    IF done<>' ' THEN EXIT; END;  (* is winner *)
  END;
  IF done='X' THEN WriteString('You won!');
  ELSIF done='O' THEN  WriteString('I won!');
  ELSE WriteString('-draw-');
  END;
  WriteLn;
  DisplayMatrix; (* shown final positions *)
END TicTacToe.
```

EXERCISES

1. Declare a character array called **Ralph** with dimensions 10, 100, and 9. Make the lowest index 0 for all dimensions.

2. Show the contents of **str** after the following code has executed.

```
VAR
  str:ARRAY[0..9] OF CHAR;

BEGIN
  str:="Sherry";
```

3. How many bytes of storage do the following arrays take up? Assume that **CHAR**s are one byte long.

a. ARRAY[0..100],[0,1] OF CHAR;

b. ARRAY[1..10],[1..10],[1..10] OF CHAR;

c. ARRAY[0..1] OF CHAR

4. What is wrong with the following code fragment?

```
VAR
  A: ARRAY[1..10] OF CHAR;
  B: ARRAY[0..9] OF CHAR;

BEGIN
  .
  .
  .
  A:=B;
```

5. Just for fun, rewrite the tic-tac-toe game so that the computer plays against itself. Try to make each game different.

Creating a Library ***MODULE***

Creating a library **MODULE** is very easy in Modula-2. It is a two-step process, where the first step is defining what you want the **MODULE** to do, and the second step is programming the **MODULE** to do it. In Modula-2, the *what* and the *how* are separated into two distinct but related **MODULE**s called the **DEFINITION** and the **IMPLEMENTATION MODULE**s.

The DEFINITION MODULE The **DEFINITION MODULE** is used to define what a library **MODULE** will do and what identifiers (procedures, variables, types, and so on) will be available for use by other pieces of the program. The general form of a **DEFINITION MODULE** is

```
DEFINITION MODULE <ModName>;
   <IMPORT-list>
   <EXPORT-list>
   <definitions>
END <ModName>.
```

The ***IMPORT-list*** is the same as that found in program **MODULE**s. The ***IMPORT-list*** should contain only those identifiers necessary for the **DEFINITION MODULE**.

The ***EXPORT-list*** introduces a new Modula-2 command. A library **MODULE** uses the **EXPORT** statement to specify exactly what identifiers (routines, variables, types, and so on) will be made known to the rest of the program. The general form of the **EXPORT** statement for global **MODULE**s is

```
EXPORT QUALIFIED <identifier-list>;
```

A **MODULE** may have only one **EXPORT** statement. The term **QUALIFIED**, which will be explained later, is necessary in a **DEFINITION MODULE**'s **EXPORT** list. Keep in mind that any identifier not in the **EXPORT** list is local to its own **MODULE** and, therefore, cannot be used or affected by code in any other **MODULE**.

In a **DEFINITION MODULE**, only **PROCEDURE** names, parameters, and return values are defined—not the actual code that does the work. Types, variables, and constants also may be defined if they will be needed by other routines.

The **DEFINITION MODULE** shown here could be used for a library that provided the control of a flight simulator.

```
DEFINITION MODULE FlightSimulator;

  EXPORT QUALIFIED Bank, Climb, Roll;

  PROCEDURE Bank(degrees: REAL);
  PROCEDURE Climb(degrees: REAL);
  PROCEDURE Roll(degrees: REAL);

END FlightSimulator.
```

The IMPLEMENTATION MODULE By itself, the **DEFINITION MODULE** is useless because it only describes what will be done. The actual code to perform the functions defined in the **DEFINITION MODULE** is found in its corresponding **IMPLEMENTATION MODULE.** An **IMPLEMENTATION MODULE** is exactly like a program **MODULE,** except that the keyword **IMPLEMENTATION** precedes the word **MODULE** on the first line. Also, a main body of code is optional.

A Simple Example

How the entire process of separate compilation works can best be shown with a simple example. Suppose that you were told to write a program that accepts whole numbers entered from the keyboard and reports whether they are even or odd to help children learn the difference. You decide to create a simple procedure called **IsEven** that will return **TRUE** if the number is even, and **FALSE** if the number is odd. Instead of simply placing this procedure in the program **MODULE**, you decide to put it in a separate file because you think it could be useful in other applications. You decide to call your library **MyLib**. Given this scenario, the program **MODULE** would look like this.

```
MODULE EvenOdd;

  FROM InOut IMPORT WriteString, ReadCard, WriteLn;

  FROM MyLib IMPORT IsEven;

  VAR
```

```
    y: BOOLEAN;
    x: CARDINAL;
BEGIN
  REPEAT
    WriteString("Enter a cardinal: ");
    ReadCard(x); WriteLn;
    y:=IsEven(x);
    IF y THEN WriteString("Is even");
    ELSE WriteString("Is odd");
    END;
    WriteLn;
  UNTIL x=0;
END EvenOdd.
```

As you can see, the line

```
FROM MyLib IMPORT IsEven;
```

is used to **IMPORT** the procedure **IsEven** from the library that you must create. Therefore, it is not possible to compile the program **MODULE** now, because the library module has not yet been developed.

The first step in creating **MyLib** is to write the **DEFINITION MODULE** for it, as shown here.

```
DEFINITION MODULE MyLib;

  EXPORT QUALIFIED IsEven;

  PROCEDURE IsEven(c: CARDINAL): BOOLEAN;

END MyLib.
```

In most implementations of Modula-2, you should give this file the name "MyLib.DEF", which indicates that it is a **DEFINITION MODULE**; however, be sure to check your user manual.

Once this has been done, the **IMPLEMENTATION MODULE** can be written. Make sure that the information in the **DEFINITION** and **IMPLEMENTATION MODULEs** match exactly. The **IMPLEMENTATION MODULE** for **MyLib** is as follows.

```
IMPLEMENTATION MODULE MyLib;

  PROCEDURE IsEven(c: CARDINAL): BOOLEAN;
  (* see if the parameter is even number *)
  BEGIN
    IF (c MOD 2) = 0 THEN RETURN TRUE;
    ELSE RETURN FALSE;
    END
  END IsEven;

END MyLib.
```

In most implementations of Modula-2, you should give this file the name "MyLib.MOD", which indicates that it is a **DEFINITION MODULE**; however, be sure to check your user manual.

Now that you have written all the necessary code, you can compile the **DEFINITION MODULE**, then the **IMPLEMENTATION MODULE**, and finally the program **MODULE**. Once all the code has been compiled, you can link the **MODULE**s together. In this way all the pieces will be joined to create your program.

Let's now review the separate compilation process, including the creation of a library. You must follow these steps:

1. Create the program **MODULE**.
2. Create a **DEFINITION MODULE**.
3. Create the corresponding **IMPLEMENTATION MODULE**.
4. Compile the **DEFINITION**, **IMPLEMENTATION**, and program **MODULE**s.
5. Link the pieces together.

Remember that you can have several different compilation units as part of your program, so you may have to compile several different library **MODULE**s prior to linking.

What you place in each library is very important. The general rule is to place logically connected routines together. This way you can easily find the routines, and you will probably not have to recompile your libraries when a change needs to be made.

Decoupling Code and Definition

Now that you know how to create a library, it is important that you understand a few key points. First, in Modula-2, the definition of what the routines in a library are going to do and how they actually do it are separate. This separation is a feature of the language that makes it possible to *decouple* a routine function from its implementation. This means that the routine can be recoded, improved, or otherwise changed without affecting the way another program interfaces to it. In essence, the actual procedure becomes a "black box" that you do not need to know about, because you only need access to its definition.

Decoupling also occurs on another level. A **MODULE** is somewhat like a **PROCEDURE** in its scope rules. Anything defined inside a **MODULE** is known only to that **MODULE** and may not be accessed or modified by code in any other **MODULE** unless it has been explicitly **EXPORT**ed. Thus, each piece of a program can be decoupled from the rest of the program except for those **EXPORT**ed identifiers. This is very important for large projects where side effects and identifier name conflicts can be especially troublesome.

EXPORTing RECORDS And Enumerations

When a **RECORD** is **EXPORT**ed, the names of fields of the **RECORD** also are **EXPORT**ed. For example, given the **RECORD**

```
Rec : RECORD
        f1: CHAR;
        f2: REAL;
END;
```

if **Rec** were **EXPORT**ed, then the field names **f1** and **f2** also would be **EXPORT**ed.

The same holds true for enumeration types. For example, given

```
TYPE
   Etype=(left, right, up, down);
VAR
   E: Etype;
```

then **EXPORT**ing **E** implies that the identifiers **left**, **right**, **up**, and **down** also are **EXPORT**ed.

Initializing IMPLEMENTATION MODULEs

As you may have noticed in the preceding example, the **IMPLEMENTATION MODULE MyLib** contained no **BEGIN** statement or main body of code. As mentioned earlier, a main body of code is optional in a library **MODULE**. In fact, the only reason that you would want to have a main body of code is to perform some initialization necessary to the routines in the library. For example, you might want to initialize an array or set the value of a global variable.

When initialization code is used in a **MODULE**, it will be executed before the program code is executed. When the Modula-2 compiler **IMPORT**s from a **MODULE**, it automatically includes any initialization code found in that **MODULE**.

To see how this works, consider a library that contains two routines, **Push** and **Pop**, that are used to manipulate a stack. As you probably know, a stack is simply a first-in, last-out list. This means that the first item placed on the stack is the last item taken off. It is similar to a stack of plates at a cafeteria. Shown here are the **DEFINITION** and **IMPLEMENTATION MODULE**s for the stack routines.

```
DEFINITION MODULE Stack;

  EXPORT QUALIFIED Push, Pop;

  PROCEDURE Push(c:CHAR): BOOLEAN;
  PROCEDURE Pop(VAR c: CHAR): BOOLEAN;

END Stack.

IMPLEMENTATION MODULE Stack;

  FROM InOut IMPORT WriteString;

  CONST
    StackSize = 10;   (* arbitrary size - change
                         to fit your needs *)

  VAR
    stack: ARRAY[0..StackSize] OF CHAR;
    tos: CARDINAL;         (* top of stack *)

  PROCEDURE Push(c: CHAR): BOOLEAN;
  (* return false if stack is full *)
  BEGIN
    IF (tos+1)>StackSize THEN RETURN FALSE
    ELSE INC(tos)
    END;
    stack[tos]:=c;
    RETURN TRUE;
  END Push;

  PROCEDURE Pop(VAR c: CHAR): BOOLEAN;
  (* return false if stack is empty *)
  BEGIN
    IF tos=0 THEN RETURN FALSE END;
    c:=stack[tos];
    DEC(tos);
    RETURN TRUE;
  END Pop;
```

```
BEGIN  (* initialization code *)
  tos:=0;  (* initialize *)
  WriteString("Stack code initialized");
END Stack.
```

These routines will maintain a stack of **CHAR**; if you want to use a different data type, simply change the type declarations. The stack routines use an array to hold the items, and the variable **tos** is used to index the appropriate items. As you can see, the main body of code in the **IMPLEMENTATION MODULE** is used to set the top of stack variable to zero—its initial state. The **WriteString** statement is for demonstration only and would not normally appear in initialization code.

A sample program that illustrates the use of the **Stack MODULE** is shown here.

```
MODULE Stest;

FROM InOut IMPORT WriteString, Read, Write, WriteLn;

FROM Stack IMPORT Push, Pop;

VAR
    c: CHAR;
    ok: BOOLEAN;

BEGIN
  REPEAT
    WriteString("Enter a character ");
    Read(c); WriteLn;
  UNTIL NOT Push(c);

  REPEAT
    ok:=Pop(c);  (* read them back *)
    IF ok THEN Write(c); END;
  UNTIL NOT ok;

END Stest.
```

This program will read characters until the stack is full and then display the contents of the stack on the screen. When the program begins execution, the first thing that happens is that the initialization code in **Stack** is executed. This means that you will see the message

Stack code initialized

before any other messages are printed.

Exactly when initialization occurs can be important. Consider a situation in which a program uses two libraries, **A** and **B**. If **B** uses some routine found in **A** as part of its initialization code, then you must ensure that **A** is initialized before **B** is initialized. In most Modula-2 compilers, the order of initialization is the same as the order of the **IMPORT** lists. That is

```
FROM A IMPORT ...
FROM B IMPORT ...
```

means that **A** will be initialized prior to **B**. However, this is implementation dependent, and you should verify the procedure for your compiler. (In general, you should avoid libraries that have this kind of dependency because the order of initialization is not defined by Modula-2.)

Qualified References

Until now, every **IMPORT** list has had the following general form:

FROM <*library*> IMPORT <*procedure-list*>;

The **FROM** part of the statement is said to *qualify* the identifiers from the **IMPORT** list. This means that it links together the **MODULE** name and the identifier automatically throughout your program.

However, it is possible to **IMPORT** every routine from a library by using the following form of the **IMPORT** statement.

IMPORT <*library*>

Here, ***library*** is the name of the library **MODULE** to be imported. For example,

```
IMPORT InOut;
```

IMPORTs all the routines in **InOut**. Before you get too excited thinking about how much easier it will be to write your **IMPORT** statements, you should know that this approach has a second effect. If you use this method of **IMPORT**ing routines, then you must explicitly *qualify* each reference to the routines using the following form:

<ModuleName>.<identifier>

where ***ModuleName*** is the name of the **IMPORT**ed **MODULE**, and ***identifier*** is the routine or variable accessed. This is illustrated in the following code fragment.

```
IMPORT InOut;  (* get the entire module *)
.
.
.
InOut.WriteString("hello");
InOut.WriteLn;
```

As you can guess, this method is seldom used because of all the extra effort it takes each time a routine is used. However, it does have an advantage; for example, you could have your own routine called **WriteLn** that would not conflict with **InOut.WriteLn**. This is not generally recommended because it can confuse anyone else reading the code.

To summarize, when you use the longer form of the **IMPORT** statement, the compiler automatically qualifies the routines and variables for you. When you **IMPORT** an entire library, then you must qualify each routine individually.

*Transparent Versus Opaque **EXPORTing***

When you **EXPORT** a **RECORD** or enumeration type, the associated identifiers are also **EXPORT**ed if the type is fully defined in the **DEFINITION MODULE**. For example,

```
DEFINITION MODULE MyLib;

  EXPORT QUALIFIED P1, RecType;

  TYPE  (* this is a transparent type *)
    RecType = RECORD
```

```
                c: CHAR;
                i: INTEGER;
     END;

   PROCEDURE P1(R: RecType);

  END MyLib.
```

defines the type **RecType**, which means that the field identifiers **c** and **i** are also **EXPORT**ed when the type **RecType** is **EXPORT**ed.

Because **RecType** is fully defined in the **DEFINITION MODULE**, it is not defined again in the corresponding **IMPLEMENTATION MODULE**, shown here.

```
IMPLEMENTATION MODULE MyLib;

  FROM InOut IMPORT Write, WriteInt;

  PROCEDURE P1(R: RecType);
  BEGIN
    Write(R.c);
    WriteInt(R.i,5);
  END P1;

END MyLib.
```

Given this situation, the following program will compile and execute correctly.

```
MODULE Transparent;

  FROM InOut IMPORT WriteString, Read, Write, WriteLn,
                    WriteCard;

  FROM MyLib IMPORT P1, RecType;

  VAR
    x: RecType;

BEGIN
  x.i:=100;
  x.c:='a';
  P1(x);

END Transparent.
```

Here, because **RecType** is fully defined in **MyLib**'s **DEFINITION MODULE**, its individual fields may be accessed by the program. An **EXPORT** of this type is called transparent because all elements are visible to all parts of a program.

However, it is not always an advantage to have the fields of a record or the identifiers of an enumeration available for use outside the library

MODULE. In some situations, you will want to restrict certain variable manipulations only to the routines in the library. This is the case with some of the **FileSystem** variables, for example. Modula-2's solution to this problem is called *opaque export*. Opaque export is used to hide the details of a variable's type from routines outside the variable's own library.

In an opaque export, only the type name is given in the **DEFINITION MODULE TYPE** statement with the **IMPLEMENTATION MODULE** fully defining it. Thus, your program can create variables of that type, but only the library can manipulate them. For example, you can convert **RecType** in the previous example into an opaque export, as shown here.

```
DEFINITION MODULE MyLib;

  EXPORT QUALIFIED P1, RecType;

  TYPE  (* this is now an opaque export *)
    RecType;

  PROCEDURE P1(R: RecType);

END MyLib.


IMPLEMENTATION MODULE MyLib;

  FROM InOut IMPORT Write, WriteInt;

  TYPE  (* this is an opaque type *)
    RecType = RECORD
                c: CHAR;
                i: INTEGER;
    END;

  PROCEDURE P1(R: RecType);
  BEGIN
    Write(R.c);
    WriteInt(R.i,5);
  END P1;

END MyLib.
```

With these changes, the **Transparent** program will not even compile because the fields **c** and **i** are not available for the program's use. Instead, new library routines will have to be written to assign values to a variable of type **RecType**.

For most one-person projects, you will want to use transparent exporting because it usually is easier to use. However, on large, several-programmer projects, opaque exporting is recommended to help avoid accidental errors and side effects.

Local MODULEs

The last type of **MODULE** is the local **MODULE**. Its use is radically different from that of the other three types. It exists to alter the scope and lifetime of certain identifiers. A local **MODULE** essentially is a nested **MODULE**; that is, it is a **MODULE** declared inside another **MODULE**. The form of a local **MODULE** is exactly the same as that of a program **MODULE**, with two exceptions. First, it must end with a semicolon, not a period; and second, it may only **IMPORT** identifiers that are known to or declared by the outer **MODULE**.

The following program contains a local **MODULE** called **SumUp**. Inside **SumUp** is the procedure **Sum** that is used to add a series of numbers entered from the keyboard.

```
MODULE Local;
(* local MODULE example *)

  FROM InOut IMPORT WriteString, WriteLn, ReadCard, WriteCard;

  MODULE SumUp;

    IMPORT WriteString, WriteLn, ReadCard;

    EXPORT count, Sum;

    VAR
      count: CARDINAL;

    PROCEDURE Sum;  (* this procedure is *)
      VAR
        c: CARDINAL;
    BEGIN                          (* inside SumUp *)
      REPEAT
        WriteString("enter number: ");
        ReadCard(c);  WriteLn;
        count:=count+c;
      UNTIL c=0;
    END Sum;

  BEGIN
    count:=0;   (* initialize MODULE SumUp *)
  END SumUp;    (* notice that a semicolon is used here,
                   not a period *)

BEGIN
  SumUp;
  WriteString("sum is: ");
  WriteCard(count,5);
END Local.
```

Notice that **count** is initialized in **SumUp**'s code body. This code, like initialization code in **IMPLEMENTATION MODULE**s, will execute prior to any other code in the **MODULE**.

You can think of a local **MODULE** as a walled city of ancient times that had only one entrance. Anything going in or coming out of the city had to pass through the gate. In a local **MODULE**, the **IMPORT** and **EXPORT** statements define the only passageway for information to get into and out of the **MODULE**. The only identifiers from outside the **MODULE** that are known to it are those specified in the **IMPORT** list, and only the **EXPORT**ed identifiers are known outside the **MODULE**.

As you may have noticed, the **EXPORT** statement did not include the modifier **QUALIFIED**. This is not necessary for local **MODULE**s. However, the use of **QUALIFIED** may be required to avoid name conflicts. Consider the following fragment.

```
MODULE M1;
  VAR
    A,B: REAL;
 .
 .
 .
  MODULE M2;
    EXPORT A,C;
    VAR
      A,C: REAL;
        .
        .
        .
  END M2;

BEGIN
.
.
.
  A:=100.1;  (* which A does this refer to? *)
END M1.
```

This will cause a name conflict between the **A** of **M1** and the **A** of **M2**. Because **M2**'s **EXPORT** list was not qualified, the names of the variables are **EXPORT**ed without alteration. The way to avoid this situation is to replace **M2**'s **EXPORT** statement with the following:

```
EXPORT QUALIFIED A,C;
```

Of course, doing this causes you to qualify each reference to **M2**'s **EXPORT**ed items. For example,

```
M2.A:=100.12;    (* M2's A *)

A:=0.02;         (* M1's A *)
```

In actual practice, most local **MODULE** export lists are not qualified because the programmer can easily keep track of the few exported identifier names. (Remember, however, that global **MODULE**s do require the use of **QUALIFIED**.)

A local **MODULE**'s primary use is to allow *static* local variables. Recall that whenever a procedure exits, all of its variables are considered destroyed. Therefore, they cannot keep their values between procedure calls. However, a local **MODULE**, and hence all its variables and procedures, stays in existence as long as the outer **MODULE** encompassing it is in existence. In this way a variable can be local to a **MODULE**—and protected from accidental use by another part of the program—and yet keep its value between procedure calls.

For example, the following program uses a local **MODULE** to maintain a queue. A queue is a first-in, first-out list. To create a queue requires an array and two variables that determine where the beginning and the end of the queue are. Elements are placed at the end of the queue, and elements are taken off the beginning of the queue. In this version only characters may be placed in the queue; however, you could easily alter the type definitions to suit your needs.

```
MODULE QueueExample;
(* using local MODULE *)

  FROM InOut IMPORT WriteString, WriteLn, ReadCard, WriteCard,
                Read, Write;

  VAR
    ch: CHAR;
    x: CARDINAL;

  MODULE Queue;

    IMPORT WriteString, WriteLn, ReadCard;

    EXPORT OverRun, EnQueue, DeQueue;
```

```
VAR
  queue: ARRAY[0..255] OF CHAR;
  head, tail: CARDINAL;
  OverRun: BOOLEAN;  (* queue full if TRUE *)

  PROCEDURE EnQueue(ch:CHAR); (* put character in queue *)
  BEGIN
    IF (head+1)=tail THEN OverRun:=TRUE;
    ELSE
      INC(head);
      queue[head]:=ch;
      OverRun:=FALSE;
    END;

    END EnQueue;

    PROCEDURE DeQueue():CHAR; (* get character from queue *)
    BEGIN
      IF tail=head THEN
        OverRun:=TRUE;
        RETURN '*';
      ELSE
        INC(tail);
        OverRun:=FALSE;
        RETURN queue[tail-1];
      END;
    END DeQueue;


  BEGIN
    head:=0;
    tail:=0;
  END Queue;    (* notice that a semicolon is used here,
                   not a period *)

BEGIN
  (* This will place characters into the queue, except
     for 'd', which takes a character off *)
  FOR x:=1 TO 100 DO
    Read(ch);
    IF ch='d' THEN
      ch:=DeQueue();
      IF NOT OverRun THEN Write(ch); END;
    ELSE
      EnQueue(ch);
    END;
  END; (* for *)
END QueueExample.
```

When the program runs, each character that you type is placed on the queue unless it is a "d," which causes an element to be taken off the queue.

As you can see, by making the variables **head** and **tail** local to **Queue**, it is not necessary for the main **MODULE** to maintain them. Remember: If these variables were not contained in a local **MODULE**, their values would be lost between procedure calls.

Final Thoughts On MODULEs

Although Modula-2 is an excellent programming language for virtually any computing task, it really shines when applied to large projects. The main reason for this is its ability to modularize a large program into pieces that have strict controls upon their interactions.

Both through the use of library **MODULEs**, which facilitate program development, and local **MODULEs**, which can be used to reduce the number of global variables in a program, **MODULEs** give Modula-2 a unique power not found in other common programming languages.

EXERCISES

1. Given the following code fragment, what is the lifetime of the variables **count**, **start**, and **end**?

```
MODULE A;

  VAR
    count: REAL;

  MODULE B;
    VAR
      start: INTEGER;
        .
        .
        .
```

```
    END B;

    PROCEDURE Test;
      VAR
        end: BOOLEAN;
    BEGIN
          .
          .
          .
    END Test;

  .
  .
  .
```

2. Give two reason why separation compilation is useful when writing a large program.

3. What does **EXPORT** do?

4. Explain the difference between a **DEFINITION** and an **IMPLEMENTATION MODULE**.

5. What is wrong with this code fragment?

```
MODULE EX1; (* this is wrong *)

  IMPORT InOut;

BEGIN
  WriteString("hello there");
  WriteLn;
END EX1;
```

ANSWERS

1. Both **count** and **start** will be in existence throughout the entire execution of the program. However, **end** will go in and out of existence each time **Test** is called.

2. First, having several smaller **MODULE**s to work with saves compilation time during development. Second, each **MODULE** can be independently developed by a separate team.

3. **EXPORT** explicitly states what identifiers in a **MODULE** will be known to other pieces of the program.

4. A **DEFINITION MODULE** simply specifies what a library unit will do; the corresponding **IMPLEMENTATION MODULE** actually contains the code to perform the functions.

5. Because **InOut** is **IMPORT**ed without qualification, all references to its identifiers must be explicitly qualified. The corrected program is

```
MODULE EX1;  (* this is correct *)

  IMPORT InOut;

BEGIN
  InOut.WriteString("hello there");
  InOut.WriteLn;
END EX1;
```

System-Dependent Features

CHAPTER 12

One of the goals of any programming language is to be hardware independent so as to allow programs written in the language to run on a wide variety of machines—in other words, to allow portable code. However, not all programs can be independent of the computer that executes them. These types of programs are called *system programs*, and they include operating systems, device drivers, compilers, and the like. Because these types of programs by their very nature are hardware dependent, they must have some way of dealing directly with the machine. In Modula-2 this is accomplished through the use of a few special system-dependent, sometimes called *low-level,* functions and features.

To allow programs to have knowledge (and therefore access to) the hardware, Modula-2 provides the following features:

1. Type-transfer functions, which override the standard type-checking rules.

2. Memory location specifications for variables.

3. Special types and procedures found in the library **SYSTEM**.

We will examine each of these in turn.

Type-Transfer Functions

Most of Modula-2's strict type checking can be bypassed through the use of *type-transfer functions*. These functions allow the contents of one type of variable to be placed in another variable without regard to type. Type-transfer functions are created by using a standard type name as the name of the function and placing the variable to be transferred inside a set of parentheses. For example,

```
VAR
  C: CARDINAL;
  I: INTEGER;

BEGIN
  C:=10;
  I:=INTEGER(C);
.
.
.
```

causes the contents of **C** to be placed into **I**.

Unlike **VAL**, **CHR**, and **ORD**, the type-transfer functions do not do any computation; they simply transfer the bit-pattern from one type of variable into another. However, this means that both variables must be exactly the same size. (C programmers: Unlike C, which truncates or zero fills to accommodate conversions from integer to character and vice versa, Modula-2 does not and, hence, does not directly allow these kinds of transfers.)

Type-transfer functions are not restricted to the built-in data types, but also work with user-defined types. For example, the following type-transfer is perfectly valid.

```
TYPE
  Rtype1 = RECORD
         CH: CHAR;
          I: INTEGER;
  END;

  Rtype2 = RECORD
          I: INTEGER;
         CH: CHAR;
  END;

VAR
  R1: Rtype1;
  R2: Rtype2;

BEGIN
.
.
.
  R1:=Rtype1(R2);
```

The following program illustrates some type-transfer functions.

```
MODULE TypeTransfer;

  FROM InOut IMPORT WriteString, Write, WriteLn, WriteInt;

  TYPE
    str2 = ARRAY[0..1] OF CHAR;

  VAR
    B: BOOLEAN;
    I: INTEGER;
    C: CARDINAL;
    CH: CHAR;
    A: str2;

BEGIN
  (* transfer an integer constant into a CHAR *)
  CH:=CHAR(88);
  Write(CH);  (* prints X *)

  B:=TRUE;      (* display a boolean value *)
  A[0]:=CHAR(B);
  A[1]:=CHAR(0);      (* zero the high order byte *)
  WriteInt(INTEGER(A),1);

  C:=100;       (* CARDINAL to INTEGER *)
  WriteInt(INTEGER(C),10);

  I:=88;        (* ASCII code for X *)
  A:=str2(I);   (* put in a *)
  Write(A[0]);  (* display *)

END TypeTransfer.
```

As you may have noticed, the character array **A** was used to help transfer a **BOOLEAN** to an **INTEGER** for display. This was necessary because a **BOOLEAN** value is only one byte long, and an **INTEGER** is two—a type-transfer condition that is not allowed. Therefore, the type **str2** was defined to allow a conversion between the array and an **INTEGER**. Finally, the **BOOLEAN** value was assigned to the first location of **A**, and the second location was zeroed. This is necessary for 8086/8088-based processors because **INTEGERs** are stored in byte-reversed order. This code thus only works on systems that store integers in byte-reversed fashion. (Now you can see why this type of code is called *machine dependent.*)

Type-transfer functions are very important in programs such as device drivers where information must be processed several different ways. For example, the following fragment uses a type-transfer function to look for various error and termination conditions of an asynchronous serial port.

```
.
.
.
VAR
  CH: INTEGER;

BEGIN
  LOOP
    CH:=ReadPort;
    CASE BITSET(CH) OF
      1 : FramingError;   |
      3 : ParityError;    |
      14 : TimeOut; |
      15 : EXIT;
    ELSE Process(CH);
    END;
.
.
.
```

You should use the type-transfer functions only when there is no (easy) way to accomplish the same goal using **VAL**, **ORD**, or **CHR**, or if your application requires that a bit-pattern be transferred without any chance of modification. Remember, each time you use a type-transfer function, you reduce the portability of your code.

Placing Variables At Specific Memory Locations

In Modula-2 you can specify an absolute memory location for a variable. This can be very useful when you are writing routines that operate directly on video memory, for example. Also, in specialized applications it often is important to be able to access certain memory locations.

To place a variable at a specific address you simply specify the absolute address location inside square brackets immediately following the variable's name. For example, the following example places the variable **DToA** at location 5767.

```
VAR
  DToA [5767] : INTEGER;
```

If you are using an 8086/8088-based computer, then all addresses must be specified using the segment/offset format. The following code specifies that the variable **VideoMonitor** be placed at D500:0100.

```
VAR
  VideoMonitor [0D500H:0100H] : ARRAY[0..2000] OF CHAR;
```

No specific examples using absolute memory variables will be developed here because they would be extremely hardware, processor, and configuration dependent.

System-Dependent Types And Procedures

The library **SYSTEM** contains some system-dependent types and procedures that make it much easier to write hardware-specific code. (**SYSTEM** also has routines that support multitasking, the subject of Chapter 13.)

SYSTEM Types

In all Modula-2 compilers the types **WORD** and **ADDRESS** are contained in **SYSTEM**. In addition, most compilers also define **BYTE** in **SYSTEM**. These system types allow you to manipulate variables without regard to their types.

The type **BYTE** is defined as being the smallest individually accessible unit of storage. In most computers this is the same number of bits as a character. Variables of type **BYTE** have only two operations defined for them: assignment and type transfer.

The type **WORD** is defined as being the same length as a **CARDINAL**. The only operations defined for variables of type **WORD** are assignment and type transfer.

The main use of **BYTE** and **WORD** is to declare the parameters of procedures. When a parameter is declared as one of these types, then any argument of the procedure that has the same length can be passed without explicit type conversion. For example, in the following program the procedure **WriteNum** can be used with both **INTEGER** and **CARDINAL** values.

```
MODULE WordExample;

  FROM SYSTEM IMPORT WORD;

  FROM InOut IMPORT WriteInt;

  VAR
    i: INTEGER;
    c: CARDINAL;

  PROCEDURE WriteNum(n: WORD; w: CARDINAL);
  (* this will write both CARDINALs and INTEGERs *)
  BEGIN
    WriteInt(INTEGER(n),w);
  END WriteNum;

BEGIN
  WriteNum(100,3);
  WriteNum(-123,4);
END WordExample.
```

Type **ADDRESS** is defined as being a pointer that points to **WORD**; that is,

```
TYPE
  ADDRESS = POINTER TO WORD;
```

In most 8086/8088-based Modula-2 compilers, **ADDRESS** also has a second definition:

```
TYPE
  ADDRESS = RECORD
        SEGMENT: CARDINAL;
        OFFSET: CARDINAL;
  END;
```

This is necessary because of the segment/offset form of addressing used by these processors.

Variables of type **ADDRESS** are assignment-compatible with all pointer types. Therefore, when a procedure parameter is declared as a type **ADDRESS**, then the actual arguments of the procedure can be of any pointer type. This completely removes all type checking—so be careful!

Variables of type **ADDRESS** have the following operations defined:

- Assignment
- **CARDINAL** addition and subtraction
- Comparison.

Multiplication and division are not defined for **ADDRESS** variables.

To show how **ADDRESS** can be used, the following program uses the procedure **Dump** to display, in hexadecimal format, the contents of a specified region of memory. It is important to understand that this program will only work on 8086/8088-based computers because it uses the segment/offset form of addressing. (However, only a small change is required to make the program work with other addressing methods.)

```
MODULE MemoryDump;

  FROM SYSTEM IMPORT ADDRESS,ADR, WORD;

  FROM InOut IMPORT WriteString, WriteHex, ReadCard, WriteLn;

  VAR
    from, to: ADDRESS;

  PROCEDURE Dump(start, end: ADDRESS);

    VAR
      t: CARDINAL;
  BEGIN
    WriteHex(start.SEGMENT,4); WriteString(':');
    WriteHex(start.OFFSET,4); WriteString(':');
```

```
      t:=0;
      WHILE start<>end DO
        WriteHex(CARDINAL(start^),5);
        start:=start+2;
        INC(t);
        IF t=8 THEN
          t:=0;
          WriteLn;
          WriteHex(start.SEGMENT,4); WriteString(':');
          WriteHex(start.OFFSET,4); WriteString(':');
        END
      END
    END Dump;

  BEGIN
    WriteString('Enter starting segment: ');
    ReadCard(from.SEGMENT); WriteLn;
    WriteString('Enter starting offset: ');
    ReadCard(from.OFFSET); WriteLn;

    WriteString('Enter ending segment: ');
    ReadCard(to.SEGMENT); WriteLn;
    WriteString('Enter ending offset: ');
    ReadCard(to.OFFSET); WriteLn;

    Dump(from, to);
  END MemoryDump.
```

As you can see, the value of the location pointed to by an **ADDRESS** variable is dereferenced like any other pointer type by using the ^ (caret).

ADR, SIZE, and TSIZE

SYSTEM contains three very important function procedures: **ADR**, **SIZE**, and **TSIZE**.

ADR is used to return the address of any variable. Its general form is

ADR(<*VarName*>);

ADR returns a value of type **ADDRESS**. Hence, the following piece of code will assign **BufLoc** the address of the array **Buffer**.

```
VAR
  Buffer: ARRAY[0..80] OF CHAR;
  BufLoc: ADDRESS;

BEGIN
  BufLoc:=ADR(Buffer);
.
.
.
```

Table 12-1. Binary File Routines in the **FileSystem** Library

Name	Function
ReadWord	Reads a word from a file
WriteWord	Writes a word to a file
ReadByte	Reads a byte from a file
WriteByte	Writes a byte to a file
WriteNBytes	Writes the specified number of bytes
ReadNBytes	Reads the specified number of bytes

SIZE and **TSIZE** return the size, in bytes, of a variable or a type, respectively. Their general forms are

SIZE(<*VarName*>);

TSIZE(<*TypeName*>);

Both **SIZE** and **TSIZE** return a **CARDINAL**. If the size of a variant record variable or type is requested, then the largest possible size is returned.

One of the most important uses of **ADR** and **TSIZE** is in file I/O. In Chapter 8, you learned how to read and write ASCII data to a disk file. Although this was fine for text, it necessitated tedious conversions for other types of data. It is possible, however, to simply read and write data as binary values. This is accomplished through the use of the binary file routines that are part of the library **FileSystem**. These routines are summarized in Table 12-1. These routines were not discussed in Chapter 8 because they required the use of the system-dependent features discussed here. These procedures in conjunction with **ADR** and **TSIZE** greatly simplify certain file I/O routines and facilitate greater efficiency.

The general forms for **ReadByte**, **WriteByte**, **ReadWord**, and **WriteWord** are

ReadByte(<*FileVar*>), <*Bytevar*>);

WriteByte(<*FileVar*>, <*byte*>);

ReadWord(<*FileVar*>), <*WordVar*>);

WriteWord(<*FileVar*>), <*word*>);

where ***FileVar*** is the file descriptor, ***byte*** and ***word*** are the values to be written, and ***ByteVar*** and ***WordVar*** are variables that will contain the information read. As with the other file routines, the outcome of the operation is found in **FileVar.res**.

ReadNBytes and **WriteNBytes** are the most commonly used routines because each can write large blocks of data using a single statement. The general form of **WriteNBytes** is

WriteNBytes(<*FileVar*>, <*BufPtr*>, <*NumBytes*>, <*NumWritten*>);

where ***BufPtr*** is the address of a buffer that contains the information to be written, ***NumBytes*** is the number of bytes to write, and ***NumWritten*** is a **CARDINAL** variable that will contain the actual number of bytes written. The outcome of the operation can be monitored through the **FileVar.res** field as well as by checking to see that the number of bytes written agrees with the number requested. If the number of bytes actually written does not agree, then some sort of file error occurred.

The general form of **ReadNBytes** is

ReadNBytes(<*FileVar*>, <*BufPtr*>, <*NumBytes*>, <*NumRead*>);

where ***BufPtr*** is the address of a buffer that will hold the information read, ***NumBytes*** is the number of bytes to be written, and ***NumRead*** is a **CARDINAL** variable that will contain the actual number of bytes read. The outcome of the operation can be monitored through the **FileVar.res** field as well as by checking to see that the number of bytes written agrees with the number requested.

Keep in mind that the buffer is simply a place to hold information. It can be either an actual variable or an allocated region of memory. The point is that it is where information will be read from or written to.

In Chapter 8, where system-dependent functions and binary file routines were not used, you saw that it was necessary to convert a **REAL** into a string before it could be written to a disk file—a tedious and inefficient process. You can now rewrite this routine so that it writes a **REAL** directly using binary I/O. For comparison, the former method is shown here.

```
MODULE NumOutput;  (* write a REAL using conversion *)
  FROM InOut IMPORT ReadString, WriteString, WriteLn;

  FROM FileSystem IMPORT File, Response, Lookup, SetWrite,
                   Close, WriteChar;
```

```
  FROM RealConversions IMPORT RealToString;

  VAR
     okay: BOOLEAN;
     F1: File;
     fname: ARRAY[0..30] OF CHAR;
     str: ARRAY[0..30] OF CHAR;
     i,j: CARDINAL;
     r: REAL;

BEGIN

  REPEAT
    WriteString('Enter output filename: ');
    ReadString(fname);  WriteLn;
    Lookup(F1,fname ,TRUE); (* create if not there *)
  UNTIL F1.res = done;

  SetWrite(F1);

  r:= 123.34;

  (* convert a REAL into a string and write it out *)
  RealToString(r,3,10,str,okay);
  FOR j:=0 TO 9 DO WriteChar(F1,str[j]); END;

  Close(F1);
END NumOutput.
```

However, if you simply treat a **REAL** as a block of data (that is, a buffer), then the program can be written using **WriteNBytes** instead of **WriteChar**. The same program written with binary I/O thus becomes the following.

```
MODULE NumOutput;
  FROM InOut IMPORT ReadString, WriteString, WriteLn;

  FROM FileSystem IMPORT File, Response, Lookup, SetWrite,
                 Close, WriteNBytes, ReadNBytes, Reset,
                 SetRead;

  FROM SYSTEM IMPORT TSIZE, ADR;

  FROM RealInOut IMPORT WriteReal;

  VAR
     okay: BOOLEAN;
     F1: File;
     fname: ARRAY[0..30] OF CHAR;
     written, read: CARDINAL;
     r,s: REAL;

BEGIN

  REPEAT
    WriteString('Enter output filename: ');
    ReadString(fname);  WriteLn;
```

```
  Lookup(F1,fname ,TRUE); (* create if not there *)
UNTIL F1.res = done;

SetWrite(F1);

r:= 123.34;

(* write out the number *)
WriteNBytes(F1,ADR(r),TSIZE(REAL),written);
IF written<>TSIZE(REAL) THEN WriteString("write error"); END;

Close(F1);

END NumOutput.
```

As you can see, the buffer is simply the variable **r**. **ADR** is used to pass the address of **r** to **WriteNBytes**, and **TSIZE** specifies how many bytes to write. **WriteNBytes** then writes to disk the bit pattern found in **r**. This makes the code much shorter, faster, and easier to understand. To read a number in from the file, you could use the following code.

```
SetRead(F1);
ReadNBytes(F1,ADR(s),TSIZE(REAL), read);
IF read<>TSIZE(REAL) THEN WriteString("read error"); END;
```

For another example of how to use **ReadNBytes** and **WriteNBytes** to simplify file I/O, rewrite the file procedures for the mailing list program developed earlier in this book. Recall that the mailing list was comprised of an array of records of type **ADDR**, shown here.

```
TYPE
  ADDR = RECORD
      name: ARRAY [0..30] OF CHAR;
      street: ARRAY [0..30] OF CHAR;
      city: ARRAY [0..30] OF CHAR;
      state: ARRAY [0..3] OF CHAR;
      zip: ARRAY [0..10] OF CHAR;
  END;
```

The **Save** and **Load** procedures were originally written like this:

```
PROCEDURE Save;   (* save the mailing list *)
  VAR
    t,i:CARDINAL;
    f: File;
    fname: ARRAY[0..30] OF CHAR;
BEGIN
  REPEAT
    WriteString('Enter Filename: ');
    ReadString(fname);  WriteLn;
    Lookup(f,fname ,TRUE); (* create if not there *)
  UNTIL f.res = done;

  Reset(f);  (* rewrite from the beginning *)
```

```
    SetWrite(f);  (* enable write *)

    FOR i:=0 TO LSIZE DO
      IF CompareStr(mlist[i].name,"")<>0 THEN
      (* Write the record *)
         FOR t:=0 TO HIGH(mlist[i].name) DO
         WriteChar(f,mlist[i].name[t]);
        END;
        FOR t:=0 TO HIGH(mlist[i].street) DO
          WriteChar(f,mlist[i].street[t]);
        END;
        FOR t:=0 TO HIGH(mlist[i].city) DO
          WriteChar(f,mlist[i].city[t]);
        END;
        FOR t:=0 TO HIGH(mlist[i].state) DO
          WriteChar(f,mlist[i].state[t]);
        END;
        FOR t:=0 TO HIGH(mlist[i].zip) DO
          WriteChar(f,mlist[i].zip[t]);
        END;
      END; (* if *)
    END; (* for *)
    Close(f);
END Save;

PROCEDURE Load;  (* read in the list *)
  VAR
    t,i:CARDINAL;
    f: File;
    fname: ARRAY[0..30] OF CHAR;
BEGIN
  REPEAT
    WriteString('Enter Filename: ');
    ReadString(fname);  WriteLn;
    Lookup(f,fname ,FALSE); (* do not create if not there *)
  UNTIL f.res = done;

  Reset(f);  (* read from the beginning *)
  SetRead(f);  (* enable read *)

  i:=0;
  REPEAT
    (* read the record *)
     FOR t:=0 TO HIGH(mlist[i].name) DO
       ReadChar(f,mlist[i].name[t]);
     END;
     FOR t:=0 TO HIGH(mlist[i].street) DO
       ReadChar(f,mlist[i].street[t]);
     END;
     FOR t:=0 TO HIGH(mlist[i].city) DO
       ReadChar(f,mlist[i].city[t]);
     END;
     FOR t:=0 TO HIGH(mlist[i].state) DO
       ReadChar(f,mlist[i].state[t]);
     END;
     FOR t:=0 TO HIGH(mlist[i].zip) DO
       ReadChar(f,mlist[i].zip[t]);
     END;
     i:=i+1;
    UNTIL f.eof AND (i<LSIZE);  (* until end-of-file *)
    Close(f);

END Load;
```

As you can see, each field of the record is written to disk separately. However, using **TSIZE** it is possible to write the entire record with one statement. Recoded, the routines become much cleaner and more efficient.

```
PROCEDURE Save;  (* save the mailing list *)
  VAR
    i,w:CARDINAL;
    f: File;
    fname: ARRAY[0..30] OF CHAR;
BEGIN
  REPEAT
    WriteString('Enter Filename: ');
    ReadString(fname);  WriteLn;
    Lookup(f,fname ,TRUE); (* create if not there *)
  UNTIL f.res = done;

  Reset(f);  (* re-write from the beginning *)
  SetWrite(f);  (* enable write *)

  FOR i:=0 TO LSIZE DO
    IF CompareStr(mlist[i].name,"")<>0 THEN
    (* Write the record *)
      WriteNBytes(f,ADR(mlist[i].name), TSIZE(ADDR), w);
      IF w<>TSIZE(ADDR) THEN WriteString('write error'); END;
    END; (* if *)
   END; (* for *)
   Close(f);
END Save;

PROCEDURE Load;  (* read in the list *)
  VAR
    r,i:CARDINAL;
    f: File;
    fname: ARRAY[0..30] OF CHAR;
BEGIN
  REPEAT
    WriteString('Enter Filename: ');
    ReadString(fname);  WriteLn;
    Lookup(f,fname ,FALSE); (* do not create if not there *)
  UNTIL f.res = done;

  Reset(f);  (* read from the beginning *)
  SetRead(f);  (* enable read *)

  i:=0;
  REPEAT
    (* read the record *)
    ReadNBytes(f,ADR(mlist[i].name), TSIZE(ADDR), r);
    IF r<>TSIZE(ADDR) THEN WriteString('read error'); END;
    INC(i);
  UNTIL f.eof AND (i<LSIZE);  (* until end-of-file *)
  Close(f);
END Load;
```

The Portability-Efficiency Trade-off

Before you decide to use a system-dependent feature of Modula-2, remember that you will most likely be reducing the portability of your program. When you use binary file routines, this reduction will be slight, but when you use absolute memory addressing of variables and some of the type-transfer functions, it will be severe. Therefore, it is important always to have a good reason for using the low-level features of Modula-2.

The general rule is: Don't use hardware-dependent features unless your application requires it. However, most routines run faster and use less memory when you make use of the low-level features. You saw that this was especially true with binary file I/O routines. With non-ASCII data, it is difficult to justify making all those tedious and time-consuming conversions when the binary routines are available. In such cases, it is probably wise to use the low-level routines because your programs become so much more efficient.

On the other hand, it is simply poor programming practice to use the type-transfer functions when they are not necessary. **WORD** parameters also should only be used in procedures when they are required—not just to save a little code.

The bottom line is that the system-dependent features of Modula-2 must be used carefully, or they will cause you many problems.

EXERCISES

1. Can this conversion be rewritten using a type-transfer function?

```
VAR
  count: CARDINAL;
     ch: CHAR;

BEGIN
  ...
  count:=ORD(ch);
```

2. What do **ADR**, **SIZE**, and **TSIZE** do?

3. Declare **monitor** to be an **INTEGER** at location 0F000h.

4. Write a procedure that will return the square of either an **INTEGER** or a **CARDINAL**.

5. Integrate the new file routines into the mailing list program.

ANSWERS

1. No, because CHAR and CARDINAL are not the same size.

2. **ADR** returns the address of a variable; **SIZE** returns the size, in bytes, of a variable; and **TSIZE** returns the size, in bytes, of a type.

3.
```
VAR
  monitor [0F000h]: INTEGER;
```

4.
```
PROCEDURE SqrIntCard(x: WORD): CARDINAL;
BEGIN
  RETURN(CARDINAL(x)*CARDINAL(x));
END SqrIntCard;
```

Coroutines And Concurrency

CHAPTER 13

One of the most exciting (and difficult) features of Modula-2 is its support of coroutines and concurrent processes. It is rare for a language to define these concepts because, traditionally, they have been left to the operating system. However, Professor Wirth recognized the need to standardize a concurrent programming interface so that it could remain fixed and stable across a variety of environments.

Coroutines and concurrency are simple in concept but very complex in implementation—there have literally been books written about them—so the material in this chapter will only scratch the surface. Also, not all Modula-2 compilers support the entire concurrent programming environment defined by Wirth, and even in complete implementations many slight differences occur because of limitations of both the CPU and the operating system.

Because coroutines and concurrent processes may be unfamiliar to you, we will begin with a short review.

Concurrent Processes

A *process* is a task. You can think of a process as a program or a procedure. When two processes are executing simultaneously on the same computer, they are called *concurrent processes.*

Most computers in use today have only one CPU. This means that only *quasiconcurrency* is possible, because the computer simply switches between processes very rapidly, giving the appearance of concurrent execution. Some computers actually have two or more CPUs, and this allows true concurrent execution of processes. As far as Modula-2 is concerned, there is no difference; the interface is the same.

A very important point is that a process can *suspend* execution and then restart. A suspended process is not terminated—it is simply waiting. A process, such as a command input module, might suspend execution because it is waiting for input; or a process may be forced to suspend if a resource it needs—a disk drive, for example—is not available. Remember: A suspended process still exists (at least logically) in the computer; it simply is not executing.

Any environment that supports concurrency has a piece of software called the *scheduler* that has the job of monitoring all processes. It is the *scheduler* that restarts suspended processes and, in some systems, gives priority to certain processes based on some sort of priority scheme.

What Are Coroutines?

Simply stated, *coroutines* are separate processes that are part of the same program. The key difference between a procedure and a coroutine is in the way control is transferred. When one procedure calls another, the called procedure always executes from the top. However, when one coroutine transfers control to another, execution is resumed at the last point of execution prior to a previous transfer of control—which may be in the middle of the coroutine. Figure 13-1 illustrates this situation.

When one coroutine gives control over to another, then the first coroutine is suspended, and no further execution occurs until control is transferred back. In Modula-2 you can let the scheduler control what coroutine is actually executing at any given moment, or you can explicitly transfer control to various coroutines under program control.

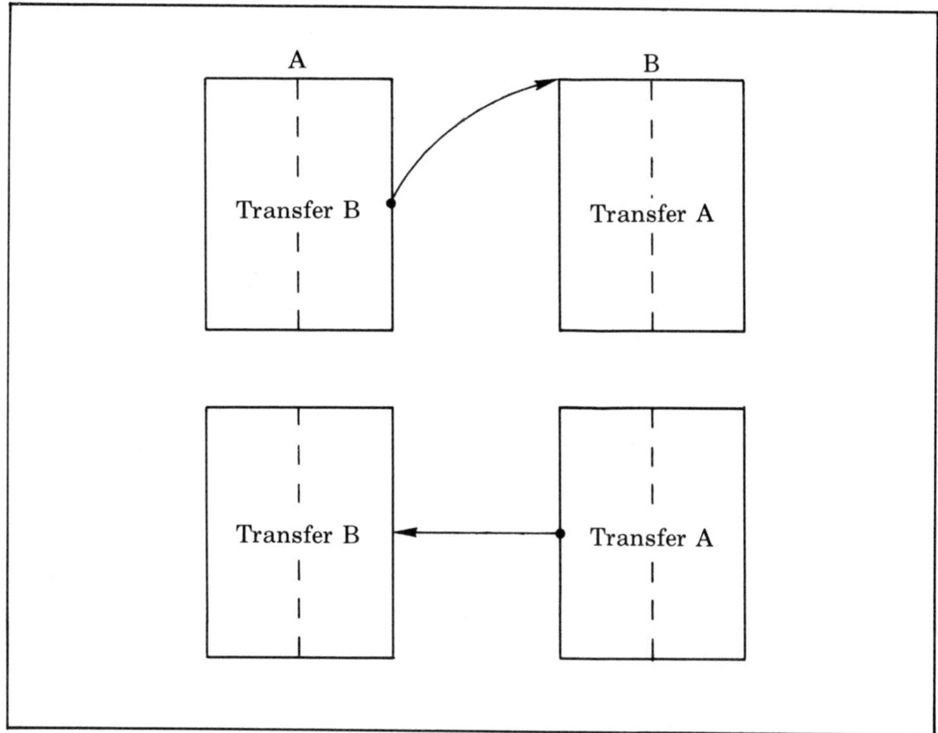

Figure 13-1. Transfer of control between coroutines

Creating Modula-2 Coroutines

In Modula-2, a coroutine has exactly the same syntax as a procedure. In fact, creating a coroutine is actually the transformation of a procedure into a process. The basic steps are as follows.

1. Create a procedure
2. Designate the procedure as a process
3. Transfer control to the process.

Before steps 2 and 3 can be accomplished, you will need to import these new procedures and types from the library **SYSTEM**:

- **PROCESS**
- **NEWPROCESS**
- **TRANSFER**.

PROCESS is a variable type. Variables of type **PROCESS** can be thought of as holding pointers that point to various coroutines. **NEWPROCESS** is the procedure used to create a new process; it is **NEWPROCESS** that transforms a procedure into a process. The procedure **TRANSFER** transfers control to the specified process. Before looking at these procedures in detail, look at a simple example.

The following program creates two processes called **Proc1** and **Proc2**. Initially control is transferred to **Proc1**. However, if you type a key on the keyboard, control is transferred to **Proc2**, where the key is read, and then control is transferred back to **Proc1**. Once **Proc1**'s loop has finished execution, control is returned to the main program, and execution terminates.

```
MODULE Coroutine;

  FROM InOut IMPORT WriteLn, WriteString, Read, Write;

  FROM Keyboard IMPORT KeyPressed;

  FROM SYSTEM IMPORT WORD, PROCESS, ADR, SIZE, NEWPROCESS,
                     TRANSFER;

VAR
  ExitPoint, p1, p2: PROCESS; (* process variables *)
  work1, work2: ARRAY[1..1000] OF CHAR;  (* workspaces *)
  buf: ARRAY[0..100] OF CHAR;
  ch: CHAR;

  PROCEDURE Proc1;
    VAR
      i: CARDINAL;
  BEGIN
    FOR i:=1 TO 100 DO
      WriteLn;
      WriteString("In Proc1 at A ");
      IF KeyPressed() THEN
        TRANSFER(p1,p2);  (* go to other procedure *)
      END;
      WriteString(" In Proc1 at B");
    END;
    TRANSFER(p1, ExitPoint);  (* clean exit *)
  END Proc1;

  PROCEDURE Proc2;
  BEGIN
    LOOP
```

```
        WriteLn;
        WriteString("In Proc2 ");
        Read(ch);                  (* clear character buffer *)
        Write(ch);
        TRANSFER(p2,p1); (* terminate program *)
      END;
    END Proc2;

   BEGIN

    NEWPROCESS(Proc1, ADR(work1), SIZE(work1), p1);
    NEWPROCESS(Proc2, ADR(work2), SIZE(work2), p2);

    TRANSFER(ExitPoint, p1);  (* start up program *)

  END Coroutine.
```

As the program executes the messages

In Procl at A In Procl at B

will continually be displayed. However, if you type **X**, for example, you will see

In Procl at A In Proc2 X In Procl at B

Enter the program and run it to fully understand its execution.

Now look at several important aspects of this program. First, three variables of type **PROCESS** were declared. They are used to perform the transfers between coroutines. In the main body of the module code, the statements

```
NEWPROCESS(Proc1, ADR(work1), SIZE(work1), p1);
NEWPROCESS(Proc2, ADR(work2), SIZE(work2), p2);
```

are used to change **Procl** and **Proc2** into processes. The general form of **NEWPROCESS** is

NEWPROCESS(*proc, workspace, WorkspaceSize, p*);

where ***proc*** is the name of the procedure that is to become a process, ***workspace*** is the address of a region of memory that will hold the process, ***WorkspaceSize*** is the size of the work space, and ***p*** is a variable of type **PROCESS** that points to the process.

Two questions arise when using **NEWPROCESS**. The first is where to get memory to hold the process, and the second is how big that region of memory should be. There are basically two ways to answer these questions. In the example, the work space was allocated by declaring an array of characters large enough to hold the code for the process and then using the **ADR** function to find the array's address. A second approach is to locate a variable, using absolute addressing, at a specific location in unused memory and then find the variable's address. Determining how big the work space should be is sometimes difficult. In the example, 1000 was chosen because it is easily more than sufficient for the small amount of code in each process—in other words, guesswork was used. Another method involves the determination of the actual amount of code in each process by first compiling the program with the process in, then with it out, and comparing the size differences. Also, some Modula-2 implementations may tell you how large each procedure is. Be sure to check your user's manual regarding this point because there may be other considerations. You can get by with a little guesswork for simple examples, but you should be very careful in real programming tasks.

Once both processes are created, the next line of code transfers control to **Proc1** using its process pointer **p1**, as shown here.

```
TRANSFER(ExitPoint, p1);   (* start up program *)
```

The general form of **TRANSFER** is

TRANSFER(*from, to*);

where ***from*** and ***to*** are variables of type **PROCESS**. The effect of this procedure is to place a pointer pointing to the current location into **from** and to move to the location pointed to by **to**. In this way coroutines can continue execution at the next line of code after a **TRANSFER**.

Notice that **ExitPoint** is a **PROCESS** variable that is used to allow a final transfer back to the main module code for clean termination. If you don't include code like this, then your program will end with a run-time error indicating that no processes are executing.

Keyboard Buffer Example

To get a better idea of how coroutines can be used effectively, consider the following program.

```
MODULE KeyBuffer;

  FROM InOut IMPORT WriteLn, WriteString, Read, EOL;

  FROM Keyboard IMPORT KeyPressed;

  FROM SYSTEM IMPORT WORD, PROCESS, ADR, SIZE, NEWPROCESS,
                     TRANSFER;

  FROM Strings IMPORT CompareStr;

VAR
  ExitPoint, p1, p2: PROCESS; (* process variables *)
  work1, work2: ARRAY[1..1000] OF CHAR;  (* workspaces *)
  buf: ARRAY[0..100] OF CHAR;
  EOC: BOOLEAN;    (* End Of Command *)

  PROCEDURE Proc1;
    VAR
      i: CARDINAL;
  BEGIN
    REPEAT      (* run until KeyBuffer terminates program *)
      WriteLn;
      WriteString("processing");
      IF KeyPressed() THEN
        TRANSFER(p1,p2);  (* go to other procedure *)
        IF(EOC) THEN WriteString(buf); END;
        EOC:=FALSE;  (* reset *)
      END
    UNTIL CompareStr(buf,"quit")=0;
    TRANSFER(p1, ExitPoint);  (* clean exit *)
  END Proc1;

  PROCEDURE KeyBuffer;
    VAR
      count: CARDINAL;
      ch: CHAR;
  BEGIN
    count:=0;
    LOOP
      Read(ch);                  (* clear character buffer *)
      IF ch<>EOL THEN
        buf[count]:=ch;
        INC(count);
```

```
        EOC:=FALSE;
        TRANSFER(p2,p1); (* go on processing *)
      ELSE
        buf[count]:=CHR(0);  (* null terminator *)
        EOC:=TRUE;          (* end of command string *)
        TRANSFER(p2,p1); (* go on processing *)
        count:=0;
      END;
    END; (* LOOP *)
  END KeyBuffer;

BEGIN

  NEWPROCESS(Proc1, ADR(work1), SIZE(work1), p1);
  NEWPROCESS(KeyBuffer, ADR(work2), SIZE(work2), p2);

  TRANSFER(ExitPoint, p1);  (* start up program *)

END KeyBuffer.
```

In this program, **Proc1** is used to simulate a process that is performing some sort of real-time activity—monitoring the flight systems of a jet plane, for example. It can be terminated only when the command **quit** is typed from the keyboard. Because **Proc1** should not stop processing while the command is being entered, control is passed to **KeyBuffer** only one character at a time. When a carriage return is entered, the command is then processed—in this case, it is displayed on the screen.

Again, enter and compile this code to better understand its operation.

IOTRANSFER

An interrupt-driven I/O device can cause a transfer through the use of **IOTRANSFER**. **IOTRANSFER** has the general form

```
IOTRANSFER(ISR, p, IntVectorNum);
```

where ***ISR*** a variable of type **PROCESS** that points to the interrupt service routine, ***p*** is of type **PROCESS** and points to the interrupted process, and ***IntVectorNum*** is the number of the interrupt vector.

Because **IOTRANSFER** is extremely machine dependent, no examples will be developed here.

Table 13-1. **Processes** Routines

Routine	Action
StartProcess	Starts a process
SEND	Sends a signal
WAIT	Suspends a process until a signal is received
Init	Initializes a signal

Using WAIT and SEND

In the examples up to now, you as programmer had explicit control over when each process was going to execute. In essence, you bypassed the scheduler. However, you can let Modula-2 execute processes on its own by simply specifying the conditions upon which each process may execute or suspend execution. When a process suspends execution, the scheduler will automatically restart another process if one is waiting to execute.

This form of concurrent programming requires the use of a new library, called **Processes**, which contains the necessary routines. These routines are listed in Table 13-1. In addition, the type **SIGNAL** is found in **Processes**.

StartProcess has the general form

StartProcess(*proc, WorkspaceSize*);

where ***proc*** is the procedure to be started, and ***WorkspaceSize*** is the number of bytes needed by the procedure. As with **NEWPROCESS**, this number may be difficult to determine, and (unfortunately) some guesswork may be needed. The effect of **StartProcess** is to immediately begin execution of *proc*—no explicit **TRANSFER** is needed.

Processes communicate with each other through variables of type **SIGNAL**. To send a signal requires the use of **SEND**, which has the general form

SEND(*signal*);

where ***signal*** is a variable of type **SIGNAL**.

Receiving a signal implies that a process is waiting for one; therefore, **WAIT** is used. It has the form

WAIT(*signal*);

SEND and **WAIT** work in the following way. When a process **WAIT**s for a signal, its execution is suspended, and another process's execution begins. If there are no other processes that can be executed, the program terminates. **SEND**ing a signal either reactivates a process that is **WAIT**ing for the signal, or does nothing if no process is **WAIT**ing. In this way, signals can be used to synchronize two or more processes.

All signals must be initialized prior to use through a call to **Init**. **Init**'s general form is

Init(*signal*);

The classic example of concurrent execution and signals is the producer/consumer process pair. In this example, one process produces something that the other process consumes. We can call the consumer C and the producer P. C must suspend processing (**WAIT**) until P has produced something. Once P has produced something, it tells C about it (**SEND**s a signal), and C can now execute. Both C and P continue along in this fashion. The program **ProCon**, shown here, implements a simple version of this, with **Consumer** printing the strings that **Producer** reads from the keyboard.

```
MODULE ProCon;

  FROM InOut IMPORT WriteLn, WriteString, Read, EOL, Write;

  FROM Keyboard IMPORT KeyPressed;

  FROM SYSTEM IMPORT WORD, PROCESS, ADR, SIZE, NEWPROCESS,
                     TRANSFER;

  FROM Processes IMPORT WAIT, SEND, StartProcess, SIGNAL,
                        Init;

VAR
  ExitPoint, p1, p2: PROCESS; (* process variables *)
  work1, work2: ARRAY[1..1000] OF CHAR;  (* workspaces *)
  buf: ARRAY[0..100] OF CHAR;
  S: SIGNAL;

  PROCEDURE Consumer;
  BEGIN
```

```
    LOOP
      WriteString("waiting ");
      WAIT(S); (* wait until characters in key buffer *)
      WriteString(buf);
    END
  END Consumer;

  PROCEDURE Producer;
    VAR
      count: CARDINAL;
      ch: CHAR;
  BEGIN
    count:=0;
    LOOP
      Read(ch);                (* clear character buffer *)
      IF ch<>EOL THEN
        buf[count]:=ch;
        Write(ch);
        INC(count);
      ELSE
        buf[count]:=CHR(0);  (* null terminator *)
        WriteLn;
        SEND(S);          (* allow other routine to execute *)
        count:=0;
      END;
    END;
  END Producer;

 BEGIN

  Init(S);

  StartProcess(Consumer,1000);
  Producer;
END ProCon.
```

Note that the order of the calls to **StartProcess** and **Producer** are very important, and if they are reversed, **Consumer** will never be executed. In this example, **Producer** does not need to be a process because it does not need to wait for a signal in order to execute.

Priorities And ***LISTEN***

A module can be given a *priority* by placing a number enclosed in square brackets immediately after the module name. For example,

```
MODULE Counter[3];
```

gives **Counter** a priority of 3. The higher the number, the higher the priority.

The module with the highest priority will execute. Execution can be temporarily suspended, however, through the use of the procedure **LISTEN**, imported from **SYSTEM**. Each time **LISTEN** is executed, a module of lower priority is allowed to execute. The use of prioritized modules and **LISTEN** have their greatest use in interrupt-driven routines.

Avoiding Deadlock

One of the most annoying and troublesome problems encountered when writing concurrent routines is *deadlock*. Deadlock is a situation in which two routines are both waiting for something only the other can provide—hence, both are suspended, and neither can run. This is similar to the old comedy routine with two men at a door both saying "after you."

The two procedures shown here will deadlock.

```
PROCEDURE A;
BEGIN
  WAIT(S);
  SEND(T);
  .
  .
  .
END A;

PROCEDURE B;
BEGIN
  WAIT(T);
  SEND(S);
  .
  .
  .
END B;
```

As you can see, **A** is suspended waiting for signal **S**, and **B** is suspended waiting for signal **T**. Neither will ever send the signal the other needs.

Although the simple situation just described is very easy to see, deadlock is most deadly when it occurs through a combination of several processes and signals. Because the actual order of execution may not be known, it is very difficult to determine why the deadlock occurred. To avoid deadlock, you must carefully think through your routines.

Final Comments On Concurrency

Both coroutines and concurrent processes are extremely important to several types of programs. They are, however, sources of frustration and trouble because the "normal" sequential execution of a program is no longer in force. Most people, including programmers, have difficulty fully grasping the actual execution path of more than two or three concurrent processes, which makes program verification extremely difficult when concurrent processes are involved. Also, debugging time is increased exponentially. Concurrent programming thus is best left to experienced programmers and used only when it is appropriate to do so.

EXERCISES

1. What is a process?

2. What is a coroutine?

3. What procedure is called to set up a new process?

4. What does **TRANSFER** do?

5. What do **SEND** and **WAIT** do and how do they relate to a concurrent environment?

6. Modify the programs in this chapter and observe the results.

ANSWERS

1. A process is a task running on a computer.

2. A coroutine is a special type of procedure that allows control to be transferred into it; execution does not need to start at the top.

3. **NEWPROCESS** or **StartProcess.**

4. **TRANSFER** allows you to explicitly transfer control between processes.

5. **SEND** sends a signal, which might restart a process. **WAIT** suspends a process until the specified signal is sent.

Efficiency And Debugging

CHAPTER 14

Now that all the features of the Modula-2 language have been covered, it is time to consider a few points that affect the way programs run. We will also look at certain programming errors and how to find them.

Efficiency

The ability to write programs that make efficient use of system resources is the mark of a professional programmer. Efficiency here refers to the speed of execution or the use of system resources, or both. System resources include RAM, disk space, printer paper, and so on—basically, anything that can be allocated and used up. Whether a program is efficient or not is sometimes a subjective judgment, and it can change from situation to situation. For example, consider a program that uses 47K of RAM to execute and consumes 2 megabytes of disk space, and whose average run time is 7 minutes. If this is a sort program running on an Apple II, then the program is probably not very efficient. However, if it is a weather forecasting program running on a Cray computer, then it is probably very efficient.

Another problem with efficiency considerations is that optimizing one aspect of a program often degrades another. For example, making the most efficient use of disk space means compacting data, which often makes disk access slower because of the overhead of the compaction. This and other efficiency trade-offs can lead to much frustration—especially for the user who is not a programmer and cannot see why one thing should affect the other.

You might be wondering how efficiency can be discussed at all. The answer lies in the fact that there are some programming practices that are *always efficient*—or, at least, always more efficient than others. Also, there are a few techniques that make programs both faster and smaller. It is these that we will look at here.

Avoiding Code Duplication

Even the best of programmers sometimes write *redundant code.* Redundant code does not refer to code that could be made into a subroutine. Rather, it is the unnecessary duplication of similar statements within a routine. To get a better idea of what redundant code is, examine this code fragment.

```
ReadInt(a);
ReadString(y);
IF a<10 THEN WriteString('Invalid input'); END;
If Length(y)=0 THEN WriteString('Invalid input'); END;
```

In this example, the statement

```
WriteString('Invalid input');
```

occurs twice. However, if you examine the code, it is apparent that it need not, because the code could be written as follows:

```
ReadInt(a);
ReadString(y);
IF (a<10) OR (Length(y)=0) THEN
  WriteString('Invalid input');
END;
```

Now not only will the object code be shorter, but the code will actually execute faster because only one **IF/THEN** statement is executed instead of two.

The preceding example is unlikely to occur in an actual program because the redundant code was close together, making it quite easy to see; duplicate statements usually are separated by numerous lines of code. Unfortunately, redundant code occurs in most computer programs.

Redundancy sometimes happens because of the method selected to code a routine. For example, following are two ways to code a function that searches an array of strings for a specific word.

```
TYPE
  str80 = ARRAY[0..79] OF CHAR;
  StrArray = ARRAY [1..100] OF str80;

PROCEDURE StrSearch1(str:StrArray, word:str80):BOOLEAN;
(* Correct, non-redundant method *)
VAR
  t:INTEGER;
BEGIN
  FOR t:=1 TO 100 DO
    IF str[t]=word THEN RETURN TRUE;
  END
  RETURN FALSE;
END StrSearch1;

PROCEDURE StrSeach2(str:StrArray, word:str80):BOOLEAN;
(* Incorrect, redundant method *)
VAR
  t:INTEGER;
BEGIN
  t:=1;
  IF str[t]=word  THEN RETURN TRUE;
  ELSE
    t:=2;
    WHILE(t<=100) DO
      IF str[t]=word THEN RETURN TRUE; END;
      t:t+1;
    END;
  END;
  RETURN FALSE;
END StrSeach2;
```

As you can see, the second method not only duplicates the **IF/THEN** comparison statements, but it also has two assignment statements, **t:=1** and **t:=2**, that are essentially duplications. The first version will not only run faster, but it will require much less memory.

In short, redundant code can be caused either by sloppiness in coding or poor judgment in choosing the way to implement a routine. Either way, it should be avoided.

Use of Procedures

The use of procedures with local variables is the basis of structured programming. Procedures with local variables are the building blocks of Modula-2 programs and one of Modula-2's strongest assets. Nothing that is discussed in this section should be construed otherwise. However, Modula-2 procedures can have ramifications for the size and speed of your code, so there are a few points about them that you should keep in mind.

First and foremost, Modula-2 is a stack-oriented language. This means that all local variables and parameters to procedures use the stack for temporary storage. When a procedure is called, the return address of the calling routine is placed on the stack as well. This enables the subroutine to return to the location from which it was called. When a procedure returns, this address, as well as all local variables and parameters, will have to be removed from the stack. The process of pushing this information is referred to as the *calling sequence,* and the popping process is called the *returning sequence.* Simply put, these sequences take time—sometimes quite a bit of time if several parameters are passed and temporary variables are used.

To best understand how a function call can slow your program, look at the two code fragments shown here.

Version 1

```
For x:=1 TO 100 DO
        t:=Compute (x);
END;

PROCEDURE Compute (q:INTEGER):REAL;
VAR
    t:REAL;
BEGIN
        RETURN ABS (Sin (q)/100/3.1416);
END Compute;
```

Version 2

```
FOR x:=1 to 100 DO
        t:=ABS (Sin(q)/
          100/3.1416);
END;
```

Although each loop performs the same function, version 2 will be much faster because the overhead of the calling and returning sequence has been eliminated through the use of inline code.

You may be thinking now that you should write programs that have just a few very large routines so that they will run fast. However, in the vast majority of cases the slight time differential will not be meaningful, and the loss of structure will be acute. Further, replacing procedures that are used by several routines with inline code will cause your program to become very large because the same code will be duplicated several times. Remember that subroutines were invented largely as a way to make efficient use of memory. In fact, this is the reason why, as a rule of thumb, making a program run faster means making it bigger, and making it smaller means making it slower.

In the final analysis, it really only makes sense to use inline code instead of a function call when speed is of absolute priority. Otherwise, the liberal use of procedures is definitely recommended.

CASE Versus *IF/ELSIF* Ladders

The following code fragments are functionally equivalent; however, one is more efficient than the other. Can you tell which?

```
CASE ch OF
   'a': f1(ch)  |
   'b': f2(ch)  |
   'c': f3(ch)  |
   'd': f4(ch);
END;
```

```
IF ch='a' THEN f1(ch)
ELSIF ch='b' THEN f2(ch)
ELSIF ch='c' THEN f3(ch)
ELSIF ch='d' THEN f4(ch)
END;
```

The code fragment on the left, which uses the **CASE** statement, is much more efficient than the one on the right because, in general, the **CASE** statement generates tighter, faster object code than does a series of **IF/ELSIF**s.

A series of **IF/ELSIF**s arranged as shown in the preceding example is referred to as an **IF/ELSIF** ladder because program execution "steps" its way down. The **IF/ELSIF** ladder is very important because it allows you to perform multi-alternative decision operations using a variety of data types that cannot be used in a **CASE** statement. However, if you are using similar, related data types, you should use the **CASE** statement instead.

INC and *DEC*

Depending upon the Modula-2 implementation, the built-in procedures **INC** and **DEC** may be faster than their corresponding assignment statements. The reason for this has to do with the way compilers handle expressions of the following type:

```
x:=x+1;

y:=y-1;
```

For technical reasons beyond the scope of this book, most compilers will cause two (or three) memory move operations to be executed for each assignment. However, the same task can be accomplished with

```
INC(x);

DEC(y);
```

which requires only one memory access operation. This means that any program that uses **INC** and **DEC** will run faster than one that uses assignment statements. This can be especially important inside loops.

Debugging

To paraphrase Thomas Edison, programming is 10 percent inspiration and 90 percent debugging. All really good programmers are good debuggers. Certain types of bugs can occur easily in Modula-2 programming, and these bugs are the topic of this section.

Pointer Problems

A very common problem in Modula-2 programs is the misuse of pointers. Pointer problems fall into two general categories: (1) misunderstanding of indirect references and the dereferencing operator and (2) the accidental use of invalid pointers. The solution to the first problem is to understand pointers in the Modula-2 language; the solution to the second is always to verify the validity of a pointer before it is used.

Following is an example of a typical error Modula-2 programmers make.

```
MODULE WRONG; (* This program is in error *)

TYPE
  PNTR = POINTER TO OBJECT;

  OBJECT = RECORD
    x: CHAR;
    y: INTEGER;
  END;

VAR
  p: PNTR;

BEGIN
  p^.x:='g';
  p^.y:=100;
END WRONG.
```

This program will most likely crash, probably taking with it the operating system as well. The reason is that the pointer **p** is never assigned a value using **New**. Rather, it contains an unknown random number that could be pointing anywhere in the memory of the computer. This is most certainly not what is wanted. To make this program correct you must add the line

```
NEW(p);
```

prior to the first use of pointer **p**.

The terrible thing about "wild" pointers is that they are hard to track down. If you make assignments to a pointer variable that does not contain a valid pointer address, then your program may appear to function correctly some of the time and crash at other times. Also, statistically, the smaller your program, the more likely it is that it will run correctly, even with a stray pointer, because very little memory is in use. As your program grows, failures will become more common, but you will be thinking about current additions or changes to your program, not about pointer errors. Hence, you will tend to look in the wrong spot for the bug. Pointer problems are marked by erratic errors—your program will work right one time and wrong another—and sometimes variables will contain garbage for no explainable reason. If these problems begin to occur, check your pointers. As a matter of procedure you should always check all pointers when bugs begin to occur.

As was mentioned in the chapter on pointers, you should always make sure that sufficient memory is available to hold the object of a pointer before issuing a call to **NEW**. Failure to do this will result in a run-time error and termination of your program. Always test available memory using the **Available** function found in **Storage**, as shown here.

```
IF Available(TSIZE(p)) THEN NEW(p)
ELSE  WriteString("Out of memory")
END;
```

Redefining Built-in Procedures

Although Modula-2 does not allow you to redefine the keywords that make up the language, it does allow you to redefine the words that reference its standard library procedures. Sometimes programmers think that it is a good idea to do this; however, it really only leads to trouble. For example, consider the following code.

```
MODULE BadIdea;

    FROM InOut IMPORT  Write, WriteLn, WriteCard, ReadString;

    FROM Strings IMPORT Length, CompareStr;

    VAR
      x: ARRAY [0..79] OF CHAR;
      count: CARDINAL;

    PROCEDURE WriteString(str:ARRAY OF CHAR);
    (* Put CRLF out after string *)
      VAR
        i: CARDINAL;
    BEGIN
      FOR i:=0 TO Length(str) DO
        Write(str[i]);
      END;
      WriteLn;
    END WriteString;

BEGIN
  count:=0;
  REPEAT
    ReadString(x);
    WriteString(x);
    INC(count);
  UNTIL CompareStr(x,"q")=0;
  WriteString('There were ');
```

```
    WriteCard(count,3);
    WriteString(' iterations.');
    WriteLn;
  END BadIdea.
```

In this example, the programmer decided to redefine the standard procedure **WriteString** to place a carriage return after each string displayed, but forgot this redefinition when printing the final message. This occurred because the redefinition of **WriteString** replaced the built-in procedure.

Although the error in this example is quite easy to see, redefinition can be very troublesome in projects involving several programmers, because other programmers will assume that the standard library procedures are being used. The only way to avoid this problem is never to give a procedure you write the same name as one in the standard library. If you are unsure, append your initials to the start of the name—for instance, use **HSWriteString** instead of **WriteString.**

IF/THEN/IF/ELSE Errors

Even very experienced programmers occasionally fall prey to the **IF/THEN/IF/ELSE** error. For example, consider the following code fragment. Are you *sure* what it does?

```
IF count<100 THEN
   IF count>50 THEN F1
ELSE F2; END;
END;
```

Don't be fooled by the improper formatting. The **ELSE** does not associate with the first **IF**, but rather with the second **IF**; that is, an **ELSE** will always be associated with the closest **IF**. So, instead of executing **F2**, if **count** is greater than 100 the program does nothing. **F2** will execute if **count** is less than 100 and less than 50. Properly formatted, this becomes clear.

```
IF count<100 THEN
   IF count>50 THEN F1
   ELSE F2
   END;
END;
```

If you want F2 to execute if count exceeds 100, you must write

```
IF count<100 THEN
   IF count>50 THEN F1 END;
ELSE F2;
END;
```

Forgetting VAR In Procedures

In the heat of programming, it is easy to forget that if an argument to a procedure is to be changed by that procedure, then the argument must be specified as a **VAR** parameter. Forgetting this can cause bizarre results and hours of frustrating debugging time. For example, consider this incorrect program.

```
MODULE WRONG;  (* incorrect program *)

   FROM InOut IMPORT WriteString, ReadInt, WriteInt;

   VAR
    t:INTEGER;

   PROCEDURE F1(x:INTEGER);
   BEGIN
     WriteString('Enter a value: ');
     ReadInt(x);
   END F1;

BEGIN
   F1(t);  (* get a value for t *)
   WriteString('t has the value: ');
   WriteInt(t);
END WRONG;
```

This program will not work because only the local variable **x** will be assigned a value, and when **F1** returns, **t** will be unmodified.

The way to make this program work is to declare **x** inside **F1** to be a VAR parameter. Then the calling variable **t** will be modified. The corrected program is shown here.

```
MODULE RIGHT;  (* correct program *)

   FROM InOut IMPORT WriteString, ReadInt, WriteInt;

   VAR
    t:INTEGER;
```

```
    PROCEDURE F1(VAR x:INTEGER);
    BEGIN
      WriteString('Enter a value: ');
      ReadInt(x);
    END F1;

  BEGIN
    F1(t);  (* get a value for t *)
    WriteString('t has the value: ');
    WriteInt(t);
  END RIGHT;
```

Although this simple program was easy to correct, when this error occurs in large programs, it can be one of the most difficult bugs to find.

General Debugging Theory

Everyone has a different approach to programming and debugging. However, certain techniques have, over time, proven to be better than others. In the case of debugging, incremental testing is considered to be the most cost- (and time-) effective method, even though it can appear to slow the development process at first. To understand what incremental testing is, first look at what it is not.

In the early days of computers, programmers were taught to prepare their programs in advance, submit them for execution, and then interpret the results. This is called *batch programming* and was necessary when computers were scarce. Batch programming helped give computers a bad image in the early 1960s because it required programmers to expend an enormous amount of time and mental energy developing a program. Because all testing had to be done in batch mode as well, it was very difficult to test all possible conditions under which a program could fail. This lack of thorough testing led to the "computer error" problems so common in many early computer installations.

Today, batch programming is seldom used because it cannot support an interactive *incremental testing* environment. Under incremental testing, an operational unit is established very early in the development process, and a working program is always available. An *operational unit* is simply a piece of working code. As new code is added to this unit, it is tested and debugged. In this way, the programmer can easily find errors because, most likely, the errors will occur in the newly added code or in the way that the new code interacts with the operational unit.

Debugging time can be computed according to this formula:

$$DebugTime=(NumOfLines+X)^2$$

where **NumOfLines** is the total number of lines of code that a bug could be in, and **X** is some constant (which is programmer dependent). As you can see, debugging time is a squared quantity. With incremental testing it is possible to restrict the number of lines of code to only those that are newly added—that is, not part of the operational unit. This situation is shown in Figure 14-1.

Incremental testing theory is based on probability and area. Area is a squared dimension. Therefore, as a program grows the area that must be searched for bugs equals N squared. As a programmer, you want the smallest possible area to deal with while debugging. With incremental testing, you can subtract the area already tested from the total area, thereby reducing the region where a bug may exist.

Large projects usually have several modules that have only minimal interaction. For these modules, several operational units can be established to allow concurrent development. In fact, Modula-2 is exceptionally well suited to these types of projects.

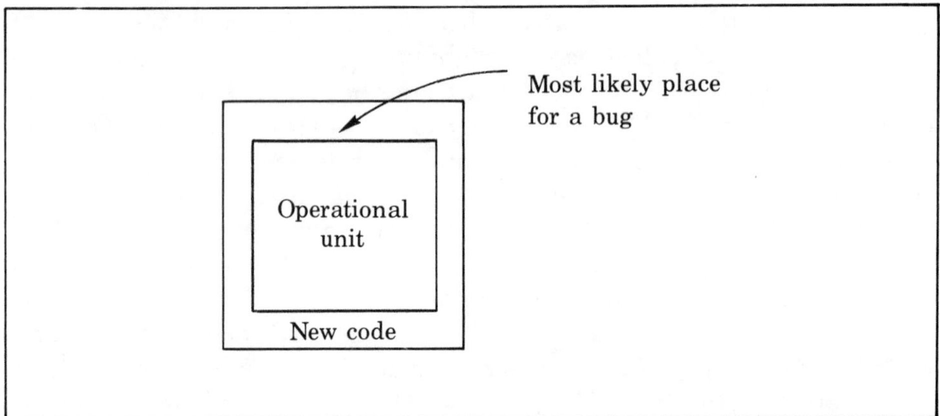

Figure 14-1. The most likely location of a bug when incremental testing is used

Incremental testing is very important because, first, it greatly reduces debugging time because it makes errors easier to find, and second, it speeds up the development process because design errors can be caught early on in the project—before all the code is written. (It should never, of course, take the place of a good design.)

Again, incremental testing is simply the process of always having working code. As soon as it is possible to run a piece of your program, you should do so, testing that section completely. As you add to the program, continue to test the new sections and the way they connect to the known operational code. In this way, you can concentrate the search for bugs to a small area of code.

Modula-2/Pascal Differences

APPENDIX A

In terms of overall appearance, Modula-2 and Pascal are very similar. Both are structured languages with similar program control statements. Because Modula-2 is Pascal's successor, most of its differences with Pascal fall into two categories: enhancements and improvements. Enhancements include features that did not exist in Pascal, like libraries and system-dependent routines that broaden the types of problems that can be solved, while improvements include minor changes intended to clean up loose ends, such as the addition of the **ELSIF** statement and the more consistent use of **BEGIN** and **END**. A third category contains features that are just different—not necessarily better one way or the other—such as the changed functions of **Write** and **WriteLn**.

In this appendix, these differences will be outlined.

MODULEs and Linking

Standard Pascal does not support the separate compilation of source files or linking. Modula-2 not only supports these features, it virtually demands them. In Modula-2, programs are thought of as modular, with each module being only a piece of the total program. The final, executable version of the program is obtained by linking all the pieces together. In Modula-2 these pieces are called **MODULE**s.

There are three types of **MODULE**s. The *program* **MODULE** is the first module executed when your program runs. For example, below are two identical programs; the one on the right is in Pascal, and the one on the left is in Modula-2.

```
MODULE Test;                PROGRAM Test;

  VAR                         VAR
    a:INTEGER;                  a:INTEGER;

BEGIN                       BEGIN
  a:=10;                      a:=10;
END Test.                   END.
```

As you can see, the first words in the programs differ. The reserved word **MODULE** is used to begin a program **MODULE**. In Modula-2, the keyword **PROGRAM** is not used.

The other two types of **MODULE**s are called **IMPLEMENTATION MODULE**s and **DEFINITION MODULE**s. They are used to create separately compiled pieces of your program, which are linked together to create the final executable program. A **DEFINITION MODULE** defines what a separately compiled **MODULE** will do, and its corresponding **IMPLEMENTATION MODULE** actually performs the operations.

Given the **MODULE** scenario, it is possible to write large programs in pieces using separate programmer teams. This makes the management of large projects much easier and is one of Modula-2's major advantages over Pascal. In fact, Professor Wirth thought that **MODULE**s were the single most important difference between Modula-2 and Pascal. In Modula-2 terminology, the separate modules are sometimes called *library modules,* or simply libraries.

IMPORT

Before a library procedure can be used, it must be explicitly requested through the use of the **IMPORT** statement. The **IMPORT** statement causes the specified procedures to be linked into your program. It is not only procedures that you write that need to be **IMPORT**ed, but also most of the standard library procedures, such as **WriteLn**, because most of Modula-2's standard procedures are found in libraries. In short, only a handful of Modula-2's standard procedures are built into the compiler.This differs greatly from Pascal, where all the standard procedures are built in.

Data Types

Modula-2 has all of Pascal's built-in data types as well as two important additions. The new type **CARDINAL** is defined as being a positive integer. For most 16-bit Modula-2 implementations, the range of **CARDINAL** values is between 0 and 65,535. Because of certain technical factors, arithmetic operations on **CARDINAL**s are faster than they are on **INTEGER**s. Hence, **CARDINAL**s are often used as loop counters to make code execute faster.

The second addition is **BITSET**, a predefined set type that generally has the same number of elements as the number of bits in a word.

Case Sensitivity

Unlike many Pascal implementations, Modula-2 is *case sensitive* with regard to identifiers—that is, uppercase and lowercase letters are different. This means that **INIT**, **Init**, and **init** are three distinct and separate names. All Modula-2 reserved words must be entered in uppercase letters.

Modula-2 identifiers must consist only of letters and digits—no special characters may be used. This differs from Pascal, which allows the underscore.

Comments

Modula-2 comments are placed between the symbols (* and *). The curly braces { } used by Pascal for comments are used by Modula-2 to denote sets.

Unlike Pascal, Modula-2 comments may be nested. This means that you can have comments within comments, making it very easy to comment out large pieces of code for debugging—even if they already contain comments.

Differences in Standard Procedures

There is little similarity between Modula-2's standard procedures and those of Pascal. However, even though functionality is different, many of the names are the same.

The most common examples of this are **Write** and **WriteLn**. In Pascal, these procedures can be used to display characters, strings, and numbers on the screen. However, in Modula-2, **Write** is used to display a character, and **WriteLn** simply outputs a carriage return/linefeed combination—it cannot take any arguments. When an entire string is to be printed, the procedure **WriteString** must be used. **WriteString** does not issue a carriage return/linefeed sequence. Because **WriteString** cannot be used to output numeric values, Modula-2 has specific procedures for this purpose, including **WriteInt**, **WriteCard**, and **WriteReal**. For example, in Pascal

```
WriteLn('This is ');
Write('the number ',1);
```

must be written in Modula-2 as

```
WriteString('This is ');
WriteLn;
WriteString('the number');
WriteCard(1,1);
```

In addition to the differences in **WriteLn** and **Write**, Modula-2's disk I/O has no relationship to Pascal's.

Perhaps the most important difference between Pascal's and Modula-2's standard procedures is that Pascal's are strictly defined, whereas Modula-2's are to a large extent implementation dependent. This means that the actual procedures included with a Modula-2 compiler are to some extent at the discretion of the implementor. However, the libraries that were created by Wirth for his initial implementation provide a de facto standard that is generally adhered to.

Code Blocks

There is a subtle but important structural difference between the program control statements in Modula-2 and Pascal that has to do with blocks of code. Program control statements include the loops **FOR**, **WHILE**, and **REPEAT**, and the **CASE** and the **IF** statements. In Pascal, **BEGIN** and **END** must be used around a group of statements to create a code block. For example,

```
WHILE X<100 DO
  BEGIN
        .
        .
        .
  END;
```

In Modula-2, however, the object of **WHILE** (and all control statements) is assumed to be a block containing one or more statements. Therefore, the same code looks like this in Modula-2:

```
WHILE X<100 DO
  .
  .
  .
END;
```

All of the loop control statements terminate with an **END**, except for the **REPEAT** loop, which uses the traditional (and necessary) **UNTIL**. Both the **CASE** and **IF** statements also work in a similar fashion.

The only places in Modula-2 that the Pascal-like **BEGIN/END** is used is for starting and ending procedure code and the main program code.

*The **FOR** Loop*

Modula-2's **FOR** loop has been expanded to allow an optional increment factor. For example, the following code will print the numbers 0 to 10 by 2's on the screen.

```
FOR X=0 TO 10 BY 2 DO
  WriteCard(X,2);
END;
```

Because the increment factor may also be negative, the **DOWNTO** is not found in Modula-2. For example, to print the numbers 10 through 0 on the screen you would write

```
FOR X=10 TO 0 BY -1 DO
  WriteCard(X,2);
END;
```

*The **CASE** Statement*

There are two differences between the **CASE** statements in Modula-2 and in Pascal. First, as stated earlier, in Modula-2 each case is assumed to be a block; therefore, multiple lines may be entered for each case without the use of a **BEGIN/END** block. Instead, a new operator, ¦, is used to separate the cases from each other.

The second difference is the inclusion in Modula-2 of an **ELSE** condition that is executed if none of the cases match. For example, the following code performs the menu selection portion of a spelling checker.

```
Read(choice);

CASE choice OF
  '1': CheckSpelling; |
  '2': Reset;
       Save;          |
  '3'| Reset;
       Load;          |
  '4': Quit;
ELSE
  Error;
END;
```

If the user types any number other than 1 through 4, the **Error** routine is executed. Notice that the ¦ does not follow the last case prior to the **ELSE**. Also, you usually will get a run-time case tag error in a CASE statement that has no ELSE and where none of the cases match.

The IF Statement

Modula-2 has a truly improved version of the **IF** statement because of the inclusion of the optional **ELSIF** test. **ELSIF** is used to replace the cumbersome **IF/ELSE IF** compound statement pair. The general form of the **IF** statement is

```
IF <condition> THEN <statement-sequence>
ELSIF <condition> THEN <statement-sequence>
.
.
.
ELSIF <condition> THEN <statement-sequence>
ELSE <default-statement-sequence>
END;
```

As you can see, it is possible to have any number of **ELSIF** conditions. You should remember, however, that one and only one statement sequence will be executed. Also, the **ELSE** is executed only if all of the conditions have been false.

If you are converting code from Pascal to Modula-2, you will be happy to know that you can still use the less structured **IF/ELSE IF** form—but it is definitely discouraged for any new programming.

*Evaluation of **BOOLEAN** Expressions*

A very important but sometimes overlooked difference between Pascal and Modula-2 is in the way **BOOLEAN** expressions are evaluated. In Modula-2, compound expressions are evaluated from left to right until a determination as to the outcome can be made. This means, in some cases, that not all of the expressions will be evaluated. Look, for example, at the following line of code.

```
IF (x<>0) AND (y DIV x = 15) THEN WriteCard(y,3) END;
```

If X equals 0, the expression is known to be false, and the second expression, **y DIV x=15**, will not be executed. It thus is unnecessary to include an extra line of code to prevent a divide-by-zero error.

LOOP and EXIT

Modula-2 contains a new loop construct, called **LOOP**, not found in Pascal. **LOOP** causes a sequence of statements to be executed continuously; that is, **LOOP** actually causes an infinite loop! The only way that a **LOOP** can be terminated is through the use of the **EXIT** command, which can be located anywhere in the loop. For example, the following code will print the ASCII number of the characters typed at the keyboard until a "q" is struck.

```
LOOP
  Read(ch);
  WriteCard(ORD(ch),3);
  IF ch='q' THEN EXIT END;
END;
```

It is possible to have many **EXIT**s inside one **LOOP**, thus enabling multiple exit points.

At first glance, the **LOOP** statement may seem destructured because it does not have a clearly defined exit point. However, there are many programming situations that really don't fit nicely into the other three loop statements. Properly applied, **LOOP** is an important addition.

Arrays as Procedure Parameters

One of Pascal's most glaring problems is its restriction that array dimensions of a procedure argument be the same as those declared in the procedure's parameter list. This makes it impossible to have truly general routines that use arrays as parameters. In Modula-2 this situation is remedied through the use of *open array parameters.* An open array parameter is a parameter that has only the type of its elements defined, not the actual dimensions or boundaries. Once this is done, arrays of various sizes can be passed to the same procedure. For example,

```
PROCEDURE String(str: ARRAY OF CHAR);
```

declares **str** as an array of characters, but does not specify how long it is, or what its boundaries are.

Functions and Return Values

Modula-2 has dropped the reserved word **FUNCTION**, which is used in Pascal to denote a procedure that returns a value. In Modula-2, whether a procedure returns a value or not, it is still called a **PROCEDURE**.

To make a procedure into a function, you must specify what data type will be returned. This is done exactly as it is done in Pascal. To return a value you *do not* assign it to the procedure name (as in Pascal), but rather you use the **RETURN** statement. For example, the following procedure returns **TRUE** or **FALSE**.

```
PROCEDURE Sample(count: CARDINAL): BOOLEAN;
BEGIN
  IF count<100 THEN RETURN TRUE
  ELSE RETURN FALSE
  END;
END Sample;
```

Concurrency

Modula-2 supports coroutines and concurrent processes; Pascal does not. Modula-2 concurrency allows the writing of sophisticated systems programs that would not be possible using Pascal. Although not applied to most programming tasks, concurrency support is a very important feature of Modula-2.

Modula-2 Standard Procedures

APPENDIX B

Most of Modula-2's standard procedures are not built into the compiler itself, but rather are found in various library modules supplied with the compiler. Although Modula-2 compiler implementors can provide whatever library routines they want, most supply at least those libraries described by Professor Wirth. Therefore, it is these libraries and their procedures that are summarized in this appendix. Remember, however, that your compiler may use somewhat different names for both the libraries and the procedures. The descriptions in this appendix are for quick reference and are not intended to take the place of the complete descriptions found elsewhere in this book.

Conversions

The **Conversions** library contains the routines to convert **INTEGERs** and **CARDINALs** to strings.

```
PROCEDURE ConvertCardinal(number, width: CARDINAL;
                          VAR str: ARRAY OF CHAR);
```

ConvertCardinal will convert the **CARDINAL** value **number** into a string of minimum width **width** and place the result in **str**.

```
PROCEDURE ConvertInteger(number: INTEGER; width: CARDINAL;
                         VAR str: ARRAY OF CHAR);
```

ConvertInteger will convert the **INTEGER** value **number** into a string of minimum width **width** and place the result in **str**.

FileSystem

FileSystem contains the procedures and types necessary to perform both ASCII and binary disk file I/O.

```
TYPE
  Response= (done, notdone, notsupported, callerror, unknownmedium,
             unknownfile, paramerror, toomanyfiles eom, userdeverror);
```

Response is used to determine the outcome of the various disk file operations as shown in Table B-1.

```
TYPE
  File= RECORD
          .
          .
          .
          eof: BOOLEAN;
          res: Response;
          .
          .
          .
  END;
```

File is used to create file descriptor variables. The only fields of general use to the programmer are **eof**, which indicates that the end of the file has

Table B-1. Disk File Operations

Response	Meaning
done	Successful completion
notdone	An error not specified by the other fields
notsupported	Internal use
callerror	File in improper state for requested operation; for example, trying to write to a read-only file
unknownmedium	Drive does not exist
unknownfile	File specified for deletion cannot be found
paramerror	Invalid parameter
toomanyfiles	Attempted to open more files than supported by the system
eom	End of medium reached
userdeverror	Internal use

been reached, and **res**, which is used to indicate the status of each operation.

```
PROCEDURE Again(VAR f: File);
```

Again causes the next read operation to read the same character again from the specified file.

```
PROCEDURE Close(VAR f: File);
```

Close flushes the specified file's buffer and closes the file.

```
PROCEDURE Create(VAR f: File; medium: ARRAY OF CHAR);
```

Create is used to create a temporary file. Here, **medium** is the name of the disk drive, and **f** is a file descriptor. **Create** is seldom used by most applications.

```
PROCEDURE Delete(VAR f: File; FileName: ARRAY OF CHAR);
```

Delete removes a file from the medium. **FileName** is the name of the file to delete, and **f.res** holds the outcome of the operation.

PROCEDURE GetPos(VAR f: File; High, Low: CARDINAL);

GetPos returns the current byte location of the specified file. The location is returned in **High** and **Low**, which represent the high- and low-order words of a long integer. The location is computed using this formula:

$$position=(High*2^{16})+Low$$

PROCEDURE Length(VAR f: File; High, Low: CARDINAL);

Length returns the length, in bytes, of the specified file. The length is returned in **High** and **Low**, which represent the high- and low-order words of a long integer. The length is computed by the formula:

$$length=(High*2^{16})+Low$$

PROCEDURE Lookup(VAR f: File; FileName: ARRAY OF CHAR;
new: BOOLEAN);

Lookup is used to open a file named **FileName** and initialize the file descriptor **f**. If the file does not exist and **new** is **TRUE**, then the file will be created; otherwise, it is not created, and an error is returned in **f.res**.

PROCEDURE Rename(VAR f: File, NewName: ARRAY OF CHAR);

Rename is used to change the name of a file. The file descriptor **f** must reference a valid file, and **NewName** is the name to change to.

PROCEDURE ReadByte(VAR f; File; VAR wd: BYTE);

ReadByte reads one byte from the current position of the specified file and places it in **wd**. The file's current position is then advanced to the next byte. This procedure usually is used with binary files.

PROCEDURE ReadChar(VAR f: File; VAR ch: CHAR);

ReadChar reads one character from the current position of the specified file and places it in **ch**. The file's current position is then advanced to the next character. This procedure usually is used with ASCII files.

```
PROCEDURE ReadNBytes(VAR f: File; buffer: ADDRESS;
                     numbytes: CARDINAL;
                     VAR numread: CARDINAL);
```

ReadNBytes is used to read **numbytes** of bytes from the specified file and place them in the buffer pointed to by **buffer**. The actual number of bytes read is returned in **numread**. **ReadNBytes** usually is used with binary files.

```
PROCEDURE ReadWord(VAR f; File; VAR wd: WORD);
```

ReadWord reads one word from the current position of the specified file and places it in **wd**. The file's current position is then advanced to the next word. This procedure usually is used with binary files.

```
PROCEDURE Reset(VAR f: File);
```

Reset sets the specified file to open and positions the file pointer at the top of the file.

```
PROCEDURE SetPos(VAR f: File; High, Low: CARDINAL);
```

SetPos is used to support random-access file I/O. The specified file will be positioned at the byte location specified by **High** and **Low**, which represent the high- and low-order words of a long integer. The location is computed using this formula:

$$position = (High*2^{16})+Low$$

```
PROCEDURE SetModify(VAR f: File);
PROCEDURE SetOpen(VAR f: File);
PROCEDURE SetRead(VAR f: File);
PROCEDURE SetWrite(VAR f: File);
```

These procedures set the type of operations that can be performed on the specified file. **SetRead** enables read-only operations, **SetWrite** enables write-only operations, and **SetModify** enables read-write operations. **Set-Open** sets a file to idle—no operations are allowed, but the file is still open.

```
PROCEDURE WriteByte(VAR f: File; b: BYTE);
```

WriteByte writes the byte in **b** to the specified file and advances the current file position to the next byte. **WriteByte** usually is used with binary files.

```
PROCEDURE WriteChar(VAR f: File; ch: CHAR);
```

WriteChar writes the character in **ch** to the specified file and advances the current file position to the next character. **WriteChar** usually is used with ASCII files.

```
PROCEDURE WriteNBytes(VAR f: File; buffer: ADDRESS;
                      numbytes: CARDINAL;
                      VAR written: CARDINAL);
```

WriteNBytes writes **numbytes** of bytes from the buffer pointed to by **buffer** to the specified file. The number of bytes actually written is returned in **written**. This procedure usually is used with binary files.

```
PROCEDURE WriteWord(VAR f: File; wd: WORD);
```

WriteWord writes the word in **wd** to the specified file and advances the current file position to the next word. **WriteWord** usually is used with binary files.

InOut

InOut contains the standard, high-level procedures for performing console I/O on strings, characters, and integers. It also supports the redirection of I/O to disk files.

```
VAR
  Done: BOOLEAN;
```

Done is used to indicate the success or failure of certain routines.

```
PROCEDURE CloseInput;
```

CloseInput closes the current input file and returns input to the console.

```
PROCEDURE CloseOutput;
```

CloseOutput closes the current output file and returns output to the console.

```
PROCEDURE OpenInput(extension: ARRAY OF CHAR);
```

OpenInput is used to redirect input to a user-specified file. If **extension** is not null and the user does not specify an extension explicitly, then **extension** will be the extension for the file name specified. If the file is found, **Done** is set to **TRUE**, and all input is taken from the specified file until a call to **CloseInput** is executed.

```
PROCEDURE OpenOutput(extension: ARRAY OF CHAR);
```

OpenOutput is used to redirect output to a user-specified file. If **extension** is not null and the user does not specify an extension explicitly, then **extension** will be the extension for the file name specified. If the file is found, **Done** is set to **TRUE**, and all output is sent to the specified file until a call to **CloseOutput** is executed.

```
PROCEDURE Read(VAR ch: CHAR);
```

Read reads the next character from the current input device. **Done** is **TRUE** unless the end of the file is encountered.

```
PROCEDURE ReadCard(VAR i: CARDINAL);
```

ReadCard reads a **CARDINAL** from the current input device.

PROCEDURE ReadInt(VAR i: INTEGER);

ReadInt reads an **INTEGER** from the current input device.

PROCEDURE ReadString(VAR str: ARRAY OF CHAR);

ReadString reads a string from the current input device. The read operation is terminated when any character with an ASCII value of 32 (a space) or less is encountered.

PROCEDURE Write(ch: CHAR);

Write writes a character to the current output device.

PROCEDURE WriteCard(c, width: CARDINAL);

WriteCard writes the cardinal **c** of minimum field width **width** to the current output device. Leading blanks are output if necessary.

PROCEDURE WriteHex(c, width: CARDINAL);

WriteHex writes the cardinal **c** of minimum field width **width** to the current output device in hexadecimal format. Leading blanks are output if necessary.

PROCEDURE WriteInt(i: INTEGER; width: CARDINAL);

WriteInt writes the integer **i** of minimum field width **width** to the current output device. Leading blanks are output if necessary.

PROCEDURE WriteOct(c, width: CARDINAL);

WriteOct writes the cardinal **c** of minimum field width **width** to the current output device in octal format. Leading blanks are output if necessary.

PROCEDURE WriteLn;

WriteLn writes a carriage return/linefeed sequence to the current output device.

```
PROCEDURE WriteString(str: ARRAY OF CHAR);
```

WriteString writes a string to the current output device.

MathLib

MathLib contains several routines that perform special mathematical functions, such as sine and cosine. In addition, it contains procedures to convert between **REAL**s and **INTEGER**s.

```
PROCEDURE arctan(r: REAL): REAL;
PROCEDURE cos(r: REAL): REAL;
PROCEDURE exp(r: REAL): REAL;
PROCEDURE ln(r: REAL): REAL;
PROCEDURE sin(r: REAL): REAL;
PROCEDURE sqrt(r: REAL): REAL;
```

These routines return the values their names imply.

```
PROCEDURE real(i: INTEGER): REAL;
```

The **real** procedure returns the **REAL** equivalent of **i**.

```
PROCEDURE entier(r: REAL): INTEGER;
```

The **entier** procedure returns the **INTEGER** equivalent of **r**. Truncation may occur.

NumberConversions

NumberConversions contains the routines necessary to convert between strings and **CARDINAL**s and **INTEGER**s.

```
PROCEDURE CardToString(c: CARDINAL;
                       VAR str: ARRAY OF CHAR;
                       width: CARDINAL);
```

CardToString is used to convert the **CARDINAL** value **c** to a string of width **width** and place the result in **str**.

```
PROCEDURE IntToString(i: INTEGER;
                      VAR str: ARRAY OF CHAR;
                      width: CARDINAL);
```

IntToString is used to convert the **INTEGER** value **i** to a string of width **width** and place the result in **str**.

```
PROCEDURE StringToCard(str: ARRAY OF CHAR;
                       VAR c; VAR OK: BOOLEAN);
```

StringToCard converts the number contained in **str** to a **CARDINAL** and places the result in **c**. **OK** is **TRUE** if the conversion is successful.

```
PROCEDURE StringToInt(str: ARRAY OF CHAR;
                      VAR i; VAR OK: BOOLEAN);
```

StringToInt converts the number contained in **str** to an **INTEGER** and places the result in **i**. **OK** is **TRUE** if the conversion is successful.

Processes

Processes contains many of the routines that support Modula-2's concurrent programming environment. Also, the type **SIGNAL**, which allows communication between processes, is defined.

```
PROCEDURE Awaited (sig: SIGNAL): BOOLEAN;
```

Awaited determines whether any process is waiting for the specified signal **sig**. It will return **TRUE** if a process is waiting and **FALSE** otherwise.

```
PROCEDURE Init(VARsig: SIGNAL);
```

Init is used to intialize a signal. This must be done prior to the signal's use.

```
PROCEDURE SEND(VAR sig: SIGNAL);
```

SEND sends the specified signal **sig**. If no process is waiting for the signal, then **SEND** has no effect; otherwise, the waiting process will resume execution.

```
PROCEDURE StartProcess(p: PROC; workspace: CARDINAL);
```

StartProcess is used to start the new process **p** with **workspace** number of bytes of work space. Control is transferred to the process after the call.

```
PROCEDURE WAIT(VAR sig: SIGNAL);
```

WAIT suspends execution of the current process and waits for the specified signal. If no other processes are running, then a call to **WAIT** terminates the program.

RealConversions

RealConversions contains two routines that allow **REAL**s to be converted into strings and vice versa.

```
PROCEDURE RealToString(r: REAL;
                       numdig, width: INTEGER
                       VAR str: ARRAY OF CHAR;
                       VAR OK: BOOLEAN);
```

RealToString converts the **REAL** value **r** to a string with **numdig** number of digits to the right of the decimal point and a maximum field width of **width**. If the conversion is successful **OK** returns **TRUE**, and the result is placed in **str**.

```
PROCEDURE StringToReal(str: ARRAY OF CHAR;
                       VAR r: real;
                       VAR OK: BOOLEAN);
```

StringToReal converts the number in **str** to a **REAL** value and places the result in **r**. If the conversion is successful, **OK** will have the value **TRUE**.

RealInOut

RealInOut contains the procedures to read and write **REAL** numbers to the current I/O device, which usually is the console. These routines are not found in **InOut**.

```
PROCEDURE ReadReal(VAR r: REAL);
```

ReadReal reads a real number from the current input device and places the result in **r**.

```
PROCEDURE WriteReal(r: REAL; width: CARDINAL);
```

WriteReal writes **r** to the current output device. The minimum field width is specified by **width**.

Storage

Storage contains the procedures necessary to support dynamic allocation. All memory is allocated from the heap, which conceptually lies between the program memory and the stack.

```
PROCEDURE ALLOCATE(VAR ptr: ADDRESS; size: CARDINAL);
```

ALLOCATE is used to allocate **size** number of bytes from the heap. The address of the first byte is returned in **ptr**.

```
PROCEDURE DEALLOCATE(VAR ptr: ADDRESS; size: CARDINAL);
```

DEALLOCATE releases **size** number of bytes pointed to by **ptr**.

```
PROCEDURE Available(size: CARDINAL): BOOLEAN;
```

Available returns **TRUE** if there are at least **size** number of free bytes of memory left in the heap.

Strings

The **Strings** library contains several routines that allow easy manipulation and comparison of strings. Keep in mind that all strings are arrays of characters and must begin their indexing at zero.

```
PROCEDURE Assign(VAR source, dest: ARRAY OF CHAR);
```

Assign copies the contents of **source** into **dest**.

```
PROCEDURE Concat(str1, str2: ARRAY OF CHAR;
                 VAR dext: ARRAY OF CHAR);
```

Concat concatenates **str1** and **str2** and places the result in **dest**.

```
PROCEDURE CompareStr(str1, str2: ARRAY OF CHAR);
```

CompareStr compares two strings and returns 0 if they are equal, 1 if str1 is greater than str2, and −1 if str1 is less than str2.

```
PROCEDURE Copy(source: ARRAY OF CHAR;
               index, len: CARDINAL;
               VAR dest: ARRAY OF CHAR);
```

Copy copies a substring of **len** characters, starting at **index**, from **source** to **dest**.

```
PROCEDURE Delete(VAR str: ARRAY OF CHAR;
                 index, len: CARDINAL);
```

Delete removes a substring of length **len**, starting at **index**, from **str**.

```
PROCEDURE Insert(substr: ARRAY OF CHAR;
                 VAR str: ARRAY OF CHAR;
                 index: CARDINAL);
```

Insert inserts the string **substr** into **str** at **index**.

```
PROCEDURE Length(str: ARRAY OF CHAR): CARDINAL;
```

Length returns the length of **str**.

```
PROCEDURE Pos(substr, str: ARRAY OF CHAR): CARDINAL;
```

Pos returns the position of **substr** in **str**. If **substr** is not in **str**, then the value returned is greater than that of **HIGH(str).**

SYSTEM

SYSTEM contains various types and procedures necessary to do system-level programming. The actual contents of **SYSTEM** vary widely among implementations, but the types and routines presented here should be common to all.

```
TYPE
   BYTE;
   WORD;
   ADDRESS=POINTER TO WORD;
   PROCESS;
```

BYTE and **WORD** have their implied meanings. They represent 8- and 16-bit quantities on most 16-bit computers. **ADDRESS** is simply a memory address. These types are used to create variables that directly access the computer's hardware—bypassing Modula-2's normal type-checking facilities. **PROCESS** is used to handle concurrent processing.

```
PROCEDURE ADR(VarName): ADDRESS;
```

ADR returns the address of any variable.

```
PROCEDURE IOTRANSFER(VAR ISR, from: PROCESS;
                         IntVectNum: CARDINAL);
```

IOTRANSFER is used to transfer control to the interrupt service routine **ISR**. The current process is **from**, and the interrupt vector number is **IntVectNum**.

```
PROCEDURE LISTEN;
```

LISTEN temporarily lowers the priority of the current process. This allows other, lower-priority processes to execute.

```
PROCEDURE NEWPROCESS(proc: PROC;
                         ProcessAddr: ADDRESS;
                         WorkSpace: CARDINAL;
                         VAR process: PROCESS);
```

NEWPROCESS is used to create a new process. The procedure **proc** becomes the process, **ProcessAddr** is the address of **proc**, **WorkSpace** is the number of bytes required by the process, and **process** is a variable that is used to transfer control between processes.

```
PROCEDURE SIZE(VarName): CARDINAL;
```

SIZE returns the size, in bytes, of the specified variable.

```
PROCEDURE TSIZE(TypeName): CARDINAL;
```

TSIZE returns the size, in bytes, of the specified type.

```
PROCEDURE TRANSFER(VAR from, to: PROCESS);
```

TRANSFER is used to transfer program control between processes.

Terminal

Terminal contains a subset of **InOut** with the following additions.

```
PROCEDURE KeyPressed(): BOOLEAN;
```

KeyPressed returns **TRUE** if a key has been struck at the console; otherwise, it returns **FALSE**.

```
PROCEDURE ReadAgain;
```

ReadAgain causes the last character read to be read again on a subsequent call to **Read**.

Reserved Words

APPENDIX C

Modula-2 has 40 reserved words that form the language and that may not be used for any other purpose. They are

AND	EXPORT	PROCEDURE
ARRAY	FOR	QUALIFIED
BEGIN	FROM	RECORD
BY	IF	REPEAT
CASE	IMPLEMENTATION	RETURN
CONST	IMPORT	SET
DEFINITION	IN	THEN
DIV	LOOP	TO
DO	MOD	TYPE
ELSE	MODULE	UNTIL
ELSIF	NOT	VAR
END	OF	WHILE
EXIT	OR	WITH
	POINTER	

AND

The logical operator **AND** is used to combine two **BOOLEAN** expressions. The outcome of the operation is **TRUE** if and only if both expressions are **TRUE**; it is false otherwise. For example,

TRUE AND TRUE is **TRUE**, and **TRUE AND FALSE** is **FALSE.**

ARRAY

ARRAY is used to form an array declaration. The general form of a single dimension array declaration is

<*VarName*>: ARRAY [<*low*>..<*high*>] OF <*type*>;

where ***VarName*** is the name of the array variable, ***low*** and ***high*** are the lower and upper bounds of the array, and ***type*** is the base data type.

Multidimensioned array declarations have this general form:

<*VarName*>: ARRAY [*low1..high1*],
[*low2..high2*],...[*lowN..highN*] OF <*type*>;

where the lower and upper bounds of each dimension are explicitly declared.

BEGIN

BEGIN signals the beginning of either a **MODULE**'s code or a **PROCEDURE**'s code.

BY

BY is used to specify the increment in the **FOR** statement. For example, the following fragment will count from 10 to 0.

```
FOR x:=10 to 0 BY -1 DO
  .
  .
  .
END;
```

CASE

The **CASE** statement is a multiway decision path.The object of the **CASE** is compared against each case. If a match is found, then the code associated with that case is executed. If no match is found, then the code associated with the optional **ELSE** case, if one exists, will be executed. Vertical bars are used to separate cases. Only constants may be used in the case list. The general form of the **CASE** statement is

```
CASE <VarName> OF
     const1: <statement-sequence> |
     const2: <statement-sequence> |
     const3: <statement-sequence> |
     .
     .
     .
     constN: <statement-sequence>
     ELSE: <statement-sequence>
END;
```

CONST

CONST is used to declare a constant in a **MODULE** or **PROCEDURE**. For example, the following code declares **MaxEvent** to be a constant equal to 100.

```
CONST
  MaxEvent = 100;
```

Notice that an equal sign, not a colon, is used in a constant declaration.

DEFINITION

DEFINITION is used to declare a **DEFINITION MODULE**. It is placed directly before the reserved word **MODULE** and indicates that only the definition of what will be done is described in the **MODULE**; the actual code to do the work is in the **IMPLEMENTATION MODULE**. Together these modules support separate compilation and linking.

DIV

DIV is the **INTEGER** and **CARDINAL** division operator. The / can only be used with **REAL** numbers.

DO

DO is used with the **FOR, WITH**, and **WHILE** statements. See these statements for specific information.

ELSE

ELSE is used to form the optional else clause of the **IF** statement. The statement sequence that follows the **ELSE** is executed only if the **IF** condition and any **ELSIF** conditions are **FALSE**. See **IF** for details.

ELSIF

ELSIF is an optional clause of the **IF** statement that takes the place of the traditional **IF/THEN/ELSE/IF** compound statements. See **IF**.

END

END is used to terminate statement sequences, **PROCEDURES**, and **MODULEs**.

EXIT

EXIT is used to force the exit from a **LOOP** loop. When it is encountered, the loop is terminated, and execution resumes at the first line of code after the **LOOP's END** statement. See **LOOP** for examples.

EXPORT

EXPORT is used to allow other **MODULE**s to have knowledge of and access to **PROCEDURE**s, **CONST**ants, **VAR**iables, and **TYPE**s contained in the current **DEFINITION MODULE**. Only one **EXPORT** statement may be used per **MODULE**. **EXPORT** is used only with **DEFINITION MODULE**s. In this case, the modifier **QUALIFIED** is required to ensure that name conflicts do not occur. For example, this fragment **EXPORT**s **Counter**, **Payee**, and **YTD**.

```
DEFINITION MODULE AccountPayable;

EXPORT QUALIFIED Counter, Payee, YTD;
.
.
.
END AccountPayable;
```

FOR

The **FOR** loop repeats a statement sequence a predetermined number of times. Its general form is

FOR <*ControlVar*>:=<*expression*> TO <*expression*>
BY <*expression*> DO
<*statement-sequence*>
END;

The **BY** is optional. If it is not present, then the ***ControlVar*** is incremented each time the loop repeats; otherwise, ***ControlVar*** is increased (or decreased) by the value of the **BY** expression. In this way, it is possible to count by increments other than 1 or to run the loop backward by using a negative value.

This code prints the numbers 1 to 10 on the screen.

```
FOR x:=1 TO 10 DO
  WriteInt(x, 3);
END;
```

This code will print the numbers 10 through 1.

```
FOR x:=10 TO 1 BY -1 DO
  WriteInt(x, 3);
END;
```

Pascal programmers note: **DOWNTO** is not used in Modula-2.

FROM

FROM is used to indicate in which library a specified **PROCEDURE**, **CONST**ant, **VAR**iable, or **TYPE** is found. See **IMPORT**.

IF

The **IF** statement has three basic forms. The simplest is

IF <*expression*> THEN <*statement-sequence*> END;

If the expression is **TRUE**, then the statement sequence will be executed; otherwise, execution resumes with the first line of code following the **END**.

The optional **ELSIF** can be added to allow one or more alternatives to be checked for. The general form of the **IF/ELSIF** is

IF <*expression*> THEN <*statement-sequence*>
ELSIF <*expression*> THEN <*statement-sequence*>
ELSIF <*expression*> THEN <*statement-sequence*>
ELSIF <*expression*> THEN <*statement-sequence*>
.
.
.
END;

If the **IF** expression is **TRUE**, then its statement sequence is executed, and all of the **ELSIF**s are skipped. If the **IF** expression is **FALSE**, then the **ELSIF**s are executed until one is found to be **TRUE**; its statement sequence is then executed. If none of the expressions are **TRUE**, then no action is taken.

The final option is the **ELSE**, which provides for a statement sequence that will be executed if the **IF** and **ELSIF** conditions are **FALSE**. The general form for the **ELSE** is

IF <*expression*> THEN <*statement-sequence*>
ELSIF <*expression*> THEN <*statement-sequence*>
ELSIF <*expression*> THEN <*statement-sequence*>
ELSIF <*expression*> THEN <*statement-sequence*>
.
.
.
ELSE <*statement-sequence*>
END;

IMPLEMENTATION

IMPLEMENTATION is used to declare an **IMPLEMENTATION MODULE**. This module holds the actual code that performs the functions described in its corresponding **DEFINITION MODULE**. These two modules are used to create libraries and to permit separate compilation and linking.

IMPORT

IMPORT is used to tell the compiler where to find certain **TYPE**s, **CONST**ants, **VAR**iables, and **PROCEDURE**s. The most common form of the **IMPORT** statement is

FROM <*library*> IMPORT <*identifier-list*>

where ***library*** is the name of the library that holds the identifiers specified in the list. For example, to use **WriteLn** from **InOut**, you must have this **IMPORT** statement:

```
FROM InOut IMPORT WriteLn;
```

IN

IN is a set operator used to determine whether a specified element is a member of a set. The general form is

<*element*> IN <*set*>

IN is **TRUE** if ***element*** is a member of ***set***; otherwise, it is **FALSE**.

LOOP

LOOP is used to create an endless loop. There is no provision for termination built into the statement. The only way a **LOOP** can be left is through the use of the **EXIT** command, which causes immediate termination of the loop when it is encountered. The general form of the **LOOP** statement is

```
LOOP
    <statement-sequence>
END;
```

For example, the following loop will run until a "q" is typed.

```
LOOP
  Read(ch);
  IF ch='q' THEN EXIT END;
END;
```

MOD

The **MOD** operation is used to compute the remainder of an integer division. For example, 10 DIV 3 equals 3 with a remainder of 1. Therefore 10 MOD 3 equals 1.

MODULE

The **MODULE** is central to Modula-2 because it is in **MODULE**s that all program activity occurs. There are four kinds of **MODULE**s:

- Program
- DEFINITION
- IMPLEMENTATION
- Local.

It is beyond the scope of this appendix to cover each of these fully; however, they all have a general form similar to that of the program

MODULE. The general form of a program **MODULE** is shown here.

MODULE <*name*>;

<*IMPORT-list*>
<*CONST-definitions*>
<*TYPE-definitions*>
<*VAR-declarations*>
<*PROCEDURE-declarations*>

BEGIN
<*statement-sequence*>
END <*name*>.

NOT

NOT is a logical operator used to reverse the state of a **BOOLEAN** expression; that is, **NOT TRUE** is **FALSE**, and **NOT FALSE** is **TRUE**.

OF

OF is used in the array declaration statement. See **ARRAY**.

OR

OR is the logical *OR* operator. The outcome of an *OR* operation is **TRUE** if at least one operand is **TRUE**. For example, **TRUE OR FALSE** is **TRUE**, but **FALSE OR FALSE** is **FALSE**.

POINTER

POINTER is used to declare pointer variables. A pointer variable is simply a variable that holds the address of another variable. The following code declares a **ptr** to be a pointer to an **INTEGER**.

```
VAR
  ptr: POINTER TO INTEGER;
```

PROCEDURE

PROCEDURE is used to declare a procedure. There are two types of **PROCEDURE**s: those that return values, and those that do not. The general form of a **PROCEDURE** with no return value is

```
PROCEDURE <name>(<parameter-list>);
    CONST <list>;
    TYPE <list>;
    VAR <declarations>
    PROCEDURE <declarations>
BEGIN
    <statement-sequence>
END <name>;
```

As you can see, it is possible to have **PROCEDURE**s inside **PROCEDURE**s. In general, all values declared inside a **PROCEDURE** are known only within that **PROCEDURE**. This helps make standalone subroutines possible.

To enable a return value, only the first line of a **PROCEDURE** need be changed, as shown here.

```
PROCEDURE <name>(parameter-list>): <type>;
```

Here, **type** is the type of value the **PROCEDURE** will be returning. The return value must be specified explicitly using the **RETURN** statement.

QUALIFIED

The **QUALIFIED** modifier is used with the **EXPORT** statement to link the **MODULE** name with the **EXPORT**ed identifiers. Its use is mandatory for separately compiled **MODULE**s and optional for local **MODULE**s.

RECORD

A **RECORD** is a conglomerate data type that allows several different variables to be linked together and accessed as a unit. The general form of a **RECORD** is

<*RecName*> = RECORD
<*Var1*>: <*type*>;
<*Var2*>: <*type*>;
<*Var3*>: <*type*>;
.
.
.
<*VarN*>: <*type*>;
END;

Individual elements of a record are accessed using the dereferencing operator ".". For example, given

```
TYPE
  Rec = RECORD
        I: INTEGER;
        R: REAL;
  END;

VAR
  x: REC;
```

the following assignments are valid.

```
x.I:=10;
x.R:=10.10;
```

REPEAT

The **REPEAT** loop is the only loop in Modula-2 that will always execute at least once. This is because the loop test condition is at the bottom of the loop. The general form of the **REPEAT** loop is

REPEAT
<*statement-sequence*>
UNTIL <*expression*>;

The expression following the **UNTIL** must evaluate to a **BOOLEAN** value. The loop will run until ***expression*** becomes **TRUE**. For example, this loop will repeat until a "q" is typed.

```
REPEAT
  Read(ch);
UNTIL ch='q';
```

RETURN

RETURN is used to return a value from a **PROCEDURE**. The general form is

RETURN <*expression*>;

where the expression must be the same type as that specified in the **PROCEDURE** declaration. For further details, see **PROCEDURE**.

SET

SET is used to declare a **SET** type. A set is a grouping of values of a subrange or an enumeration. **SET** variables can only be operated on by the set's operators and procedures. For example, the following code creates a **SET** of digits.

```
TYPE
  digits = [0..9];
  DigSet = SET OF digits;
```

THEN

See **IF**.

TO

See **FOR**.

TYPE

TYPE tells the compiler that **TYPE** definitions will follow. A **TYPE** definition is used either to create a new type of data or to give a new name to an existing type.

UNTIL

See **REPEAT**.

VAR

VAR tells the compiler that variable declarations will follow.

WHILE

The **WHILE** loop has the general form

WHILE <*expression*> DO
    <*statement sequence*>
END;

Here, ***expression*** must evaluate to a **BOOLEAN** value. The **WHILE** loop will run while ***expression*** is **TRUE**. For example, this loop will repeat until a "q" is typed.

```
Read(ch);
WHILE ch<>'q' DO
  Read(ch);
END;
```

WITH

WITH is used to dereference **RECORD** automatically, thus eliminating the need for the dereferencing operator. Its general form is

WITH <*RecName*> DO
<*statement-sequence*>
END;

The following code fragment illustrates the use of **WITH**.

```
TYPE
  RecType = RECORD
              index: INTEGER;
              ratio: REAL;
  END;

VAR
  rec: RecType;

BEGIN
  WITH rec DO
    ratio:=10.1;
    index:=1;
  END;
  .
  .
  .
```

INDEX

80386/80286 Assembly Language Programming
by William H. Murray and Chris Pappas

This comprehensive guide enables serious programmers to take full advantage of the unique design of the 80386 and 80286 microprocessors found in the IBM® PC AT, COMPAQ® Desk Pro 286, TANDY 6000,® and other major computer systems. Instructions for programming the 8087/80287/80387 coprocessor are also included. The authors carefully detail the use of assembler pseudo-ops; macros, procedures, and libraries; and testing and debugging techniques. You'll also find instructions for interacting with high-level languages such as BASIC, Pascal, and FORTRAN. Many practical programming examples show beginners how to implement assembly language, while experienced programmers have an invaluable reference to the 80386 and 80286 instruction set.

\$19.95p
0-07-881217-8, 400 pp., 6³/₈ x 9¹/₄

65816/65802 Assembly Language Programming
by Michael Fischer

This addition to the Osborne/McGraw-Hill ALP series is a complete handbook to assembly language programming with the 65816 and 65802 microprocessors. Serious programmers will find complete coverage of the 65816 and 65802 chip series. Assemblers, instruction sets, arithmetic operations, loops, and code conversion are presented. You'll also learn about sorting and searching, subroutines, I/O and interrupts, debugging and testing. Michael Fischer, a columnist for *Bay Area Computer Currents,* provides you with concise, comprehensive information. *65816/65802 Assembly Language Programming* is both a tutorial and a lasting reference.

\$19.95p
0-07-881235-6, 425 pp., 6³/₈ x 9¹/₄

68000 Assembly Language Programming, Second Edition, Includes 68010 & 68020
by Lance A. Leventhal, Doug Hawkins, Gerry Kane, and William D. Cramer

This classic on assembly language programming for the 68000 microprocessor has been revised to provide complete coverage of the entire 68000 family, including the 68010 and 68020 chips. Every instruction you need to program in assembly langauge is thoroughly described. Fully debugged, practical programing examples with solutions in both object code and source code are used throughout the text to illustrate techniques. The authors also discuss assembler conventions, I/O device programming, and interfacing methods. If you're designing software for the Macintosh,™ Commodore Amiga,™ Atari® ST,™ Altos® 3068, Tandy® 6000, or other 68000-based computers, you'll find essential information in this lasting reference. (*Part of the Osborne/McGraw-Hill Assembly Language Programming series.*)

\$19.95p
0-07-881232-1, 625 pp., 6³/₈ x 9¹/₄

The 8086 Book
by Russell Rector and George Alexy

". . .is far superior to any other book about the 8086." (Dr. Dobbs Journal)

Anyone using, designing, or simply interested in an 8086-based system will be delighted by this book's scope and authority. As the 16-bit microprocessor gains wider inclusion in small computers, this book becomes invaluable as a reference tool which covers the timing, architecture and design of the 8086, as well as optimal programming techniques, interfacing, special features and more.

\$18.95p
0-07-931029-X, 624 pp., 6¹/₂ x 9¹/₄

Advanced dBASE III®: Programming & Techniques
by Miriam Liskin

Experienced dBASE® programmers can improve their skills with this complete guide to designing and implementing more effective dBASE III® business applications. Nationally known columnist and consultant Miriam Liskin addresses the "real world" business environment so you can make the most of dBASE III modes of operation. Follow the development of an accounts receivable system from start to finish while Liskin outlines the strategy for planning, testing, and refining this practical financial application. You'll proceed through all the critical steps: defining your needs, establishing data files, modeling the application at command level, determining user control, writing the programs, and evaluating and documenting the system. Database managers, system designers, and other professionals can use Liskin's expertise and insights to achieve optimal dBASE III performance.

\$19.95p
0-07-881196-1, 630 pp., 7³/₈ x 9¹/₄

Available at fine bookstores and computer stores everywhere.

For a complimentary catalog of all our current publications contact: Osborne **McGraw-Hill**, 2600 Tenth Street, Berkeley, CA 94710

Phone inquiries may be made using our toll-free number.
Call 800-227-0900 or 800-772-2531 (in California).
TWX 910-366-7277.

Prices subject to change without notice.

The manuscript for this book was prepared and submitted to Osborne **McGraw-Hill** in electronic form. The acquisitions editor for this project was Jon Erickson, the technical reviewer was Seth Pratt, and the project editor was Lyn Cordell.

Text design by Judy Wohlfrom, using Century Expanded for text body and Eras demi bold for display.

Cover art by Yashi Okita. Cover supplier is Phoenix Color Corp. Book printed and bound by R. R. Donnelley & Sons Company, Crawfordsville, Indiana.